1/21

Written by ZIDROU

Illustrated by ARNO MONIN

Translation by Jeremy Melloul
Localization, Layout, and Editing by Mike Kennedy

MAGNETIC™
ISBN: 978-1-942367-83-3
Library of Congress Control Number: 2020907174

The Adoption, Published 2020 by Magnetic Press, LLC.
Originally published as *L'Adoption books 1 and 2* © 2016 Bamboo Éditions by Zidrou and Arno Monin. www.bamboo.fr

Printed in Hong Kong.

10 9 8 7 6 5 4 3 2 1

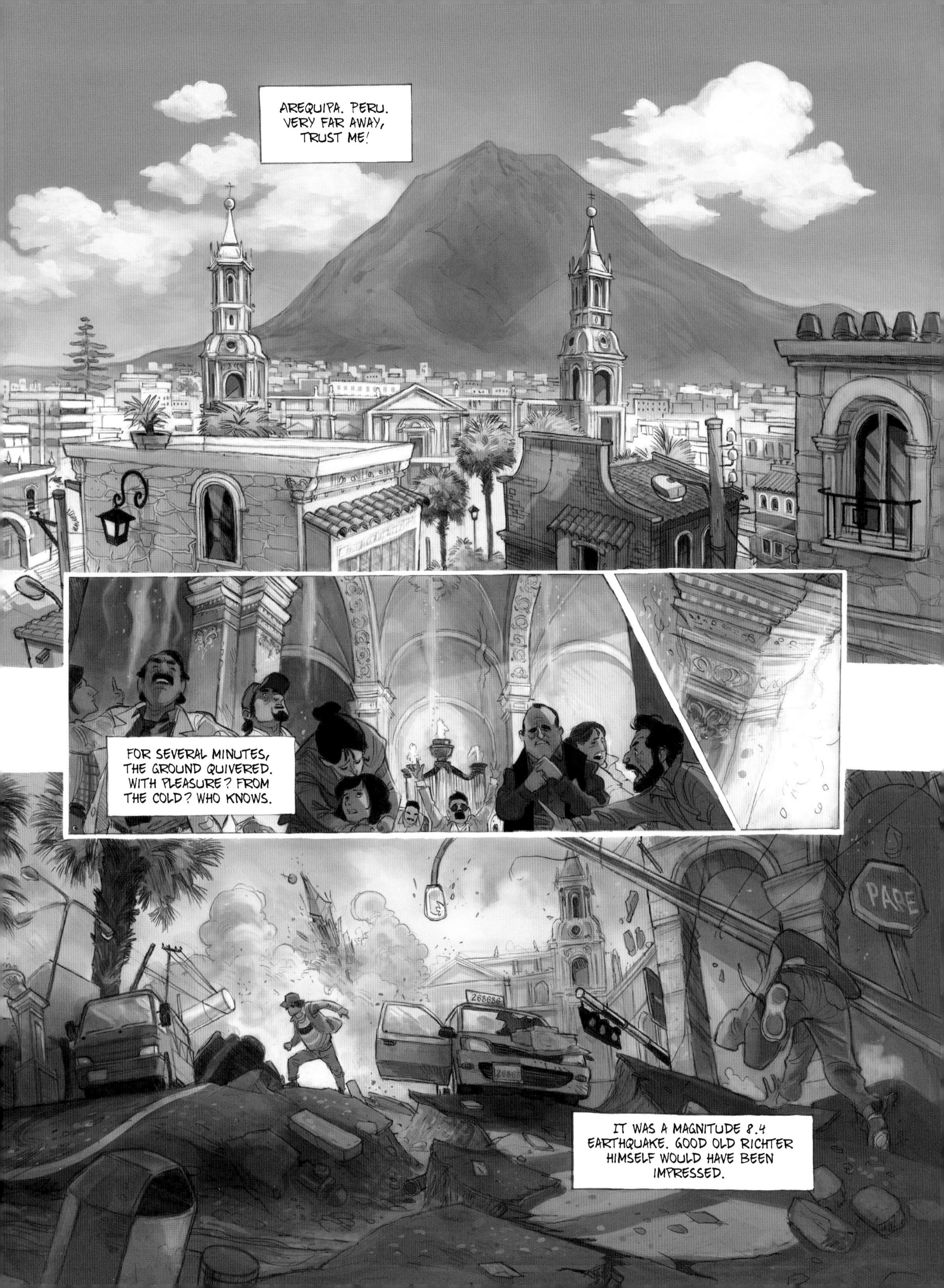
AREQUIPA. PERU. VERY FAR AWAY, TRUST ME!
FOR SEVERAL MINUTES, THE GROUND QUIVERED. WITH PLEASURE? FROM THE COLD? WHO KNOWS.
PARE
IT WAS A MAGNITUDE 8.4 EARTHQUAKE. GOOD OLD RICHTER HIMSELF WOULD HAVE BEEN IMPRESSED.

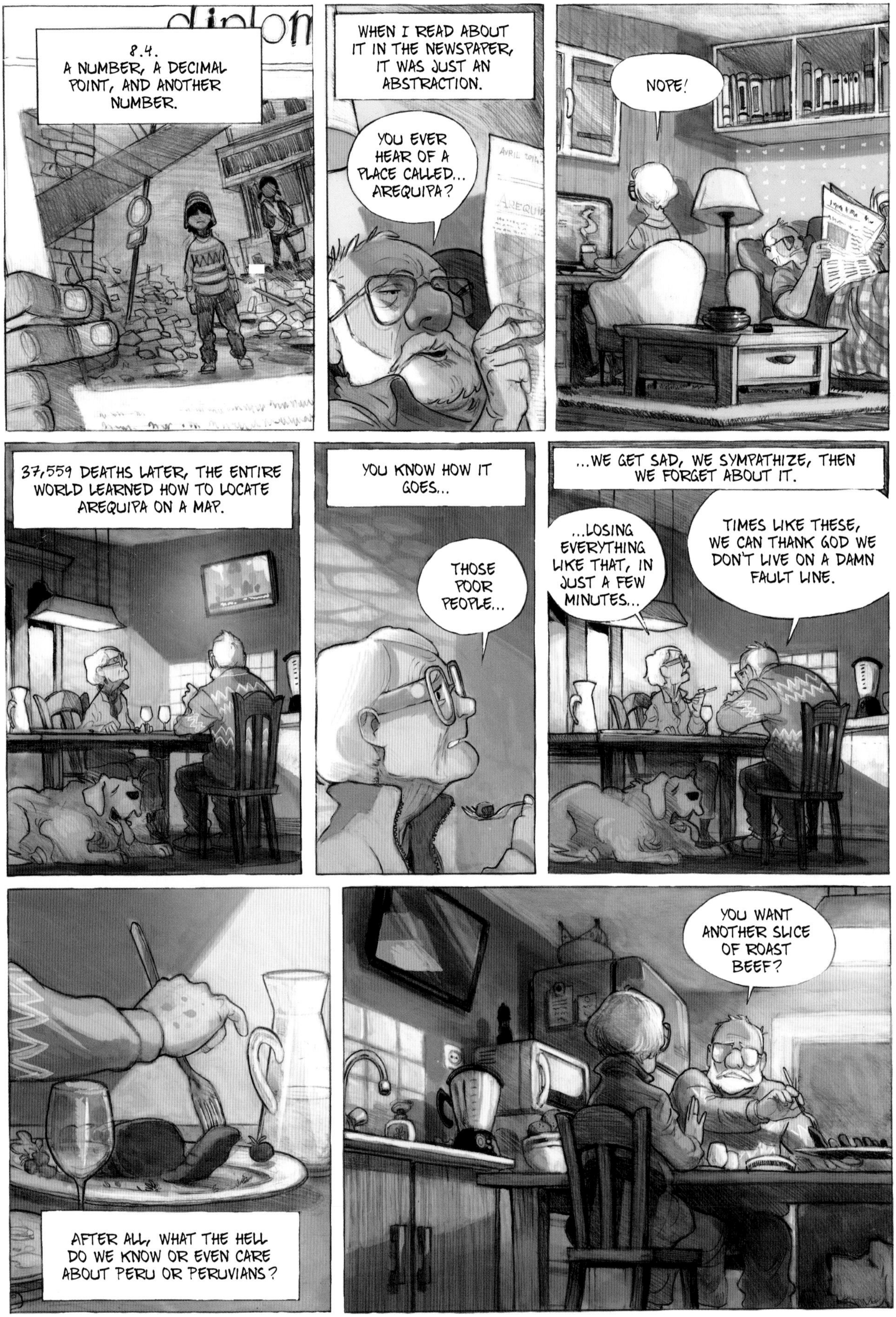
8.4.
A NUMBER, A DECIMAL POINT, AND ANOTHER NUMBER.
WHEN I READ ABOUT IT IN THE NEWSPAPER, IT WAS JUST AN ABSTRACTION.
YOU EVER HEAR OF A PLACE CALLED... AREQUIPA?
NOPE!
37,559 DEATHS LATER, THE ENTIRE WORLD LEARNED HOW TO LOCATE AREQUIPA ON A MAP.
YOU KNOW HOW IT GOES...
THOSE POOR PEOPLE...
...WE GET SAD, WE SYMPATHIZE, THEN WE FORGET ABOUT IT.
...LOSING EVERYTHING LIKE THAT, IN JUST A FEW MINUTES...
TIMES LIKE THESE, WE CAN THANK GOD WE DON'T LIVE ON A DAMN FAULT LINE.
AFTER ALL, WHAT THE HELL DO WE KNOW OR EVEN CARE ABOUT PERU OR PERUVIANS?
YOU WANT ANOTHER SLICE OF ROAST BEEF?

— QINAYA —

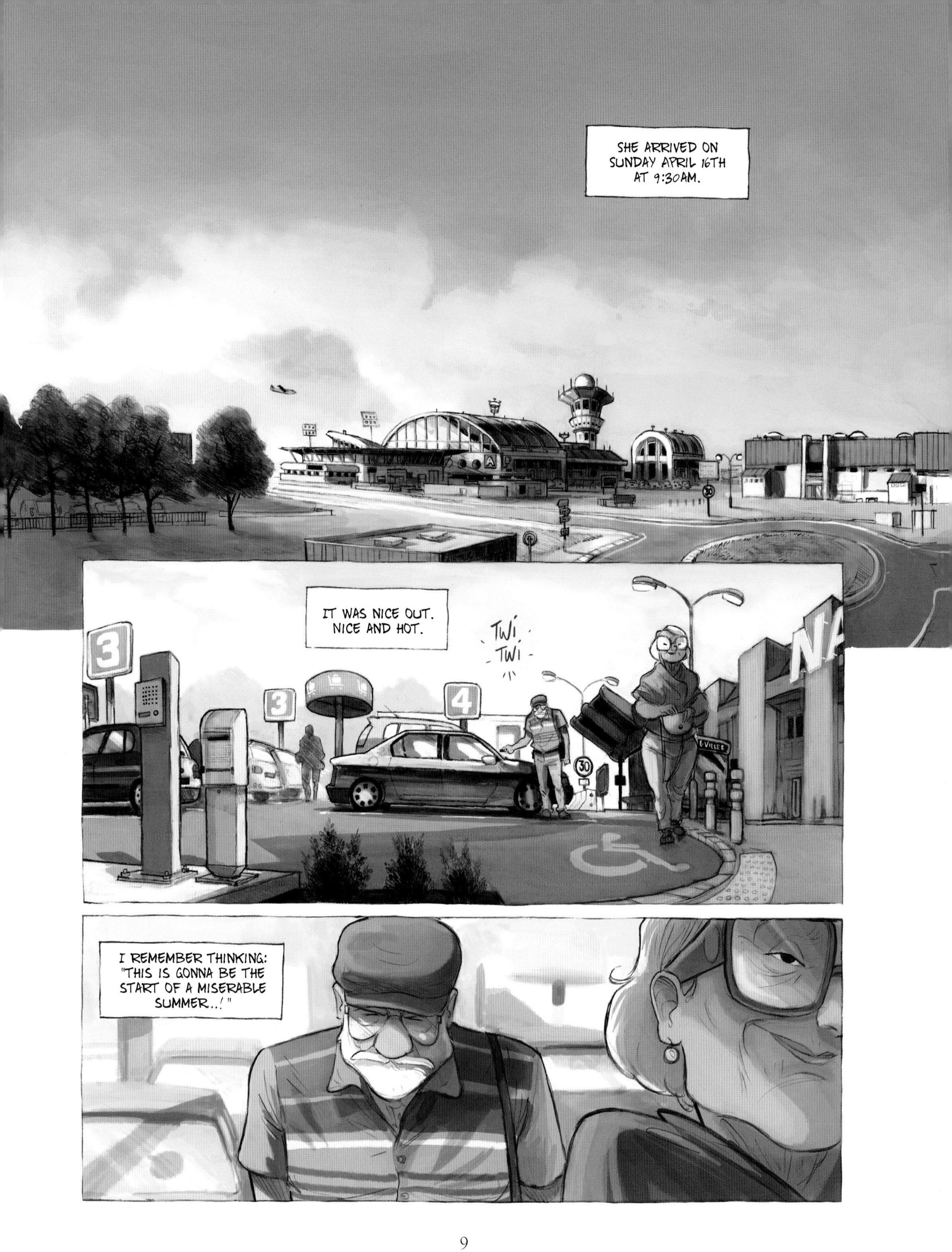
SHE ARRIVED ON SUNDAY APRIL 16TH AT 9:30AM.
IT WAS NICE OUT. NICE AND HOT.
TWI TWI
I REMEMBER THINKING: "THIS IS GONNA BE THE START OF A MISERABLE SUMMER...!"

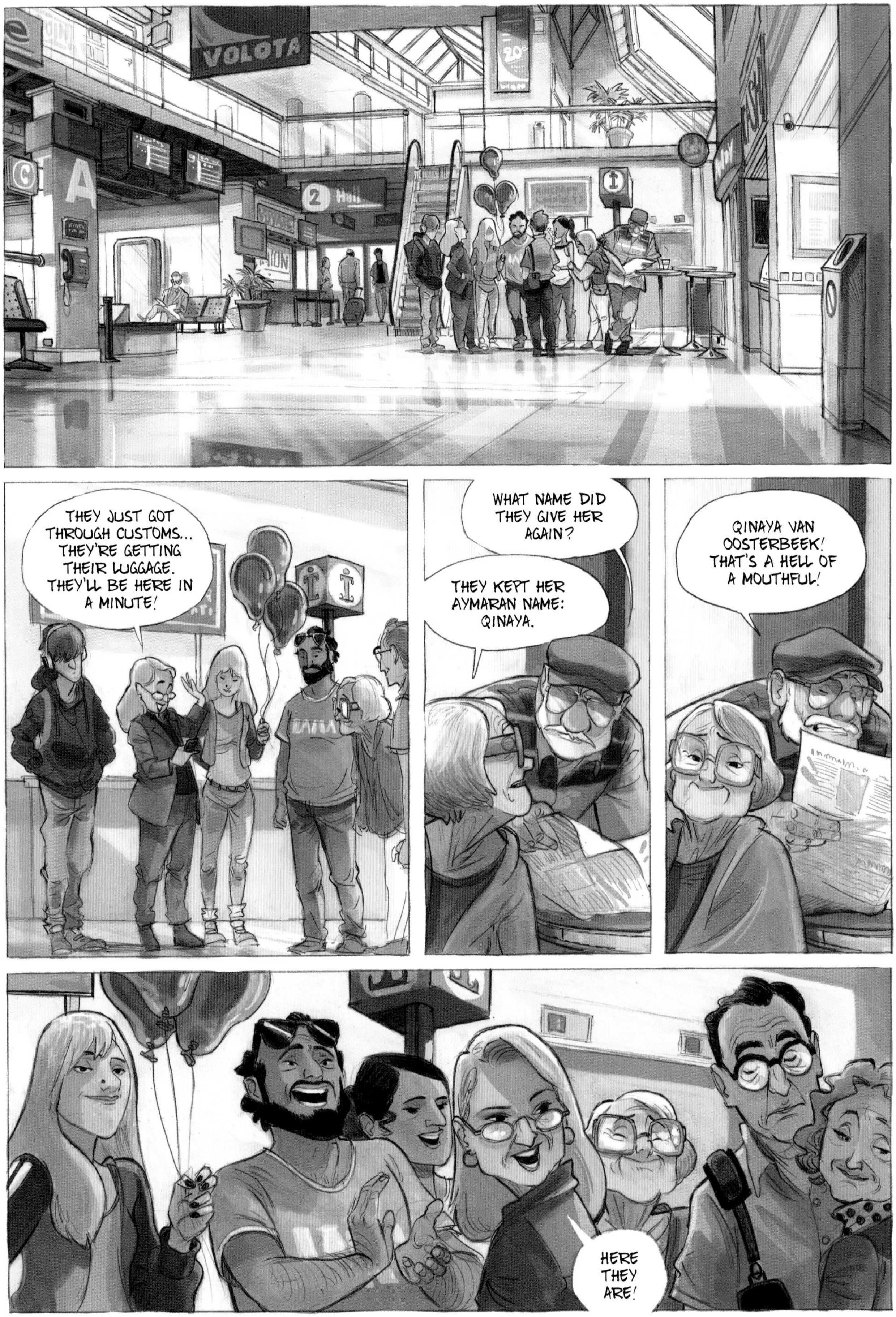
VOLOTA
THEY JUST GOT THROUGH CUSTOMS... THEY'RE GETTING THEIR LUGGAGE. THEY'LL BE HERE IN A MINUTE!
WHAT NAME DID THEY GIVE HER AGAIN?
THEY KEPT HER AYMARAN NAME: QINAYA.
QINAYA VAN OOSTERBEEK! THAT'S A HELL OF A MOUTHFUL!
HERE THEY ARE!

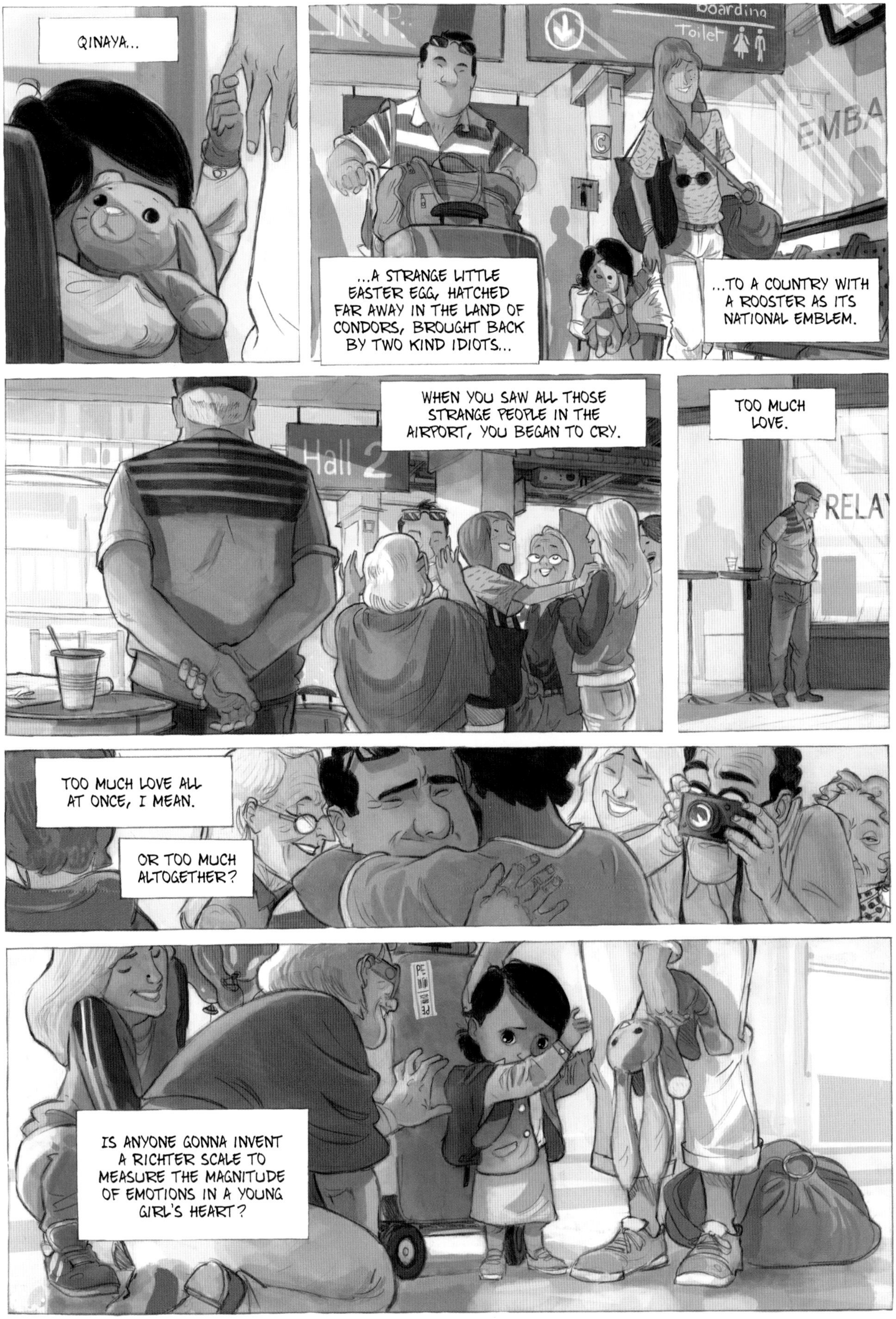
QINAYA...
...A STRANGE LITTLE EASTER EGG, HATCHED FAR AWAY IN THE LAND OF CONDORS, BROUGHT BACK BY TWO KIND IDIOTS...
...TO A COUNTRY WITH A ROOSTER AS ITS NATIONAL EMBLEM.
WHEN YOU SAW ALL THOSE STRANGE PEOPLE IN THE AIRPORT, YOU BEGAN TO CRY.
TOO MUCH LOVE.
TOO MUCH LOVE ALL AT ONCE, I MEAN.
OR TOO MUCH ALTOGETHER?
IS ANYONE GONNA INVENT A RICHTER SCALE TO MEASURE THE MAGNITUDE OF EMOTIONS IN A YOUNG GIRL'S HEART?

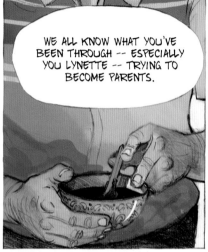

WE ALL KNOW WHAT YOU'VE BEEN THROUGH -- ESPECIALLY YOU LYNETTE -- TRYING TO BECOME PARENTS.

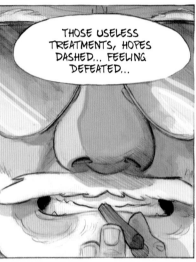

THOSE USELESS TREATMENTS, HOPES DASHED... FEELING DEFEATED...

...SAYING THIS CHILD WAS A LONG-AWAITED BLESSING WOULD BE AN UNDERSTATEMENT!

WOULDN'T YOU AGREE, BROTHER?

YOU WERE READY TO DO ANYTHING TO HAVE A CHILD! AND THEN THAT TERRIBLE TRAGEDY STRUCK PERU, LEAVING THOUSANDS OF VICTIMS...

THE HORROR! BUT FROM WHICH OUR RES... POOR ORPHA... ...BLE THAN

MAYBE SOMEONE SHOULD REMIND BRIGITTE SHE'S NOT CAMPAIGNING HERE...

...SUCH A WONDERFUL GESTURE OF LOVE. WE COULD EVEN CALL IT -- AND LET'S NOT BE AFRAID OF THE WORD -- HEROIC, PURE AND SIMPLE. ALAIN, I'M PROUD OF YOU!

TO MY CARAMEL-COLORED NIECE!

TO QINAYA!

12

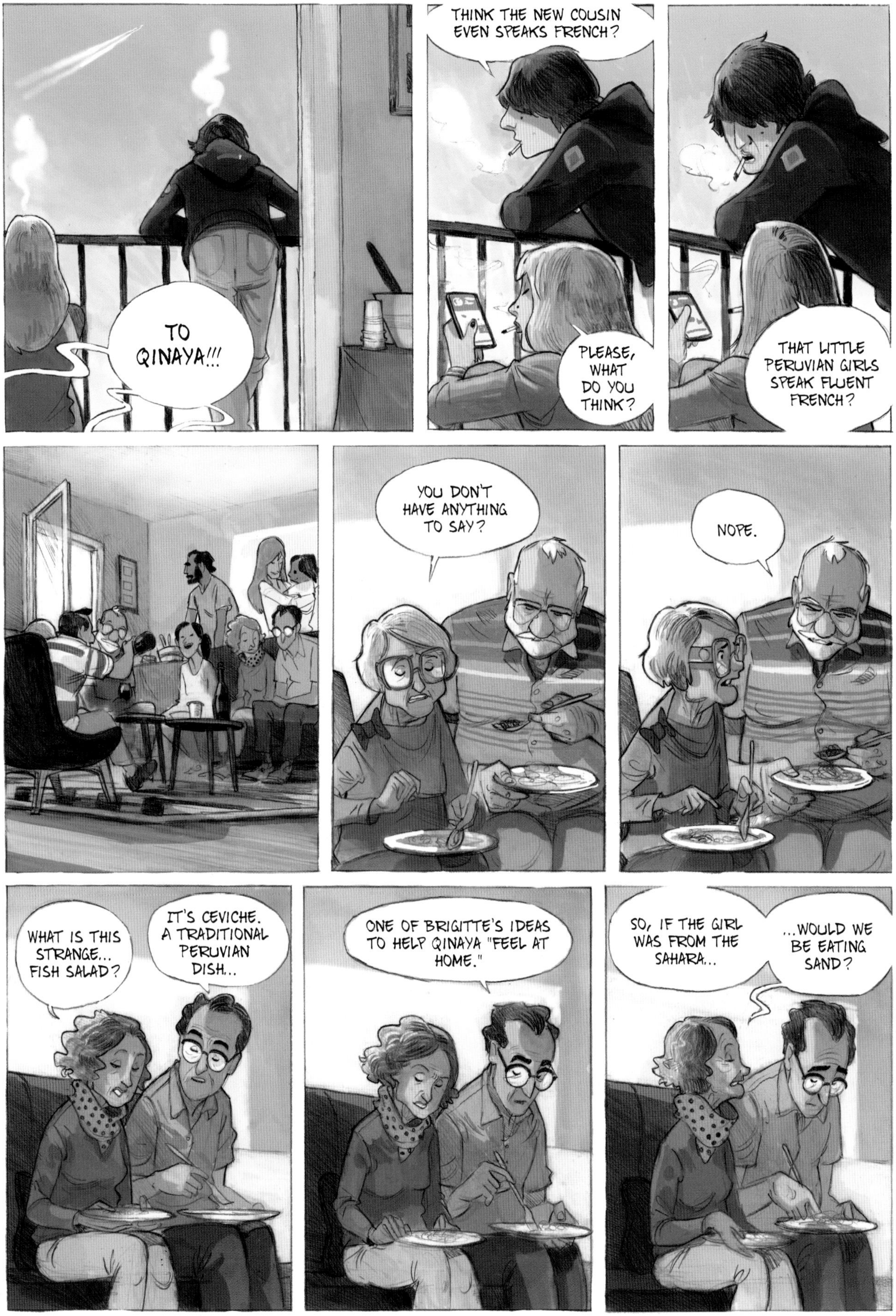

TO QINAYA!!!
THINK THE NEW COUSIN EVEN SPEAKS FRENCH?
PLEASE, WHAT DO YOU THINK?
THAT LITTLE PERUVIAN GIRLS SPEAK FLUENT FRENCH?
YOU DON'T HAVE ANYTHING TO SAY?
NOPE.
WHAT IS THIS STRANGE... FISH SALAD?
IT'S CEVICHE. A TRADITIONAL PERUVIAN DISH...
ONE OF BRIGITTE'S IDEAS TO HELP QINAYA "FEEL AT HOME."
SO, IF THE GIRL WAS FROM THE SAHARA...
...WOULD WE BE EATING SAND?

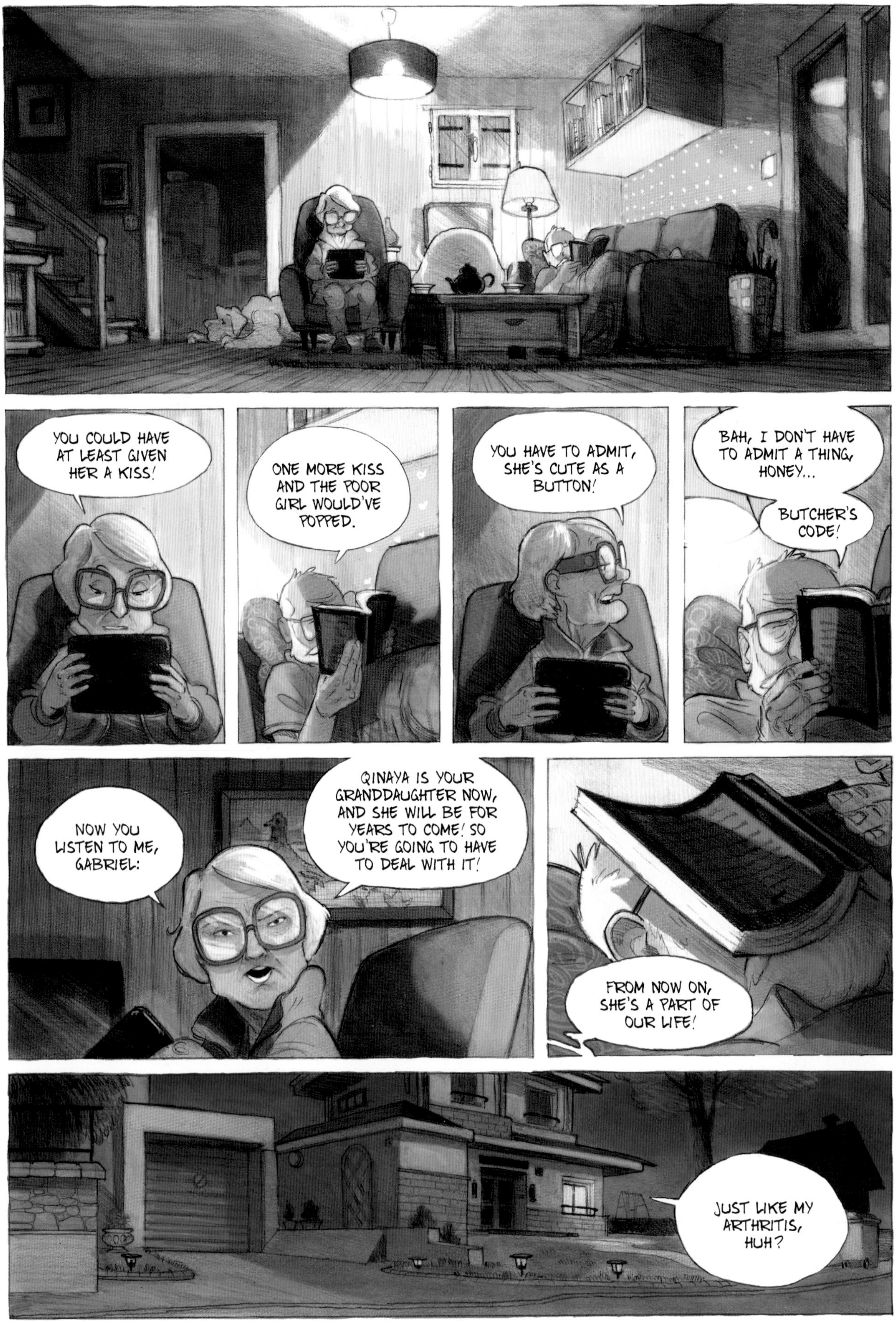
YOU COULD HAVE AT LEAST GIVEN HER A KISS!
ONE MORE KISS AND THE POOR GIRL WOULD'VE POPPED.
YOU HAVE TO ADMIT, SHE'S CUTE AS A BUTTON!
BAH, I DON'T HAVE TO ADMIT A THING, HONEY...
BUTCHER'S CODE!
NOW YOU LISTEN TO ME, GABRIEL:
QINAYA IS YOUR GRANDDAUGHTER NOW, AND SHE WILL BE FOR YEARS TO COME! SO YOU'RE GOING TO HAVE TO DEAL WITH IT!
FROM NOW ON, SHE'S A PART OF OUR LIFE!
JUST LIKE MY ARTHRITIS, HUH?

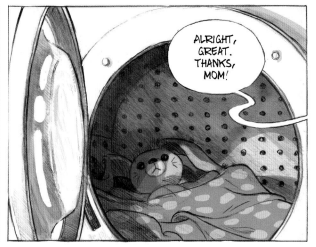

ALRIGHT, GREAT. THANKS, MOM!

YEAH, SHE CRIED A LITTLE, AT FIRST. BUT AFTER THE LONG TRIP AND ALL THE EMOTIONS... SHE SLEPT LIKE A LOG.

TO BE HONEST. SHE ONLY JUST WOKE UP.

SEVEN HOURS, YEAH.

RIGHT NOW, IN AREQUIPA, IT'S... YEAH, THAT'S RIGHT...

ELEVEN IN THE MORNING.

NOT A WORD, NO.

BUT YOUR GRANDDAUGHTER ALREADY BAPTIZED THE NEW SHEETS YOU GOT HER FROM IKEA!

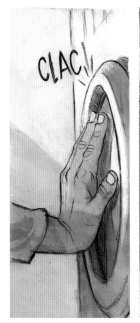

CLAC!

SO WHAT IF IT WAS A GIFT, MOM?

WET PAJAMAS? WHAT...?

NO, MOM! IN FRONT OF THE TV, SHE SPILLED A BOWL OF CEREAL...!

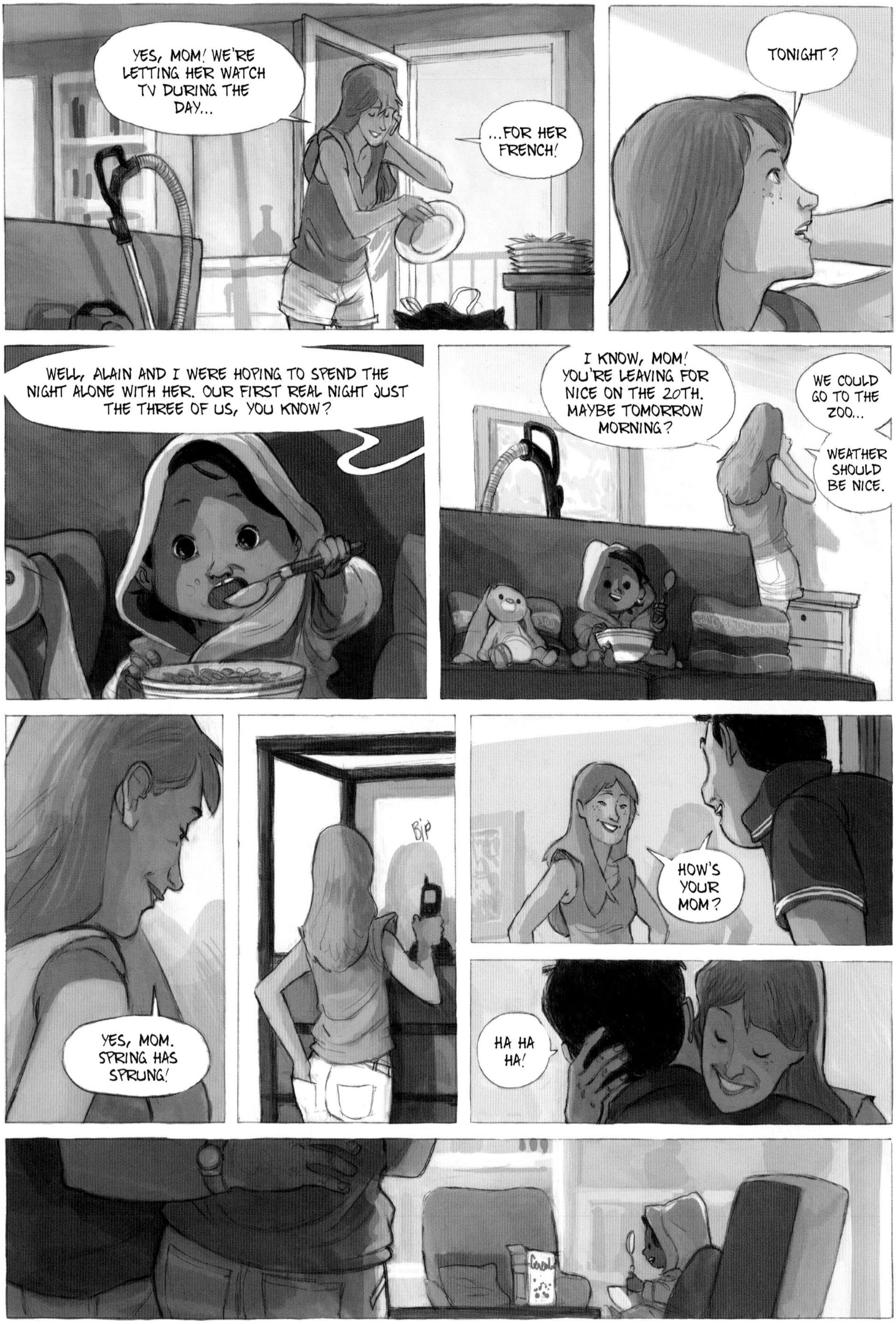
YES, MOM! WE'RE LETTING HER WATCH TV DURING THE DAY...
...FOR HER FRENCH!
TONIGHT?
WELL, ALAIN AND I WERE HOPING TO SPEND THE NIGHT ALONE WITH HER. OUR FIRST REAL NIGHT JUST THE THREE OF US, YOU KNOW?
I KNOW, MOM! YOU'RE LEAVING FOR NICE ON THE 20TH. MAYBE TOMORROW MORNING?
WE COULD GO TO THE ZOO...
WEATHER SHOULD BE NICE.
YES, MOM. SPRING HAS SPRUNG!
BIP
HOW'S YOUR MOM?
HA HA HA!

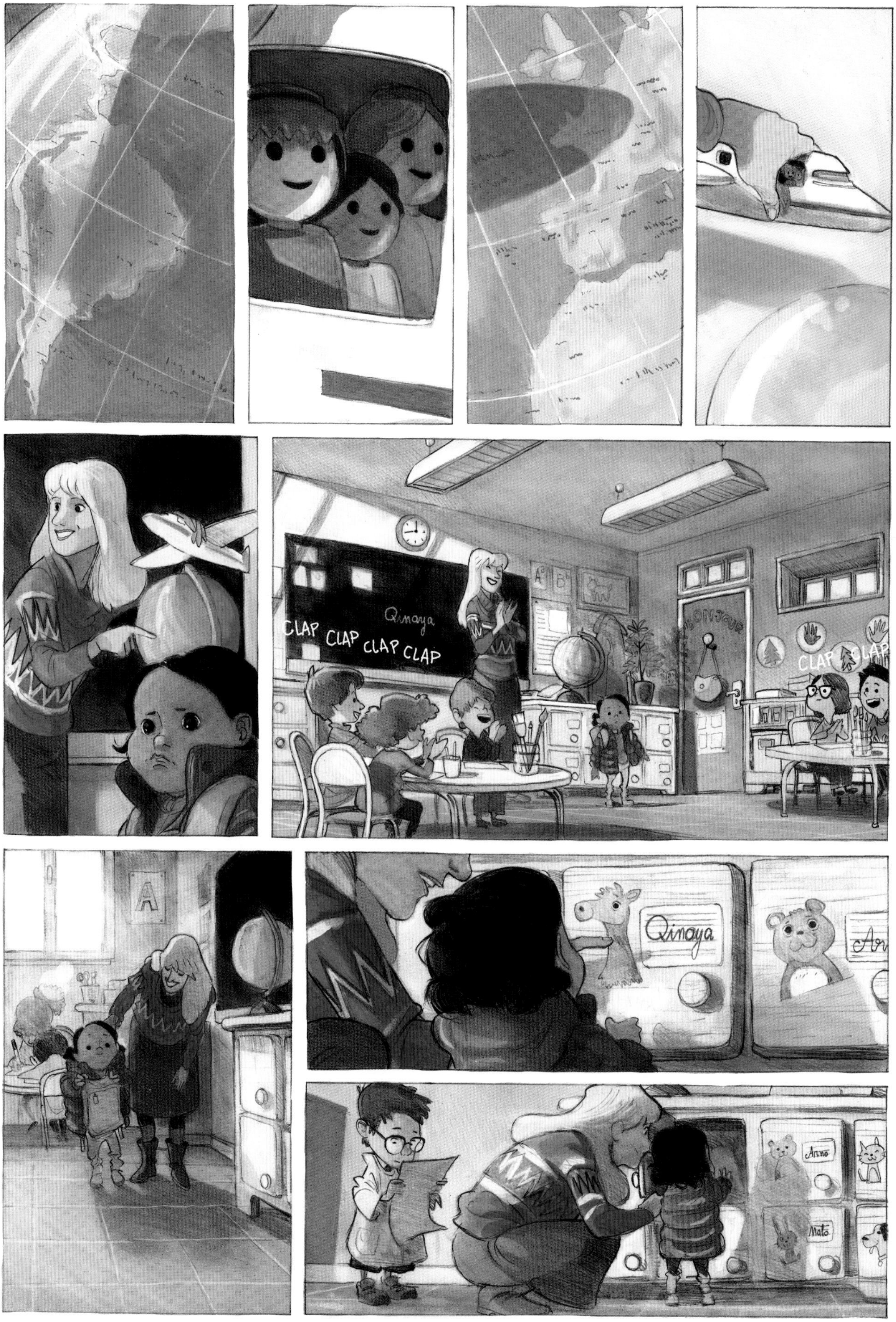

Qinaya
CLAP CLAP CLAP CLAP
BONJOUR
CLAP CLAP
Qinaya
Anno
Mato

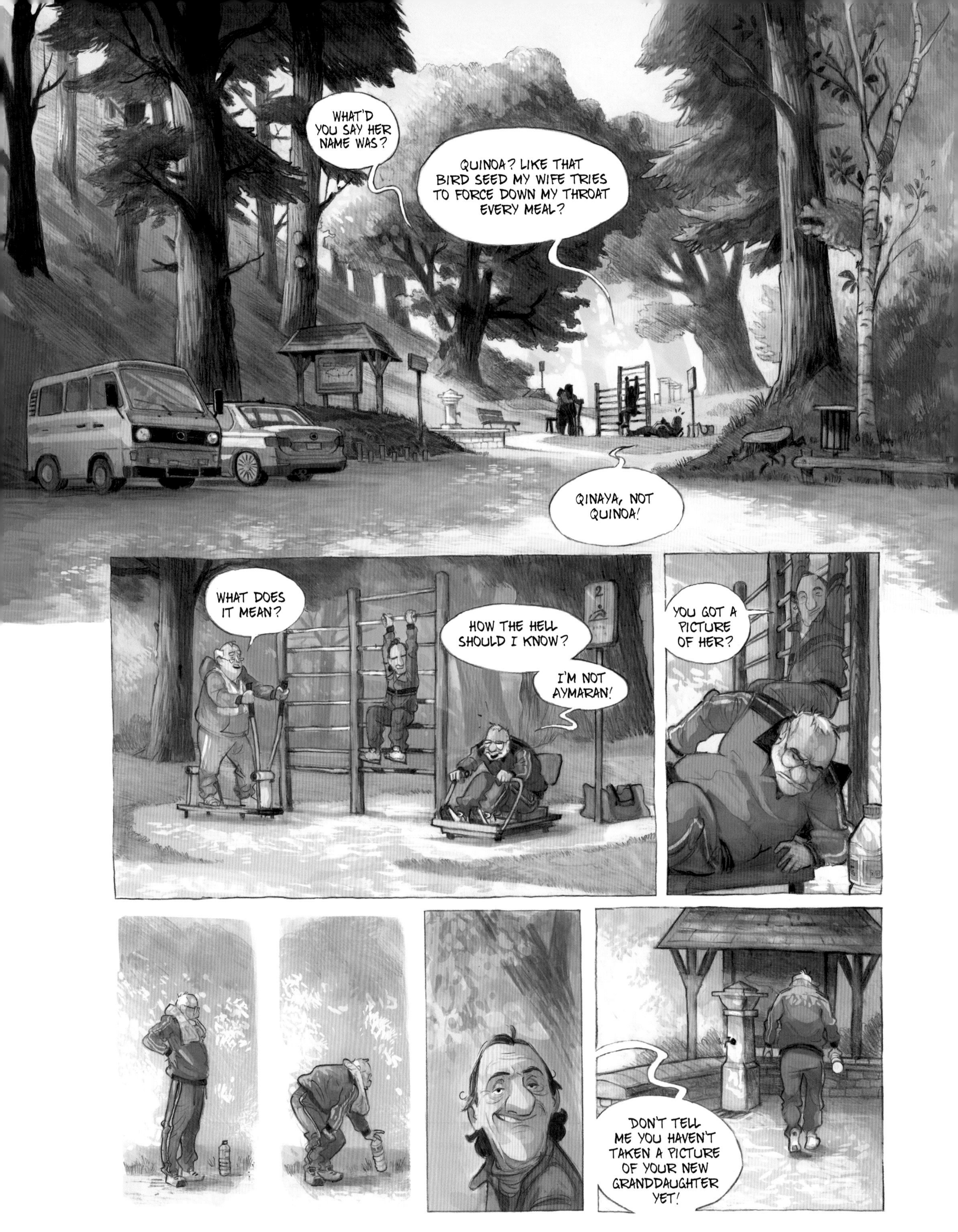
WHAT'D YOU SAY HER NAME WAS?
QUINOA? LIKE THAT BIRD SEED MY WIFE TRIES TO FORCE DOWN MY THROAT EVERY MEAL?
QINAYA, NOT QUINOA!
WHAT DOES IT MEAN?
HOW THE HELL SHOULD I KNOW?
I'M NOT AYMARAN!
YOU GOT A PICTURE OF HER?
DON'T TELL ME YOU HAVEN'T TAKEN A PICTURE OF YOUR NEW GRANDDAUGHTER YET!

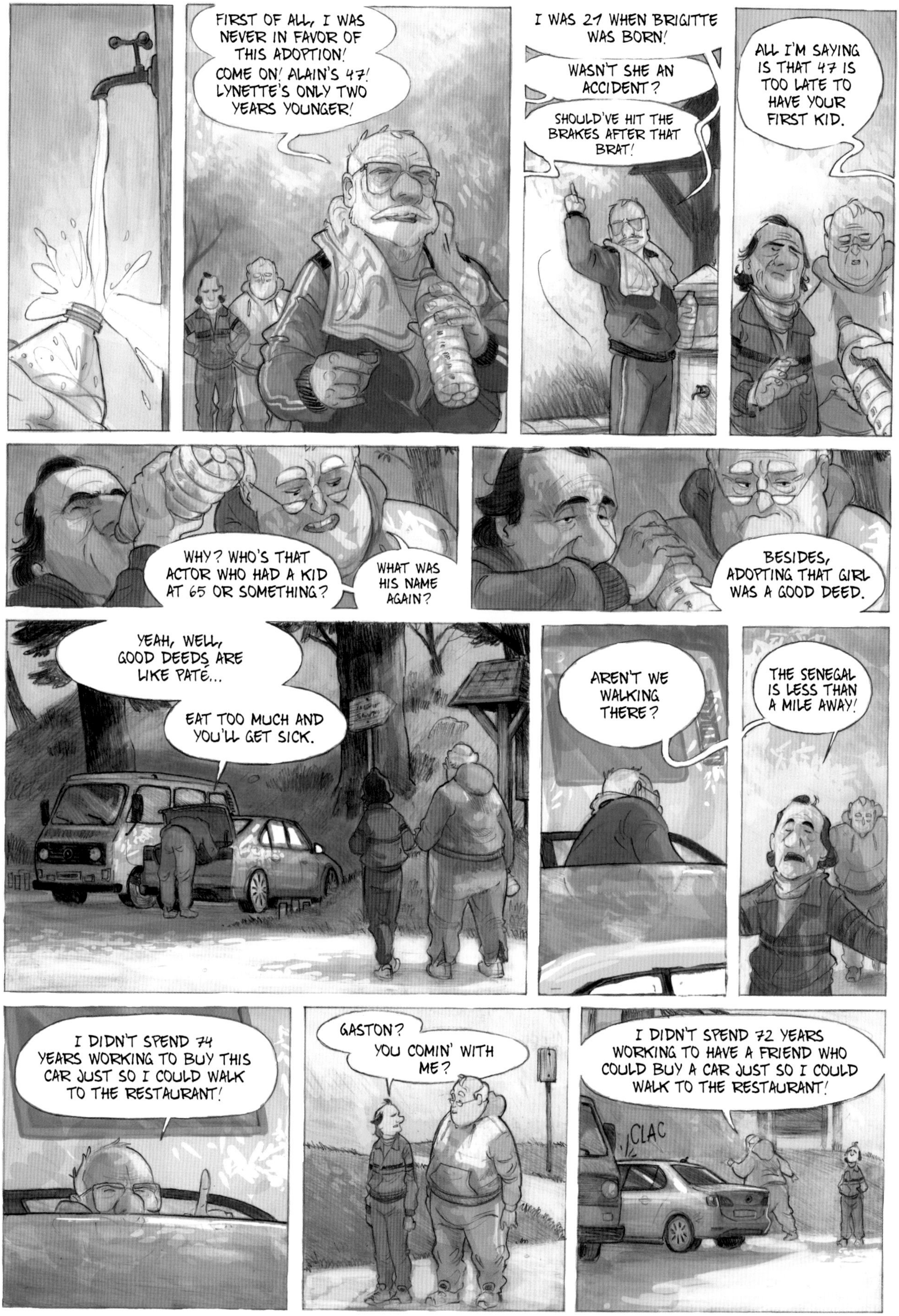
FIRST OF ALL, I WAS NEVER IN FAVOR OF THIS ADOPTION!
COME ON! ALAIN'S 47! LYNETTE'S ONLY TWO YEARS YOUNGER!
I WAS 27 WHEN BRIGITTE WAS BORN!
WASN'T SHE AN ACCIDENT?
SHOULD'VE HIT THE BRAKES AFTER THAT BRAT!
ALL I'M SAYING IS THAT 47 IS TOO LATE TO HAVE YOUR FIRST KID.
WHY? WHO'S THAT ACTOR WHO HAD A KID AT 65 OR SOMETHING?
WHAT WAS HIS NAME AGAIN?
BESIDES, ADOPTING THAT GIRL WAS A GOOD DEED.
YEAH, WELL, GOOD DEEDS ARE LIKE PATÉ...
EAT TOO MUCH AND YOU'LL GET SICK.
AREN'T WE WALKING THERE?
THE SENEGAL IS LESS THAN A MILE AWAY!
I DIDN'T SPEND 74 YEARS WORKING TO BUY THIS CAR JUST SO I COULD WALK TO THE RESTAURANT!
GASTON?
YOU COMIN' WITH ME?
I DIDN'T SPEND 72 YEARS WORKING TO HAVE A FRIEND WHO COULD BUY A CAR JUST SO I COULD WALK TO THE RESTAURANT!
CLAC

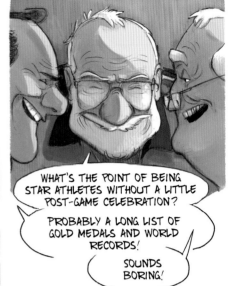

ALRIGHT, GEEGEES... ARE YA PUTTING ON EVERYTHING YA BURNT OFF?

WHAT'S THE POINT OF BEING STAR ATHLETES WITHOUT A LITTLE POST-GAME CELEBRATION?

PROBABLY A LONG LIST OF GOLD MEDALS AND WORLD RECORDS!

SOUNDS BORING!

THREE DAILY SPECIALS AND THREE DESSERTS IT IS!

ANYTHING TO DRINK WITH THAT?

A PITCHER OF--

A BOTTLE OF YOUR BEST!

GABE'S PICKIN' UP THE TAB!

HE'S A GRANDFATHER AGAIN! SINCE YESTERDAY!

OOOUUUUUUUUUH!!

COME NOW, SHOW ME A PICTURE!

HAHAH

WARF!! AAAAH PARFAIT!

BY THE WAY, LYNETTE CALLED...

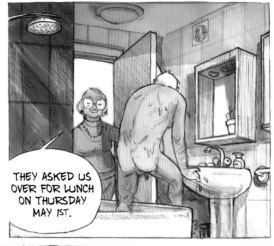

THEY ASKED US OVER FOR LUNCH ON THURSDAY MAY 1ST.

MMM, GUINEA PIG OR CEVICHE? CAN'T WAIT TO--

THE HELL IS THIS?!

OH, I BOUGHT IT FOR QUINAYA, BUT LYNETTE DOESN'T LIKE DISNEY.

IN FACT, I'M TRYING TO FIND A GIFT TO BRING HER ON THURSDAY... A PUZZLE OR PICTURE BOOK...

ANOTHER GIFT?

OH, DON'T BE A GRUMPY OLD MICHEL SIMON!

WHO?!

MICHEL SIMON, THE OLD MAN IN THAT MOVIE "THE TWO OF US"...

GRUMPY OLD MAN...?

21

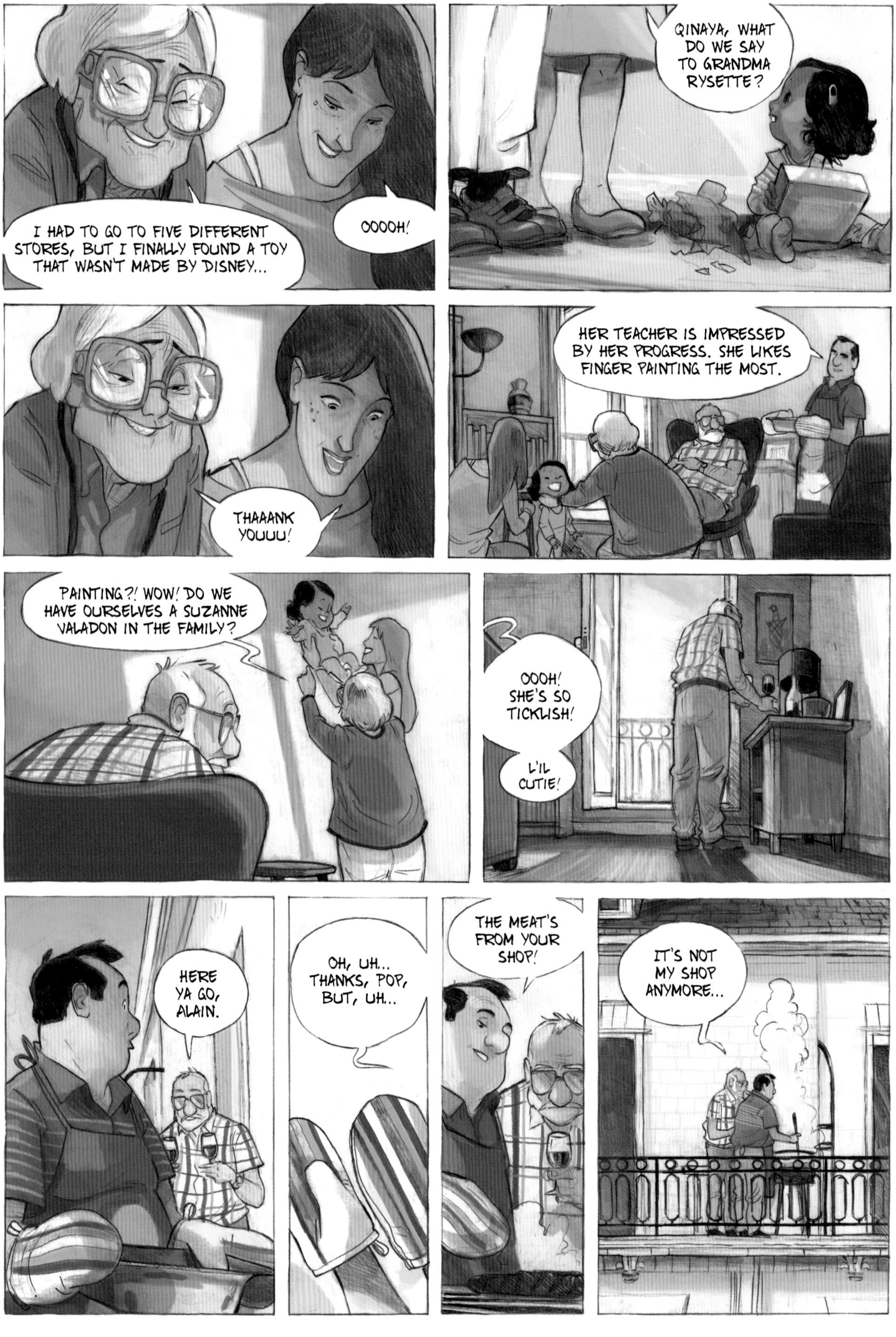
I HAD TO GO TO FIVE DIFFERENT STORES, BUT I FINALLY FOUND A TOY THAT WASN'T MADE BY DISNEY...
OOOOH!
QINAYA, WHAT DO WE SAY TO GRANDMA RYSETTE?
THAAANK YOUUU!
HER TEACHER IS IMPRESSED BY HER PROGRESS. SHE LIKES FINGER PAINTING THE MOST.
PAINTING?! WOW! DO WE HAVE OURSELVES A SUZANNE VALADON IN THE FAMILY?
OOOH! SHE'S SO TICKLISH!
L'IL CUTIE!
HERE YA GO, ALAIN.
OH, UH... THANKS, POP, BUT, UH...
THE MEAT'S FROM YOUR SHOP!
IT'S NOT MY SHOP ANYMORE...

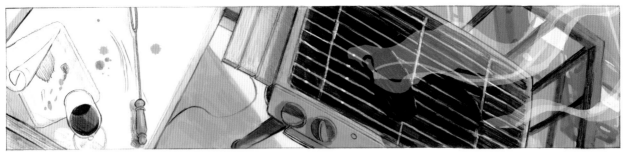

DON'T RUSH TO HELP US CLEAR THE TABLE, BOYS!

HEY, I MADE DINNER!

AND I MADE THE GUY WHO MADE DINNER!

FOUR PEOPLE IN THE KITCHEN IS TOO MANY ANYWAY!

ISN'T SHE KINDA SMALL FOR A FOUR YEAR OLD?

I MEAN... THE NEIGHBOR'S DAUGHTER JUST TURNED THREE AND SHE'S ALREADY BIGGER THAN HER...

WELL, AYMARANS RARELY BECOME NBA STARS!

23

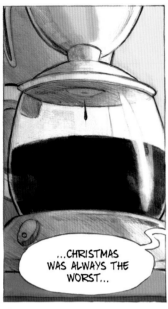

...CHRISTMAS WAS ALWAYS THE WORST...

...WHAT'S THE POINT OF CHRISTMAS WITHOUT ANY KIDS TO SHARE IT WITH?

WELL, NOW YOU CAN START CATCHING UP ON ALL THOSE HOLIDAYS!

OH! I ALMOST FORGOT! THEY HAVE THE DAY OFF FROM SCHOOL TOMORROW. YOU WANNA TAKE HER FOR THE DAY?

WOULD WE?! OF COURSE!

THANKS, THAT'LL SAVE US HAVING TO FIND A BABYSITTER. WE DON'T GET THE HOLIDAY OFF AT XANTHOS.

AND WE BOTH USED UP OUR VACATION TIME WITH THE TRIP TO PERU.

OH, WAIT! I HAVE A HAIR APPOINTMENT! THE LETO'S OLDEST DAUGHTER, YOU REMEMBER, FROM THE BOOKSTORE NEXT TO YOUR DAD'S SHOP, SHE'S GETTING MARRIED SATURDAY...

HONEY, CAN YOU WATCH THE GIRL FOR A COUPLE OF HOURS?

ME? BUT... IT'S... FRIDAY IS GEEGEE DAY!

AND I HAVEN'T BABYSAT A KID IN YEARS!

OH, IT'S LIKE RIDING BIKE. YOU NEVER FORGET HOW!

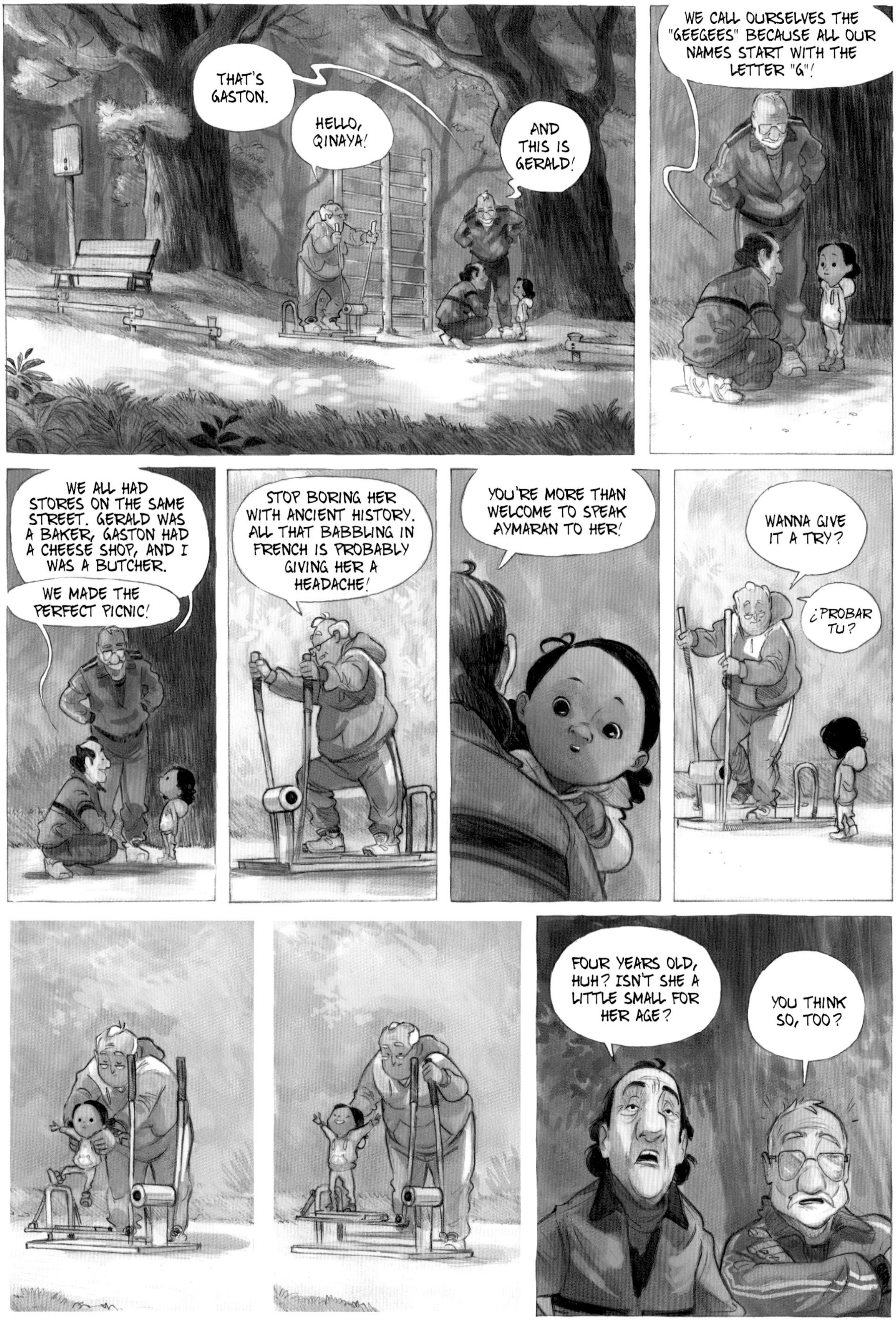
THAT'S GASTON.
HELLO, QINAYA!
AND THIS IS GERALD!
WE CALL OURSELVES THE "GEEGEES" BECAUSE ALL OUR NAMES START WITH THE LETTER "G"!
WE ALL HAD STORES ON THE SAME STREET. GERALD WAS A BAKER, GASTON HAD A CHEESE SHOP, AND I WAS A BUTCHER.
WE MADE THE PERFECT PICNIC!
STOP BORING HER WITH ANCIENT HISTORY. ALL THAT BABBLING IN FRENCH IS PROBABLY GIVING HER A HEADACHE!
YOU'RE MORE THAN WELCOME TO SPEAK AYMARAN TO HER!
WANNA GIVE IT A TRY?
¿PROBAR TU?
FOUR YEARS OLD, HUH? ISN'T SHE A LITTLE SMALL FOR HER AGE?
YOU THINK SO, TOO?

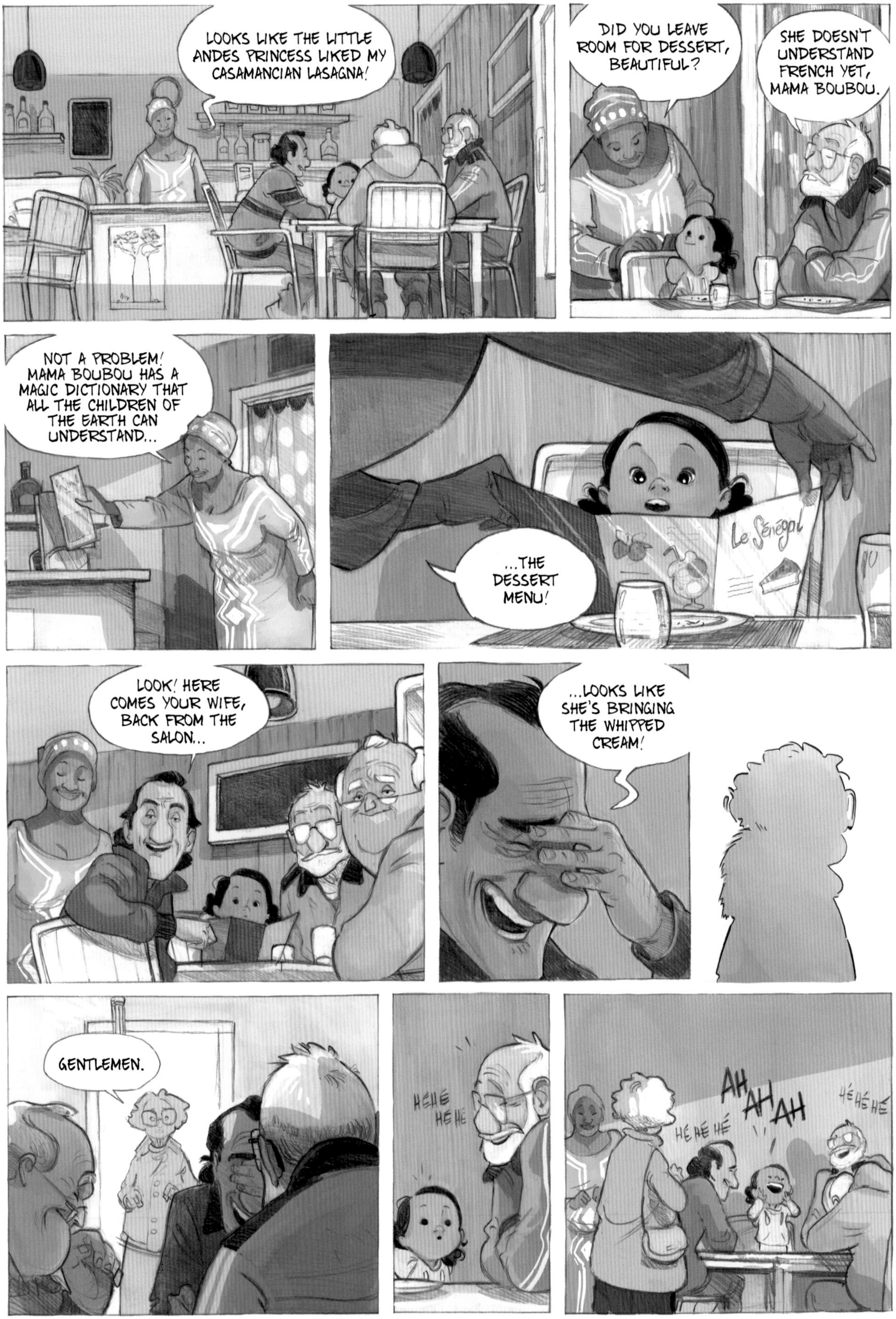
LOOKS LIKE THE LITTLE ANDES PRINCESS LIKED MY CASAMANCIAN LASAGNA!
DID YOU LEAVE ROOM FOR DESSERT, BEAUTIFUL?
SHE DOESN'T UNDERSTAND FRENCH YET, MAMA BOUBOU.
NOT A PROBLEM! MAMA BOUBOU HAS A MAGIC DICTIONARY THAT ALL THE CHILDREN OF THE EARTH CAN UNDERSTAND...
Le Sénégal
...THE DESSERT MENU!
LOOK! HERE COMES YOUR WIFE, BACK FROM THE SALON...
...LOOKS LIKE SHE'S BRINGING THE WHIPPED CREAM!
GENTLEMEN.
HÉHÉ HÉHÉ
AH AH AH
HÉ HÉ HÉ
HÉ HÉ HÉ

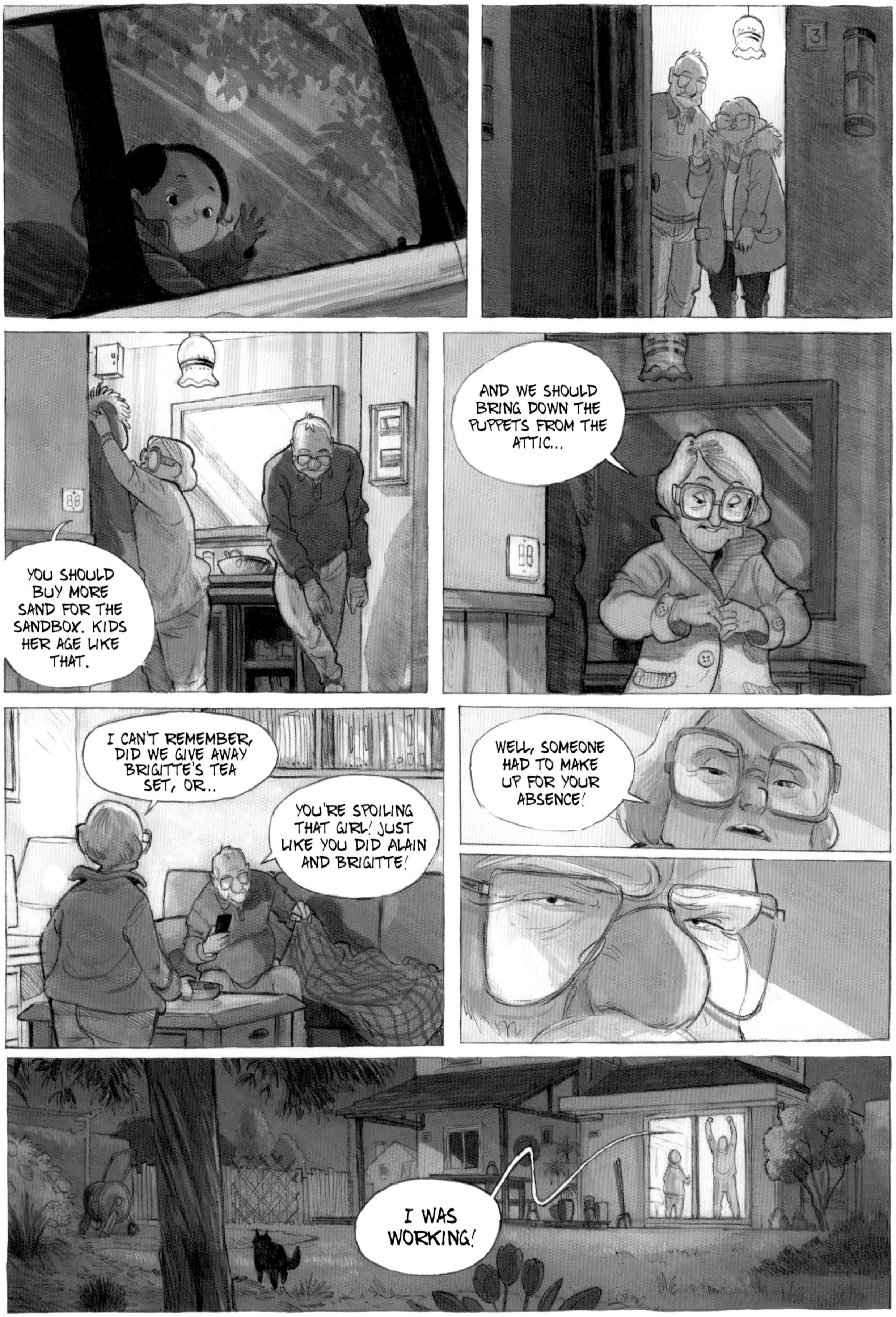
YOU SHOULD BUY MORE SAND FOR THE SANDBOX. KIDS HER AGE LIKE THAT.
AND WE SHOULD BRING DOWN THE PUPPETS FROM THE ATTIC...
I CAN'T REMEMBER, DID WE GIVE AWAY BRIGITTE'S TEA SET, OR..
YOU'RE SPOILING THAT GIRL! JUST LIKE YOU DID ALAIN AND BRIGITTE!
WELL, SOMEONE HAD TO MAKE UP FOR YOUR ABSENCE!
I WAS WORKING!

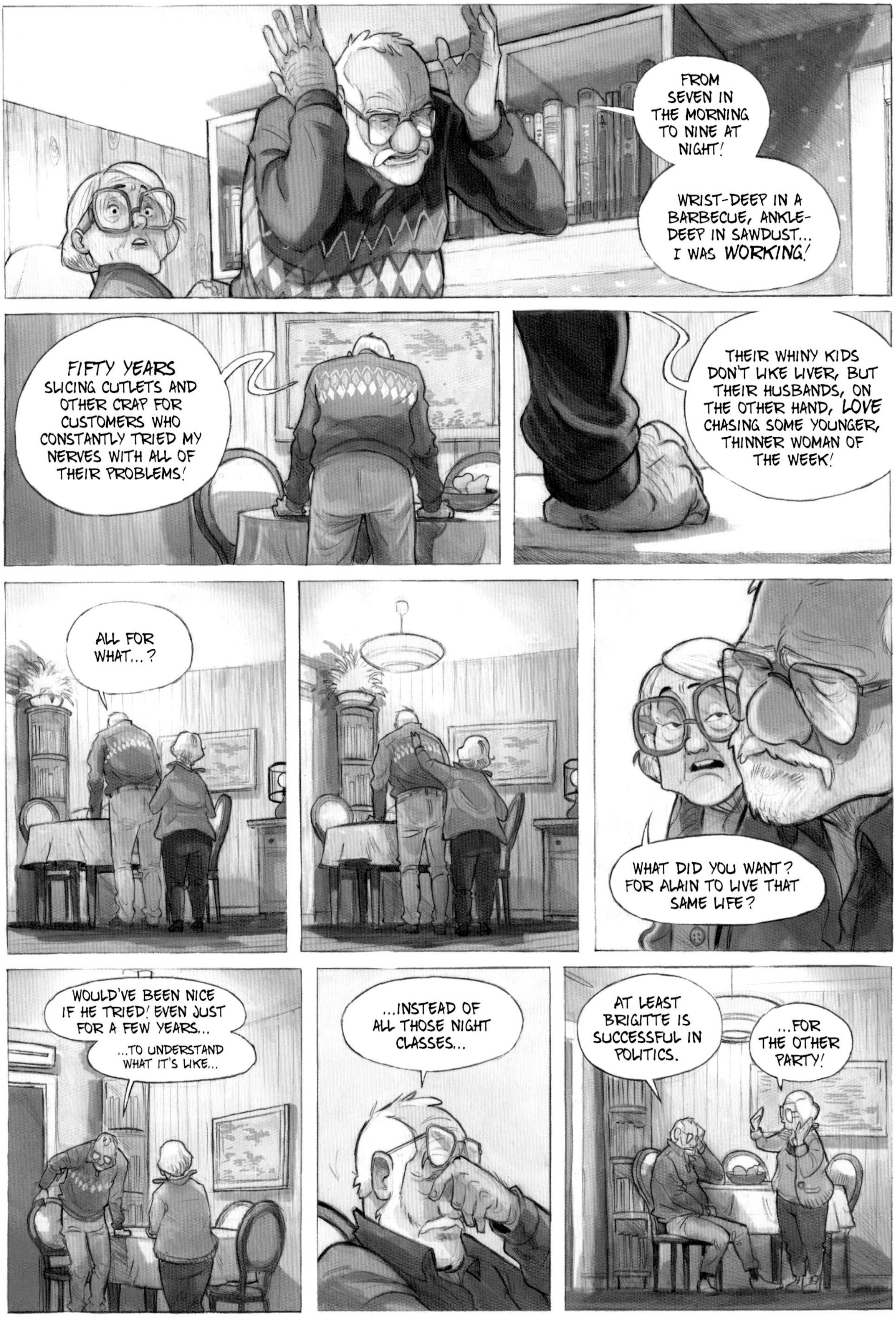
FROM SEVEN IN THE MORNING TO NINE AT NIGHT!
WRIST-DEEP IN A BARBECUE, ANKLE-DEEP IN SAWDUST... I WAS WORKING!
FIFTY YEARS SLICING CUTLETS AND OTHER CRAP FOR CUSTOMERS WHO CONSTANTLY TRIED MY NERVES WITH ALL OF THEIR PROBLEMS!
THEIR WHINY KIDS DON'T LIKE LIVER, BUT THEIR HUSBANDS, ON THE OTHER HAND, LOVE CHASING SOME YOUNGER, THINNER WOMAN OF THE WEEK!
ALL FOR WHAT...?
WHAT DID YOU WANT? FOR ALAIN TO LIVE THAT SAME LIFE?
WOULD'VE BEEN NICE IF HE TRIED! EVEN JUST FOR A FEW YEARS...
...TO UNDERSTAND WHAT IT'S LIKE...
...INSTEAD OF ALL THOSE NIGHT CLASSES...
AT LEAST BRIGITTE IS SUCCESSFUL IN POLITICS.
...FOR THE OTHER PARTY!

A BROKER FOR XANTHOS INSURANCE...

THAT'S A LIFE?!

YOUR NOSE BURIED IN PAPERWORK ALL DAY?

I DUNNO...

THAT'S NOT REAL LIFE. IT'S TOO... CLEAN!

PAPER'S FOR WRAPPING MEAT!

GABRIEL...

ALAIN? A BUTCHER?

YOU KNOW OUR SON COULD NEVER GET HIS HANDS DIRTY.

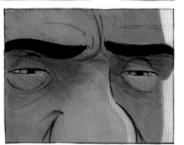

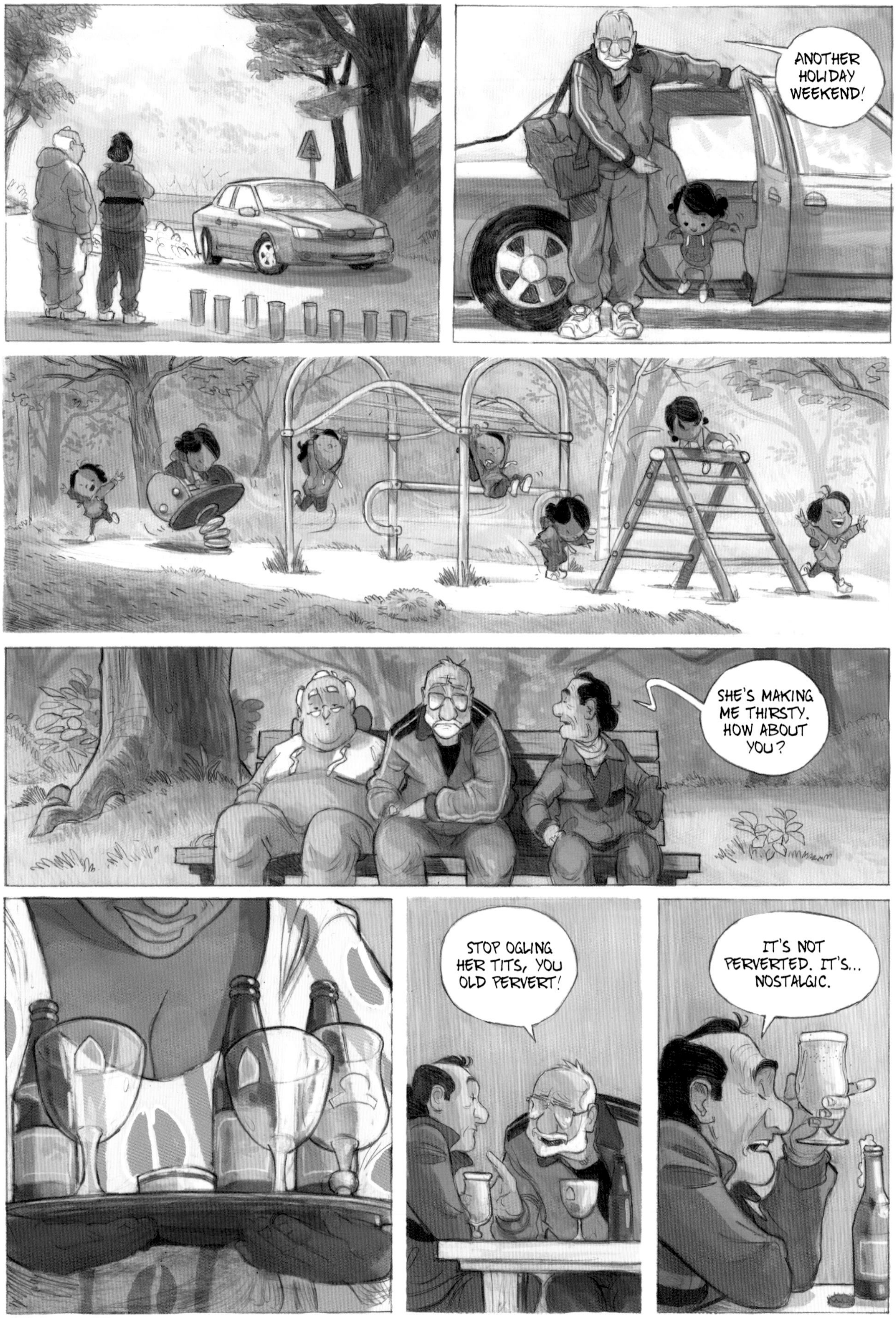
ANOTHER HOLIDAY WEEKEND!
SHE'S MAKING ME THIRSTY. HOW ABOUT YOU?
STOP OGLING HER TITS, YOU OLD PERVERT!
IT'S NOT PERVERTED. IT'S... NOSTALGIC.

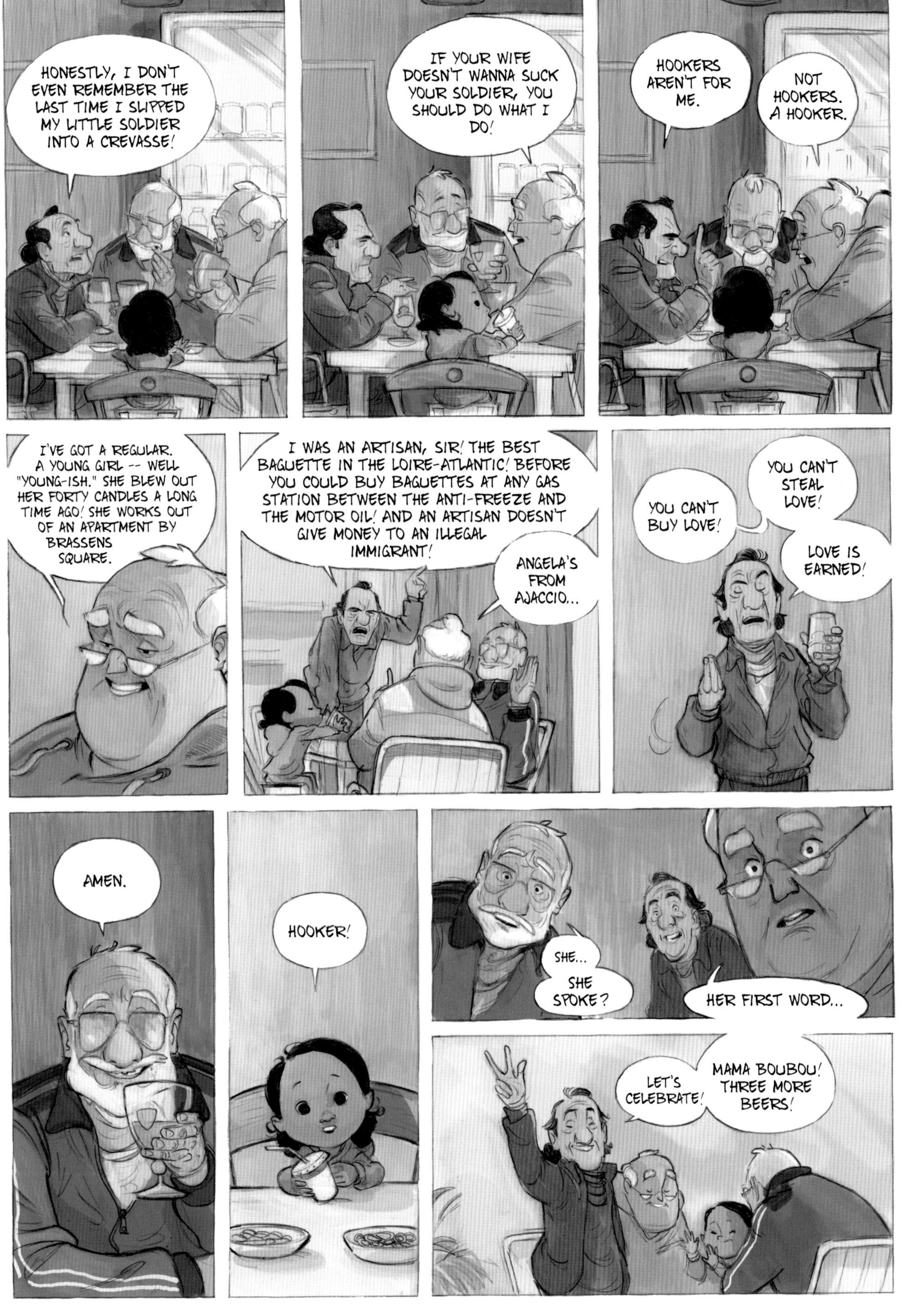
HONESTLY, I DON'T EVEN REMEMBER THE LAST TIME I SLIPPED MY LITTLE SOLDIER INTO A CREVASSE!
IF YOUR WIFE DOESN'T WANNA SUCK YOUR SOLDIER, YOU SHOULD DO WHAT I DO!
HOOKERS AREN'T FOR ME.
NOT HOOKERS. A HOOKER.
I'VE GOT A REGULAR. A YOUNG GIRL -- WELL "YOUNG-ISH." SHE BLEW OUT HER FORTY CANDLES A LONG TIME AGO! SHE WORKS OUT OF AN APARTMENT BY BRASSENS SQUARE.
I WAS AN ARTISAN, SIR! THE BEST BAGUETTE IN THE LOIRE-ATLANTIC! BEFORE YOU COULD BUY BAGUETTES AT ANY GAS STATION BETWEEN THE ANTI-FREEZE AND THE MOTOR OIL! AND AN ARTISAN DOESN'T GIVE MONEY TO AN ILLEGAL IMMIGRANT!
ANGELA'S FROM AJACCIO...
YOU CAN'T BUY LOVE!
YOU CAN'T STEAL LOVE!
LOVE IS EARNED!
AMEN.
HOOKER!
SHE...
SHE SPOKE?
HER FIRST WORD...
LET'S CELEBRATE!
MAMA BOUBOU! THREE MORE BEERS!

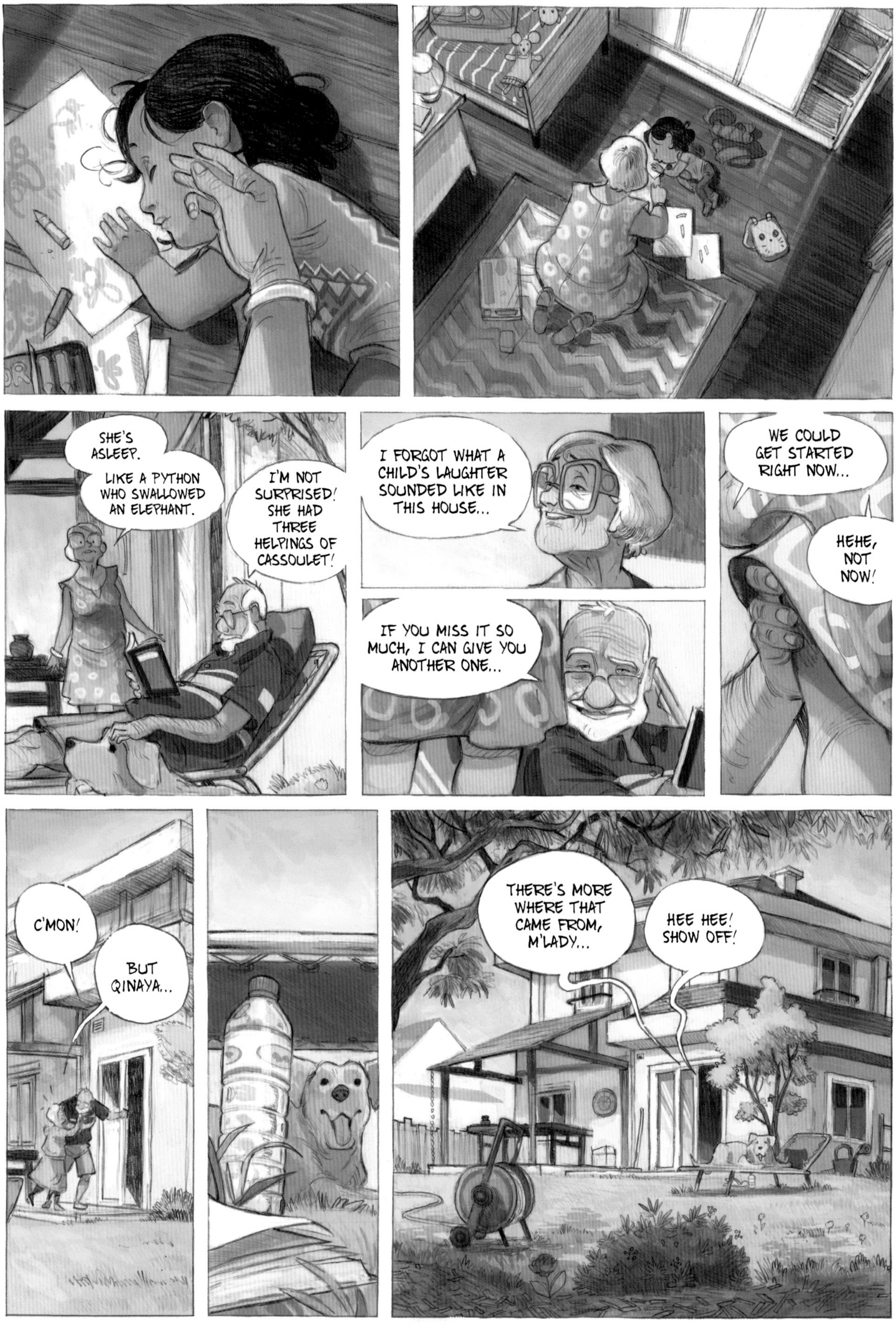
SHE'S ASLEEP.
LIKE A PYTHON WHO SWALLOWED AN ELEPHANT.
I'M NOT SURPRISED! SHE HAD THREE HELPINGS OF CASSOULET!
I FORGOT WHAT A CHILD'S LAUGHTER SOUNDED LIKE IN THIS HOUSE...
IF YOU MISS IT SO MUCH, I CAN GIVE YOU ANOTHER ONE...
WE COULD GET STARTED RIGHT NOW...
HEHE, NOT NOW!
C'MON!
BUT QINAYA...
THERE'S MORE WHERE THAT CAME FROM, M'LADY...
HEE HEE! SHOW OFF!

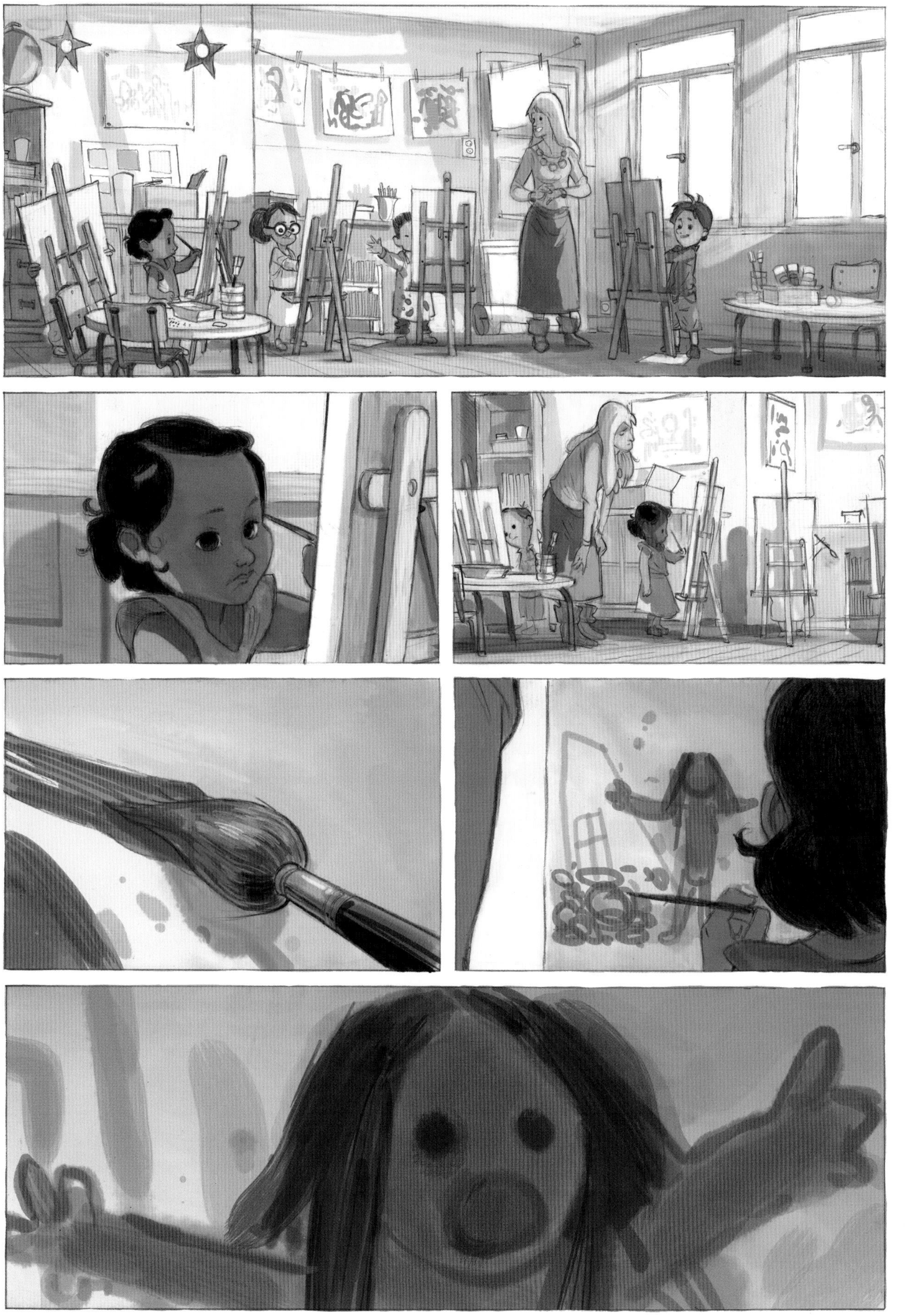

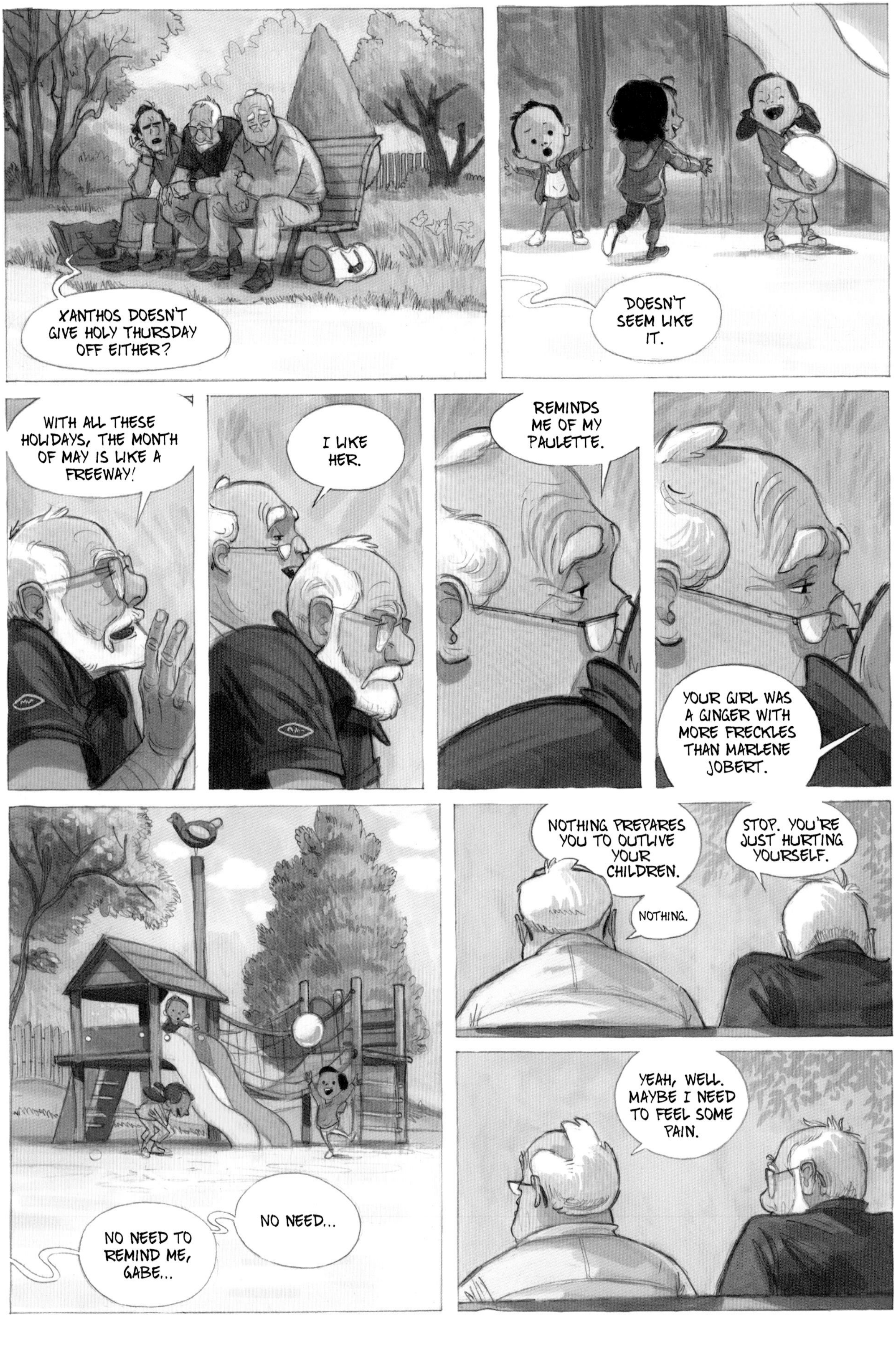
XANTHOS DOESN'T GIVE HOLY THURSDAY OFF EITHER?
DOESN'T SEEM LIKE IT.
WITH ALL THESE HOLIDAYS, THE MONTH OF MAY IS LIKE A FREEWAY!
I LIKE HER.
REMINDS ME OF MY PAULETTE.
YOUR GIRL WAS A GINGER WITH MORE FRECKLES THAN MARLENE JOBERT.
NO NEED TO REMIND ME, GABE...
NO NEED...
NOTHING PREPARES YOU TO OUTLIVE YOUR CHILDREN.
NOTHING.
STOP. YOU'RE JUST HURTING YOURSELF.
YEAH, WELL. MAYBE I NEED TO FEEL SOME PAIN.

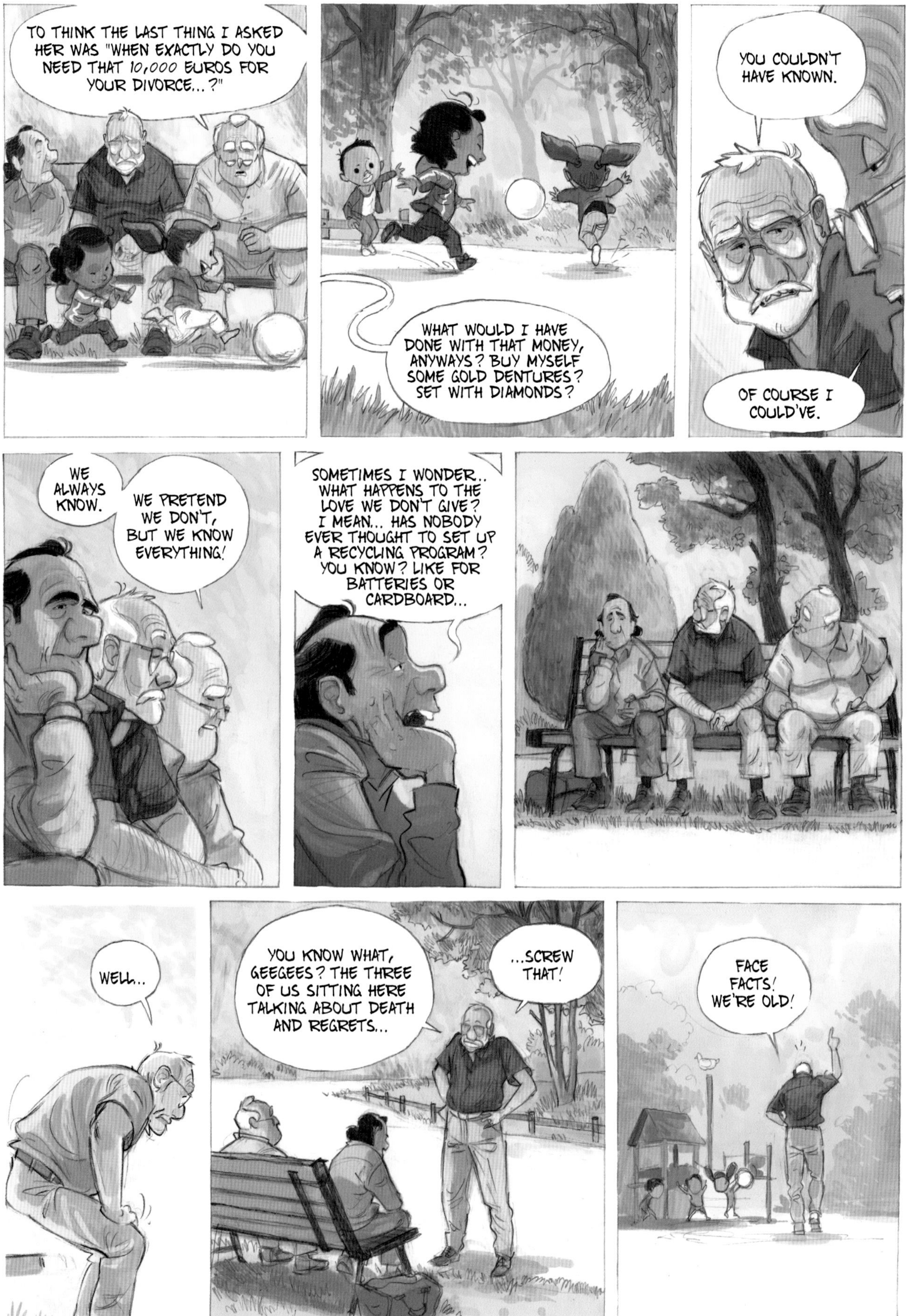
TO THINK THE LAST THING I ASKED HER WAS "WHEN EXACTLY DO YOU NEED THAT 10,000 EUROS FOR YOUR DIVORCE...?"
WHAT WOULD I HAVE DONE WITH THAT MONEY, ANYWAYS? BUY MYSELF SOME GOLD DENTURES? SET WITH DIAMONDS?
YOU COULDN'T HAVE KNOWN.
OF COURSE I COULD'VE.
WE ALWAYS KNOW.
WE PRETEND WE DON'T, BUT WE KNOW EVERYTHING!
SOMETIMES I WONDER.. WHAT HAPPENS TO THE LOVE WE DON'T GIVE? I MEAN... HAS NOBODY EVER THOUGHT TO SET UP A RECYCLING PROGRAM? YOU KNOW? LIKE FOR BATTERIES OR CARDBOARD...
WELL...
YOU KNOW WHAT, GEEGEES? THE THREE OF US SITTING HERE TALKING ABOUT DEATH AND REGRETS...
...SCREW THAT!
FACE FACTS! WE'RE OLD!

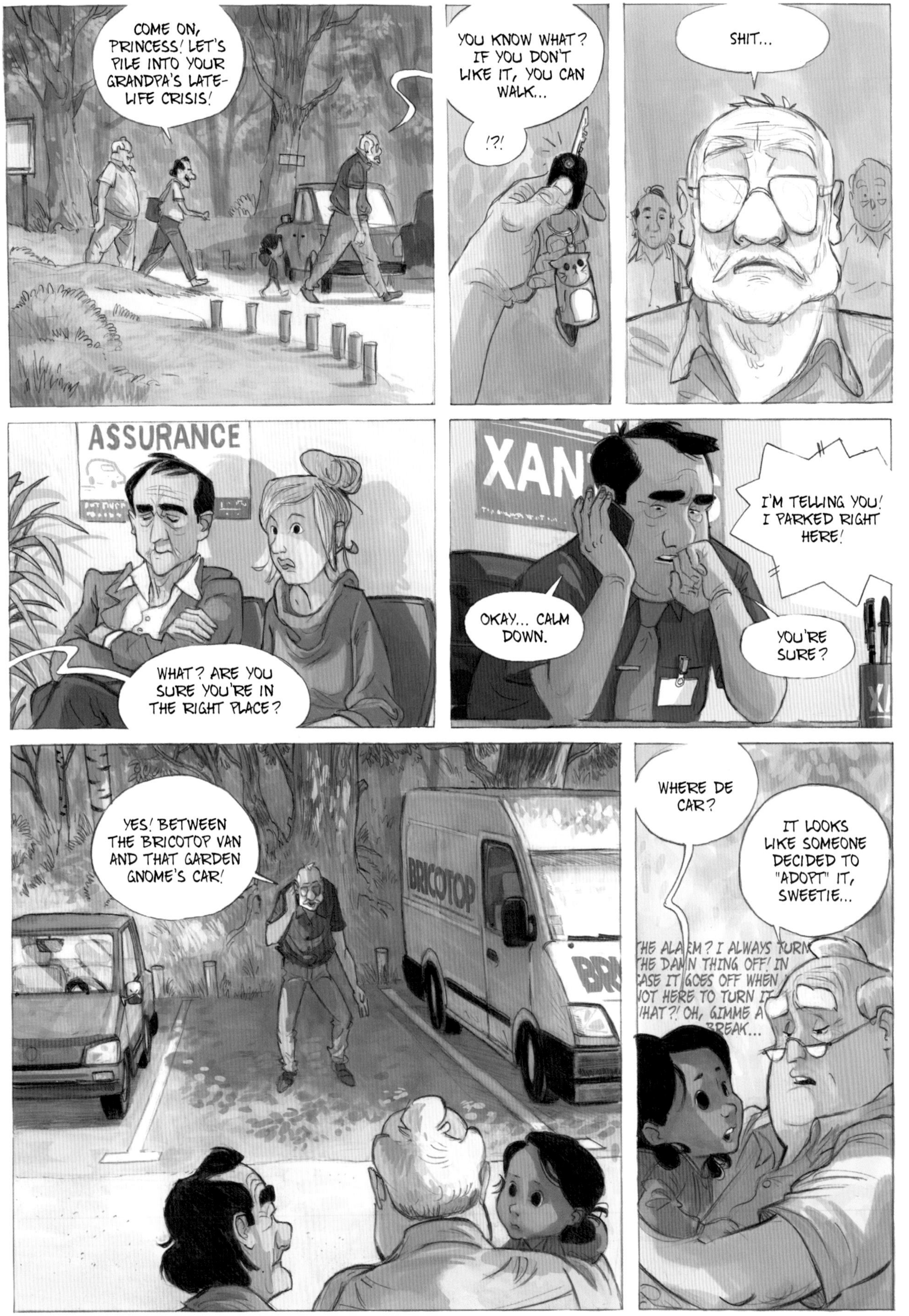

COME ON, PRINCESS! LET'S PILE INTO YOUR GRANDPA'S LATE-LIFE CRISIS!
YOU KNOW WHAT? IF YOU DON'T LIKE IT, YOU CAN WALK...
!?!
SHIT...
ASSURANCE
WHAT? ARE YOU SURE YOU'RE IN THE RIGHT PLACE?
XAN
I'M TELLING YOU! I PARKED RIGHT HERE!
OKAY... CALM DOWN.
YOU'RE SURE?
YES! BETWEEN THE BRICOTOP VAN AND THAT GARDEN GNOME'S CAR!
BRICOTOP
WHERE DE CAR?
IT LOOKS LIKE SOMEONE DECIDED TO "ADOPT" IT, SWEETIE...
THE ALARM? I ALWAYS TURN THE DAMN THING OFF! IN CASE IT GOES OFF WHEN NOT HERE TO TURN IT WHAT?! OH, GIMME A BREAK...

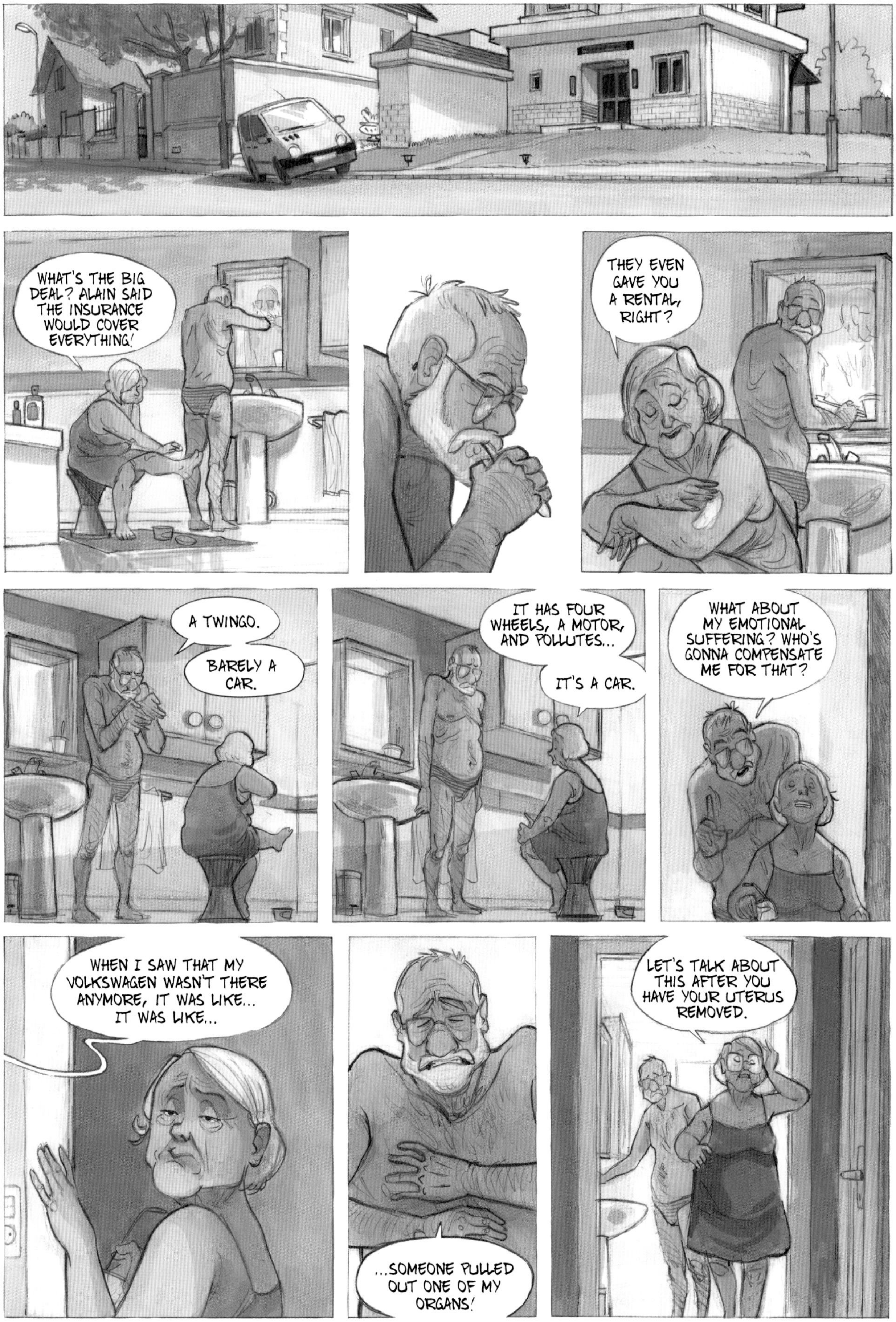
WHAT'S THE BIG DEAL? ALAIN SAID THE INSURANCE WOULD COVER EVERYTHING!
THEY EVEN GAVE YOU A RENTAL, RIGHT?
A TWINGO.
BARELY A CAR.
IT HAS FOUR WHEELS, A MOTOR, AND POLLUTES...
IT'S A CAR.
WHAT ABOUT MY EMOTIONAL SUFFERING? WHO'S GONNA COMPENSATE ME FOR THAT?
WHEN I SAW THAT MY VOLKSWAGEN WASN'T THERE ANYMORE, IT WAS LIKE... IT WAS LIKE...
...SOMEONE PULLED OUT ONE OF MY ORGANS!
LET'S TALK ABOUT THIS AFTER YOU HAVE YOUR UTERUS REMOVED.

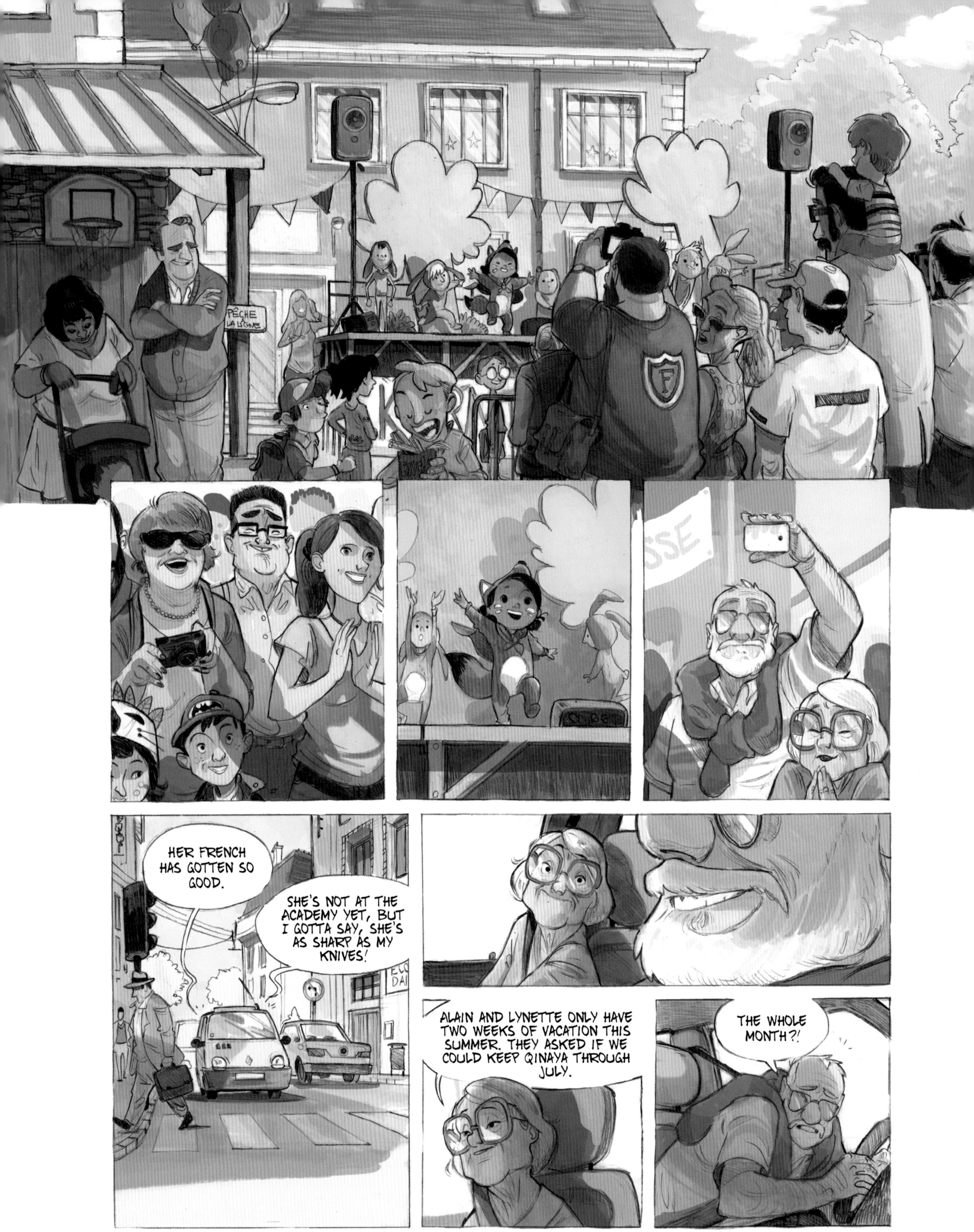
HER FRENCH HAS GOTTEN SO GOOD.
SHE'S NOT AT THE ACADEMY YET, BUT I GOTTA SAY, SHE'S AS SHARP AS MY KNIVES!
ALAIN AND LYNETTE ONLY HAVE TWO WEEKS OF VACATION THIS SUMMER. THEY ASKED IF WE COULD KEEP QINAYA THROUGH JULY.
THE WHOLE MONTH?!

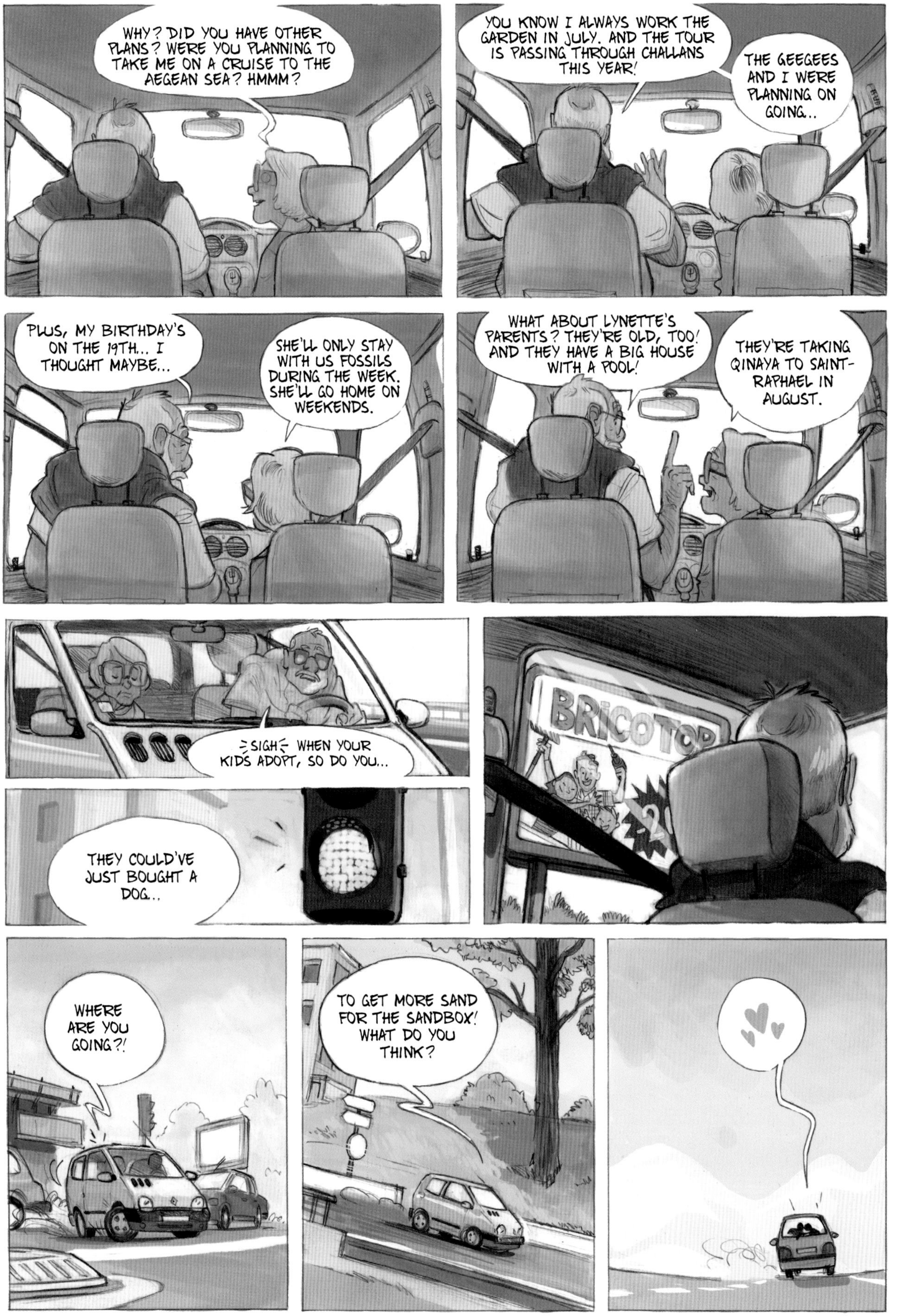
WHY? DID YOU HAVE OTHER PLANS? WERE YOU PLANNING TO TAKE ME ON A CRUISE TO THE AEGEAN SEA? HMMM?
YOU KNOW I ALWAYS WORK THE GARDEN IN JULY. AND THE TOUR IS PASSING THROUGH CHALLANS THIS YEAR!
THE GEEGEES AND I WERE PLANNING ON GOING..
PLUS, MY BIRTHDAY'S ON THE 19TH... I THOUGHT MAYBE...
SHE'LL ONLY STAY WITH US FOSSILS DURING THE WEEK. SHE'LL GO HOME ON WEEKENDS.
WHAT ABOUT LYNETTE'S PARENTS? THEY'RE OLD, TOO! AND THEY HAVE A BIG HOUSE WITH A POOL!
THEY'RE TAKING QINAYA TO SAINT-RAPHAEL IN AUGUST.
=SIGH= WHEN YOUR KIDS ADOPT, SO DO YOU...
BRICOTOP
THEY COULD'VE JUST BOUGHT A DOG..
WHERE ARE YOU GOING?!
TO GET MORE SAND FOR THE SANDBOX! WHAT DO YOU THINK?

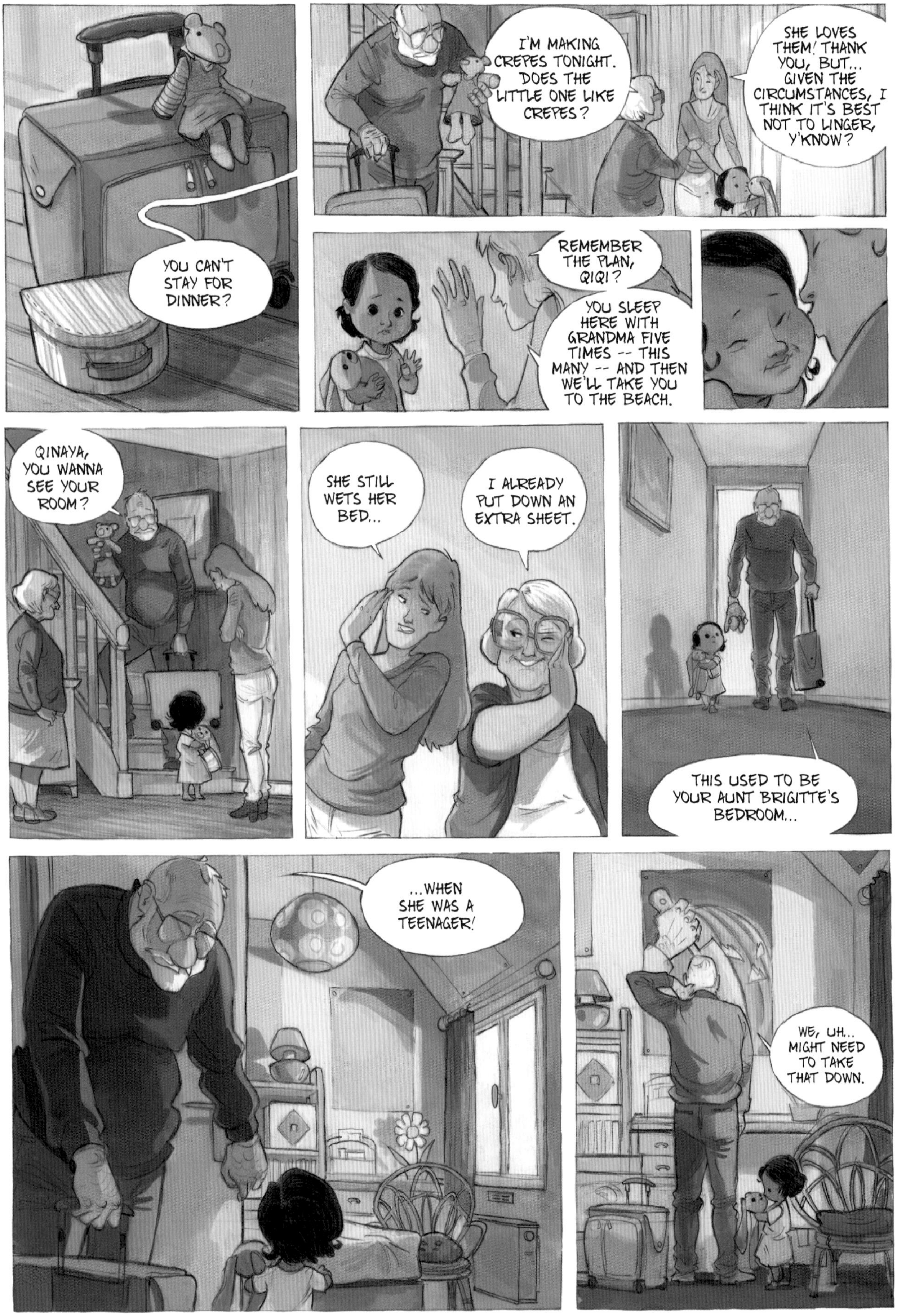
YOU CAN'T STAY FOR DINNER?
I'M MAKING CREPES TONIGHT. DOES THE LITTLE ONE LIKE CREPES?
SHE LOVES THEM! THANK YOU, BUT... GIVEN THE CIRCUMSTANCES, I THINK IT'S BEST NOT TO LINGER, Y'KNOW?
REMEMBER THE PLAN, QIQI?
YOU SLEEP HERE WITH GRANDMA FIVE TIMES -- THIS MANY -- AND THEN WE'LL TAKE YOU TO THE BEACH.
QINAYA, YOU WANNA SEE YOUR ROOM?
SHE STILL WETS HER BED...
I ALREADY PUT DOWN AN EXTRA SHEET.
THIS USED TO BE YOUR AUNT BRIGITTE'S BEDROOM...
...WHEN SHE WAS A TEENAGER!
WE, UH... MIGHT NEED TO TAKE THAT DOWN.

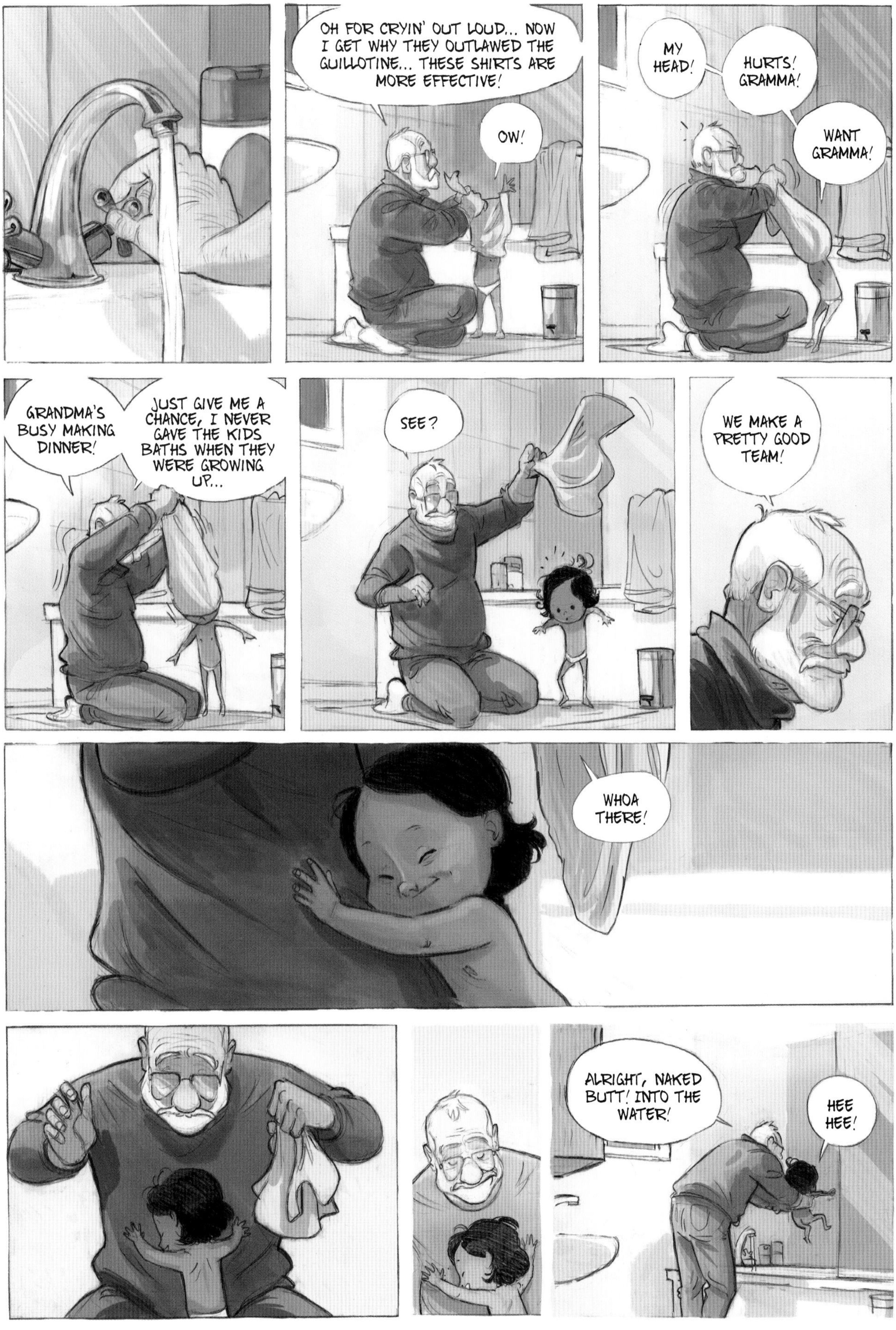

OH FOR CRYIN' OUT LOUD... NOW I GET WHY THEY OUTLAWED THE GUILLOTINE... THESE SHIRTS ARE MORE EFFECTIVE!
OW!
MY HEAD!
HURTS! GRAMMA!
WANT GRAMMA!
GRANDMA'S BUSY MAKING DINNER!
JUST GIVE ME A CHANCE, I NEVER GAVE THE KIDS BATHS WHEN THEY WERE GROWING UP...
SEE?
WE MAKE A PRETTY GOOD TEAM!
WHOA THERE!
ALRIGHT, NAKED BUTT! INTO THE WATER!
HEE HEE!

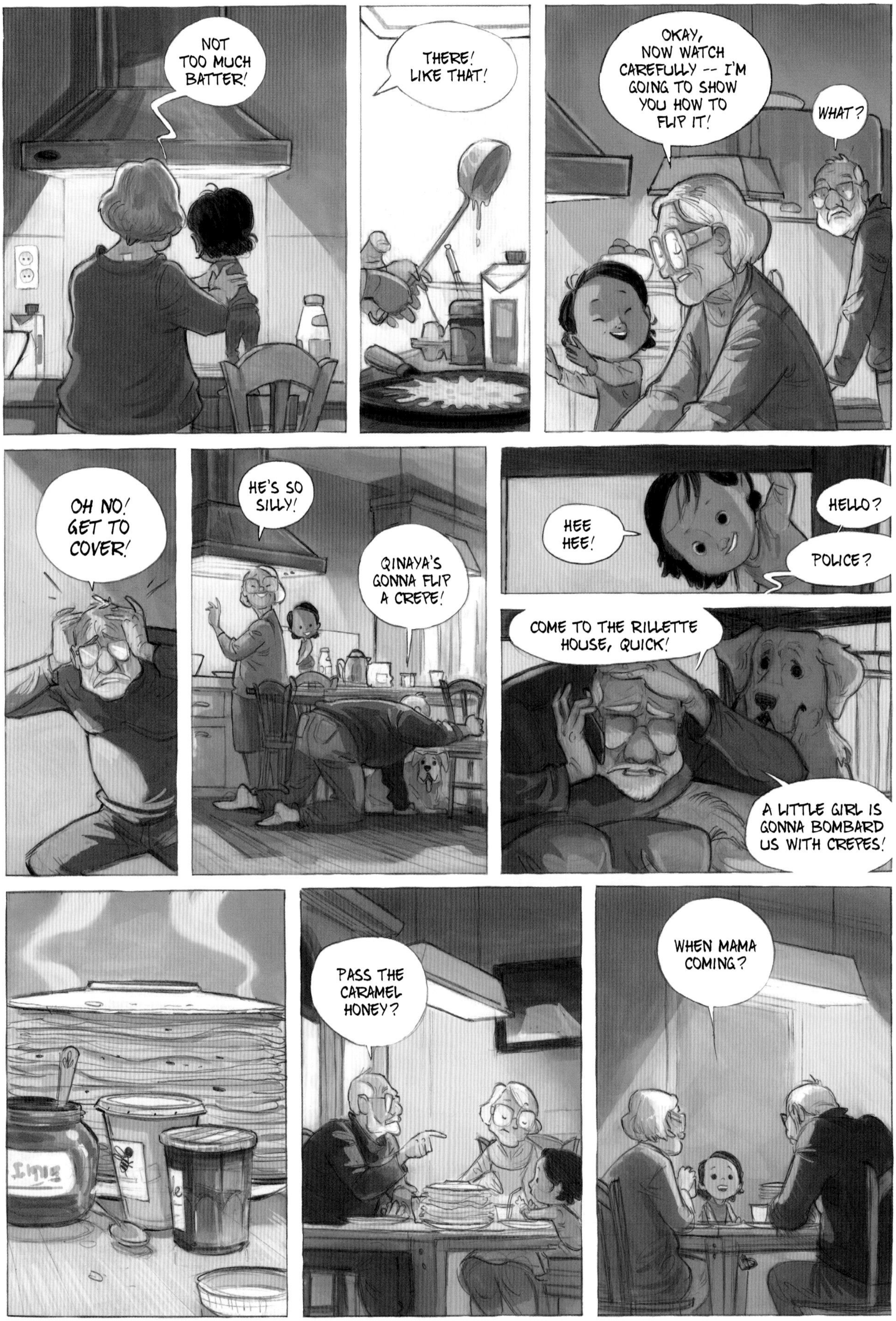
NOT TOO MUCH BATTER!
THERE! LIKE THAT!
OKAY, NOW WATCH CAREFULLY -- I'M GOING TO SHOW YOU HOW TO FLIP IT!
WHAT?
OH NO! GET TO COVER!
HE'S SO SILLY!
QINAYA'S GONNA FLIP A CREPE!
HEE HEE!
HELLO?
POLICE?
COME TO THE RILLETTE HOUSE, QUICK!
A LITTLE GIRL IS GONNA BOMBARD US WITH CREPES!
PASS THE CARAMEL HONEY?
WHEN MAMA COMING?

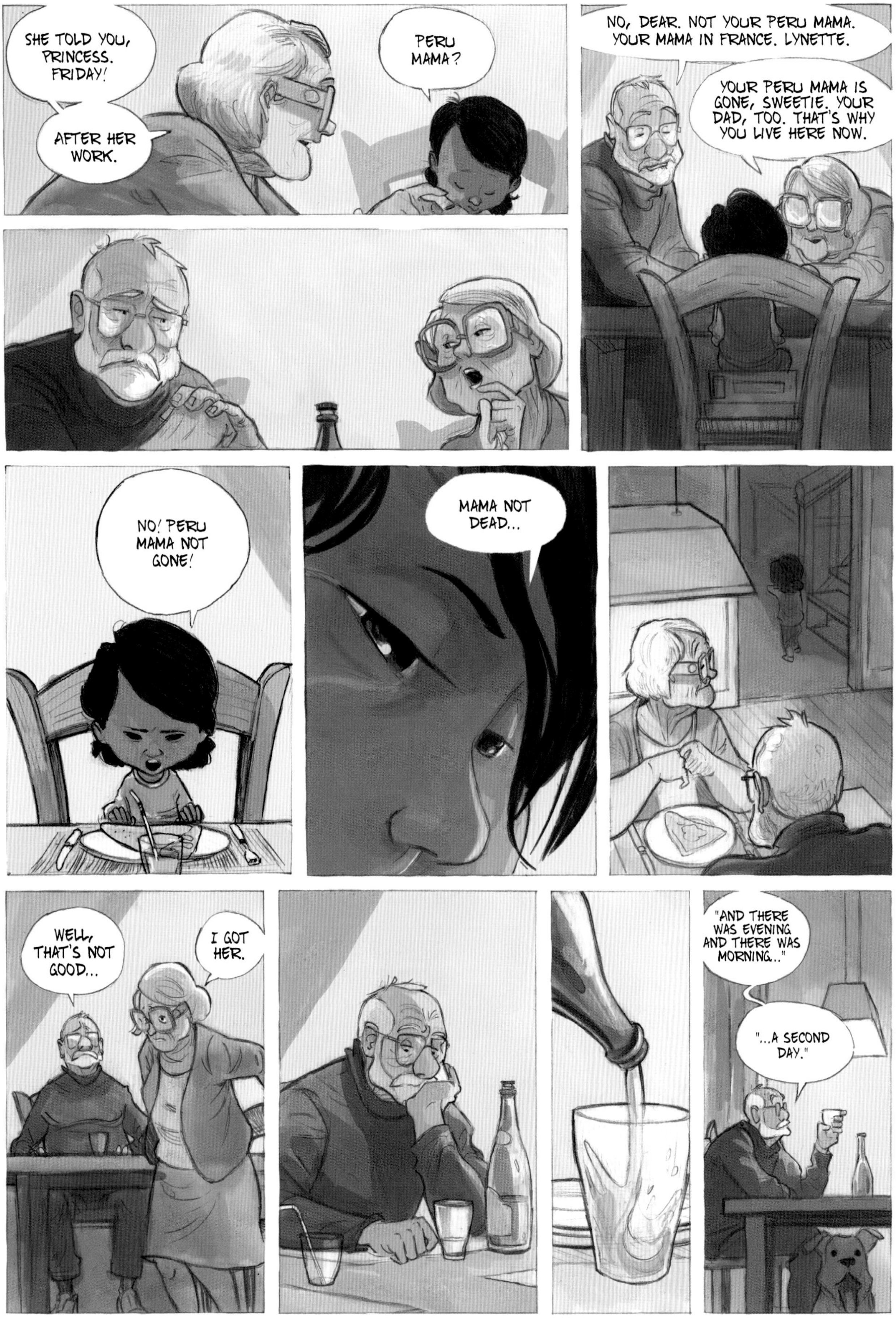
SHE TOLD YOU, PRINCESS. FRIDAY!
AFTER HER WORK.
PERU MAMA?
NO, DEAR. NOT YOUR PERU MAMA. YOUR MAMA IN FRANCE. LYNETTE.
YOUR PERU MAMA IS GONE, SWEETIE. YOUR DAD, TOO. THAT'S WHY YOU LIVE HERE NOW.
NO! PERU MAMA NOT GONE!
MAMA NOT DEAD...
WELL, THAT'S NOT GOOD...
I GOT HER.
"AND THERE WAS EVENING AND THERE WAS MORNING..."
"...A SECOND DAY."

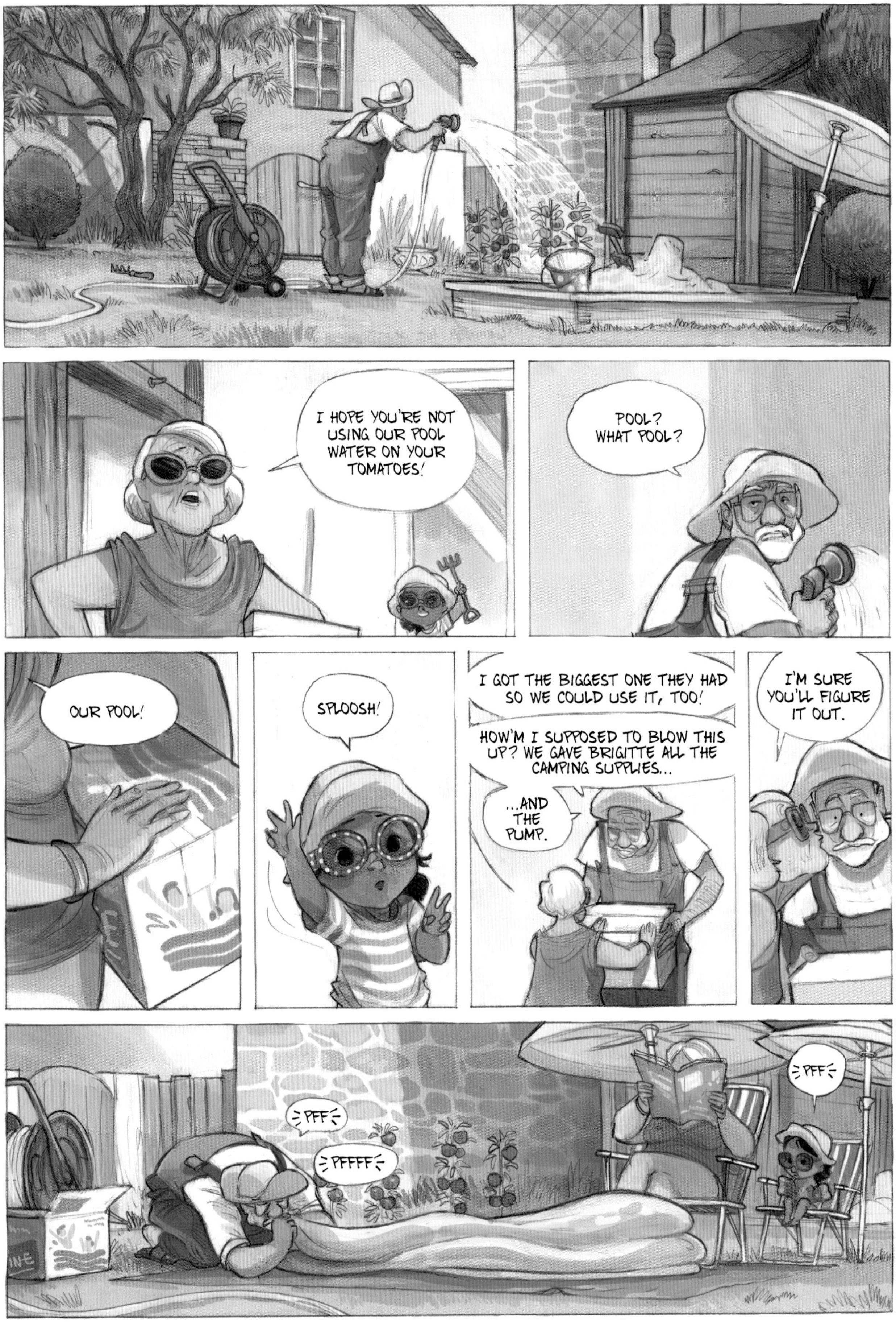
I HOPE YOU'RE NOT USING OUR POOL WATER ON YOUR TOMATOES!
POOL? WHAT POOL?
OUR POOL!
SPLOOSH!
I GOT THE BIGGEST ONE THEY HAD SO WE COULD USE IT, TOO!
HOW'M I SUPPOSED TO BLOW THIS UP? WE GAVE BRIGITTE ALL THE CAMPING SUPPLIES...
...AND THE PUMP.
I'M SURE YOU'LL FIGURE IT OUT.
PFF
PFFFF
PFF

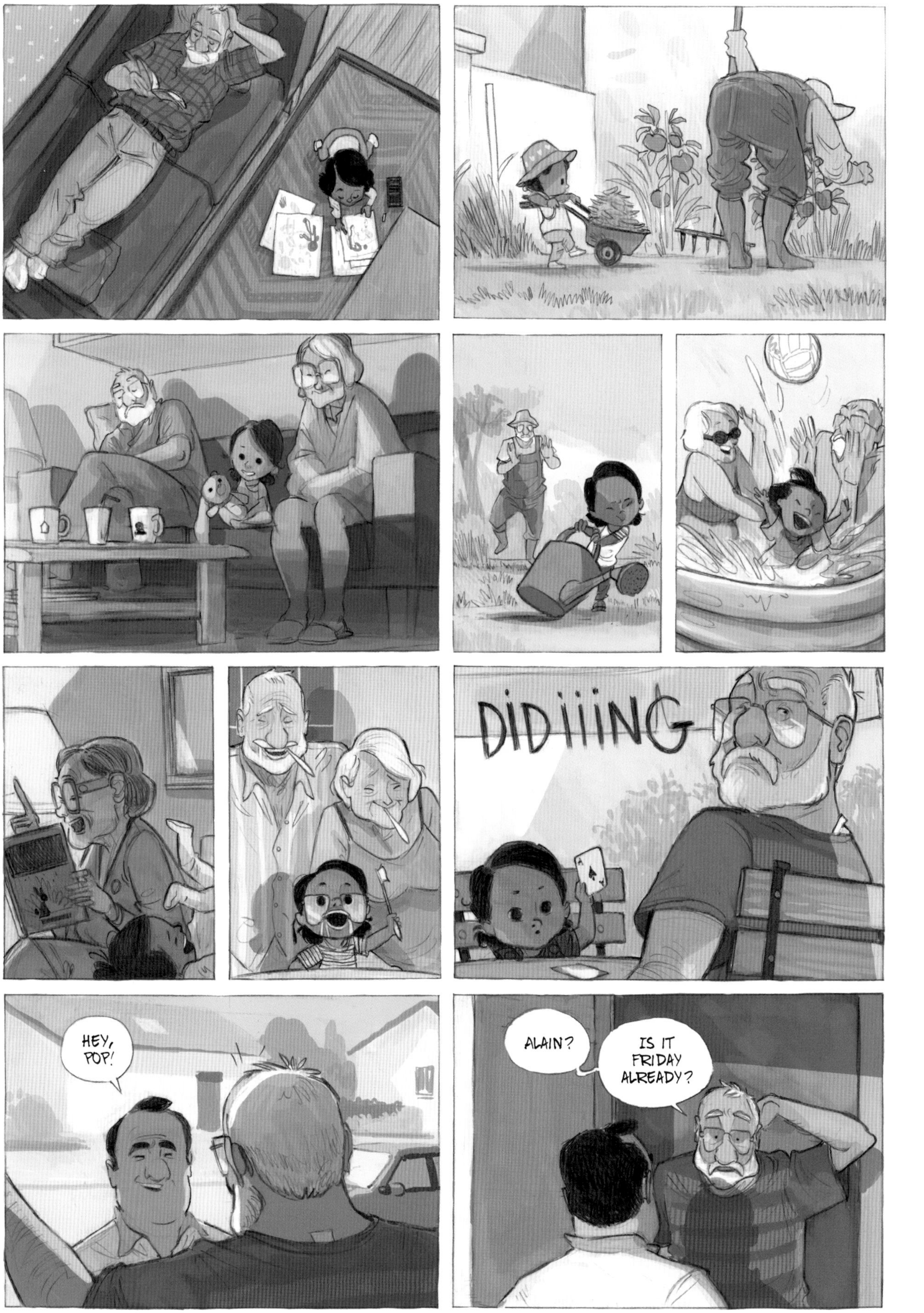
DIDiiiNG
HEY, POP!
ALAIN?
IS IT FRIDAY ALREADY?

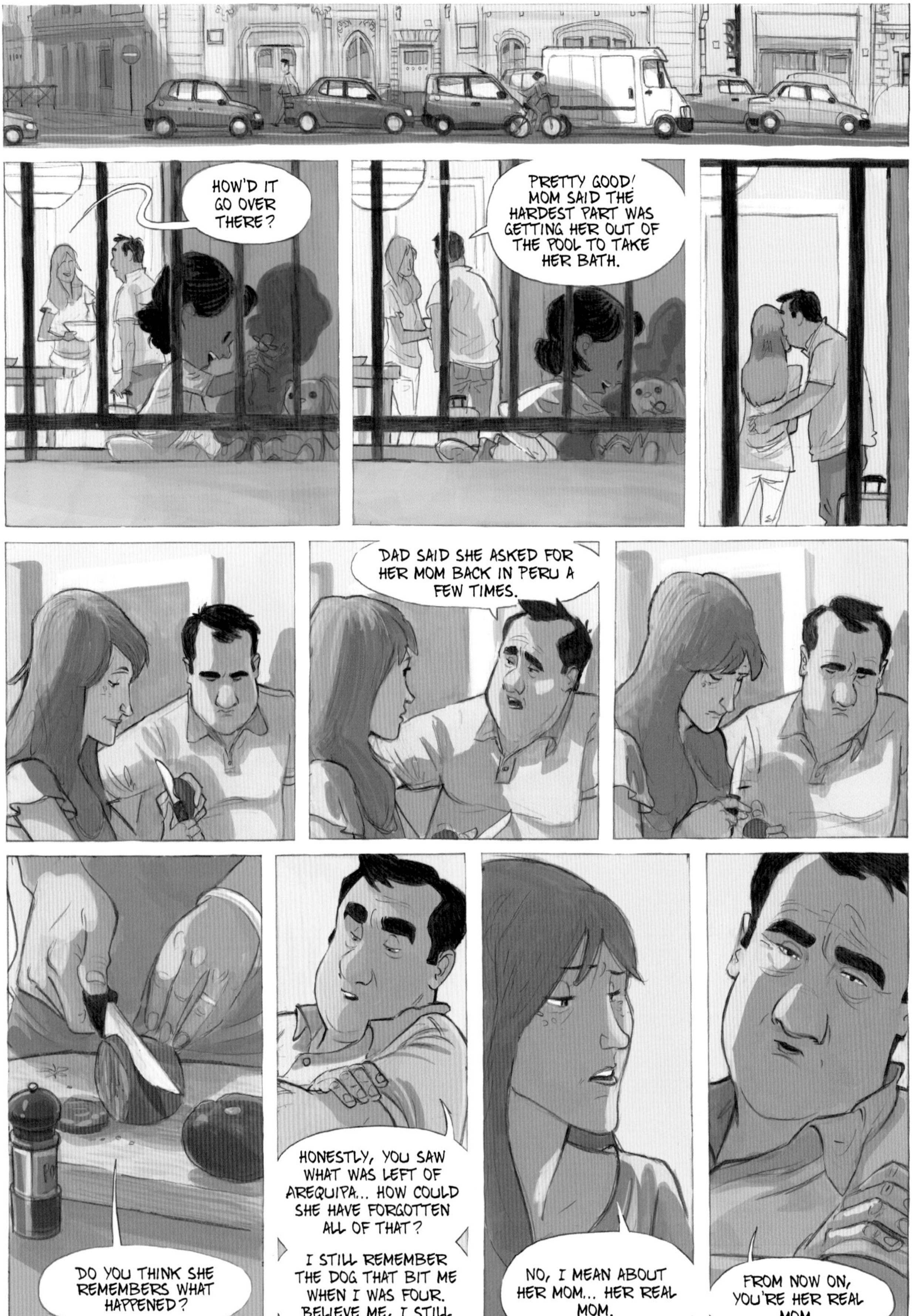
HOW'D IT GO OVER THERE?
PRETTY GOOD! MOM SAID THE HARDEST PART WAS GETTING HER OUT OF THE POOL TO TAKE HER BATH.
DAD SAID SHE ASKED FOR HER MOM BACK IN PERU A FEW TIMES.
DO YOU THINK SHE REMEMBERS WHAT HAPPENED?
HONESTLY, YOU SAW WHAT WAS LEFT OF AREQUIPA... HOW COULD SHE HAVE FORGOTTEN ALL OF THAT?
I STILL REMEMBER THE DOG THAT BIT ME WHEN I WAS FOUR. BELIEVE ME, I STILL HAVE NIGHTMARES...
NO, I MEAN ABOUT HER MOM... HER REAL MOM.
FROM NOW ON, YOU'RE HER REAL MOM.

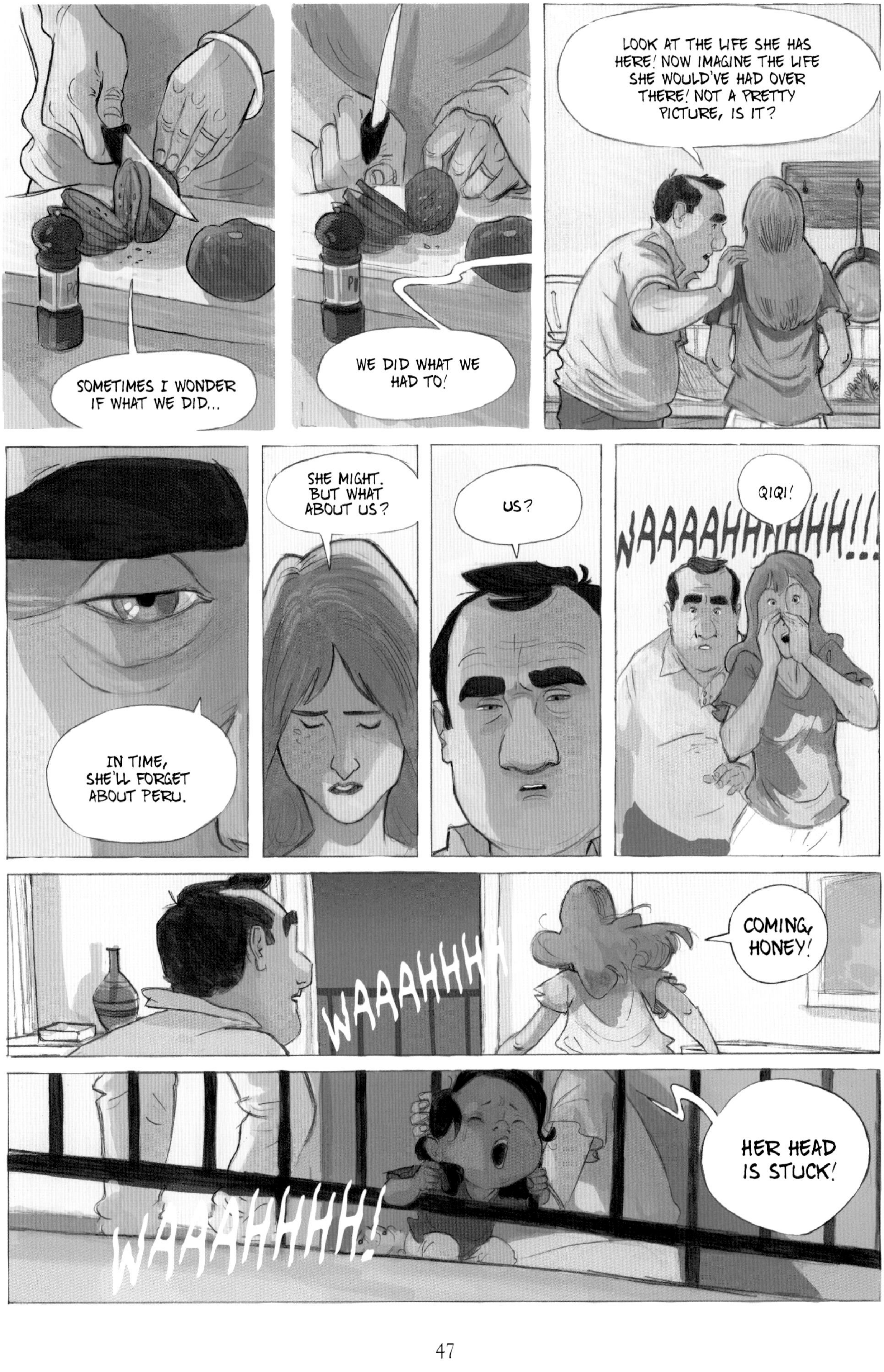
SOMETIMES I WONDER IF WHAT WE DID...
WE DID WHAT WE HAD TO!
LOOK AT THE LIFE SHE HAS HERE! NOW IMAGINE THE LIFE SHE WOULD'VE HAD OVER THERE! NOT A PRETTY PICTURE, IS IT?
IN TIME, SHE'LL FORGET ABOUT PERU.
SHE MIGHT. BUT WHAT ABOUT US?
US?
QIQI!
WAAAAHHHHHH!!!
COMING, HONEY!
WAAAHHHH
HER HEAD IS STUCK!
WAAAHHHHH!

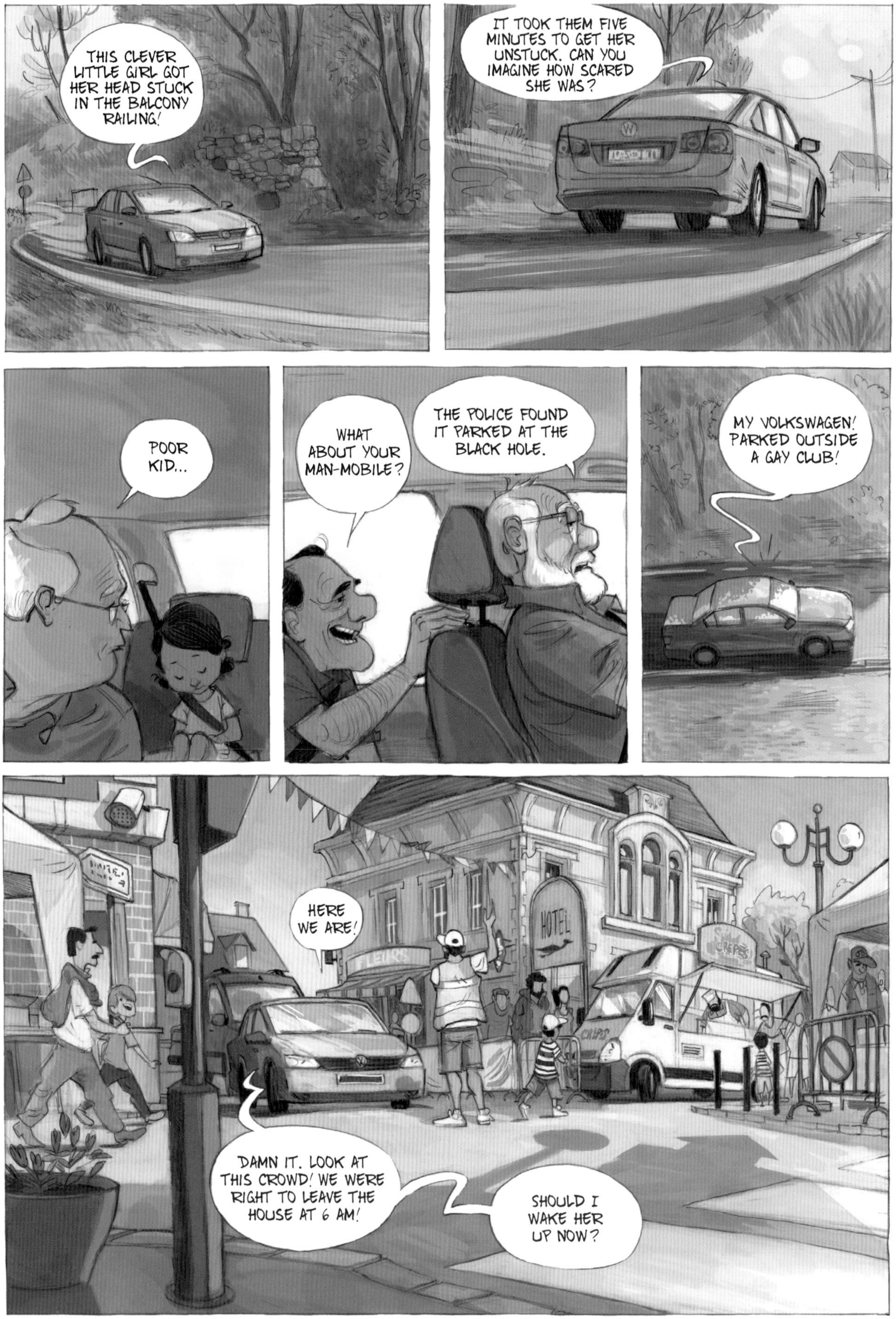
THIS CLEVER LITTLE GIRL GOT HER HEAD STUCK IN THE BALCONY RAILING!
IT TOOK THEM FIVE MINUTES TO GET HER UNSTUCK. CAN YOU IMAGINE HOW SCARED SHE WAS?
POOR KID...
WHAT ABOUT YOUR MAN-MOBILE?
THE POLICE FOUND IT PARKED AT THE BLACK HOLE.
MY VOLKSWAGEN! PARKED OUTSIDE A GAY CLUB!
HOTEL
HERE WE ARE!
DAMN IT. LOOK AT THIS CROWD! WE WERE RIGHT TO LEAVE THE HOUSE AT 6 AM!
SHOULD I WAKE HER UP NOW?

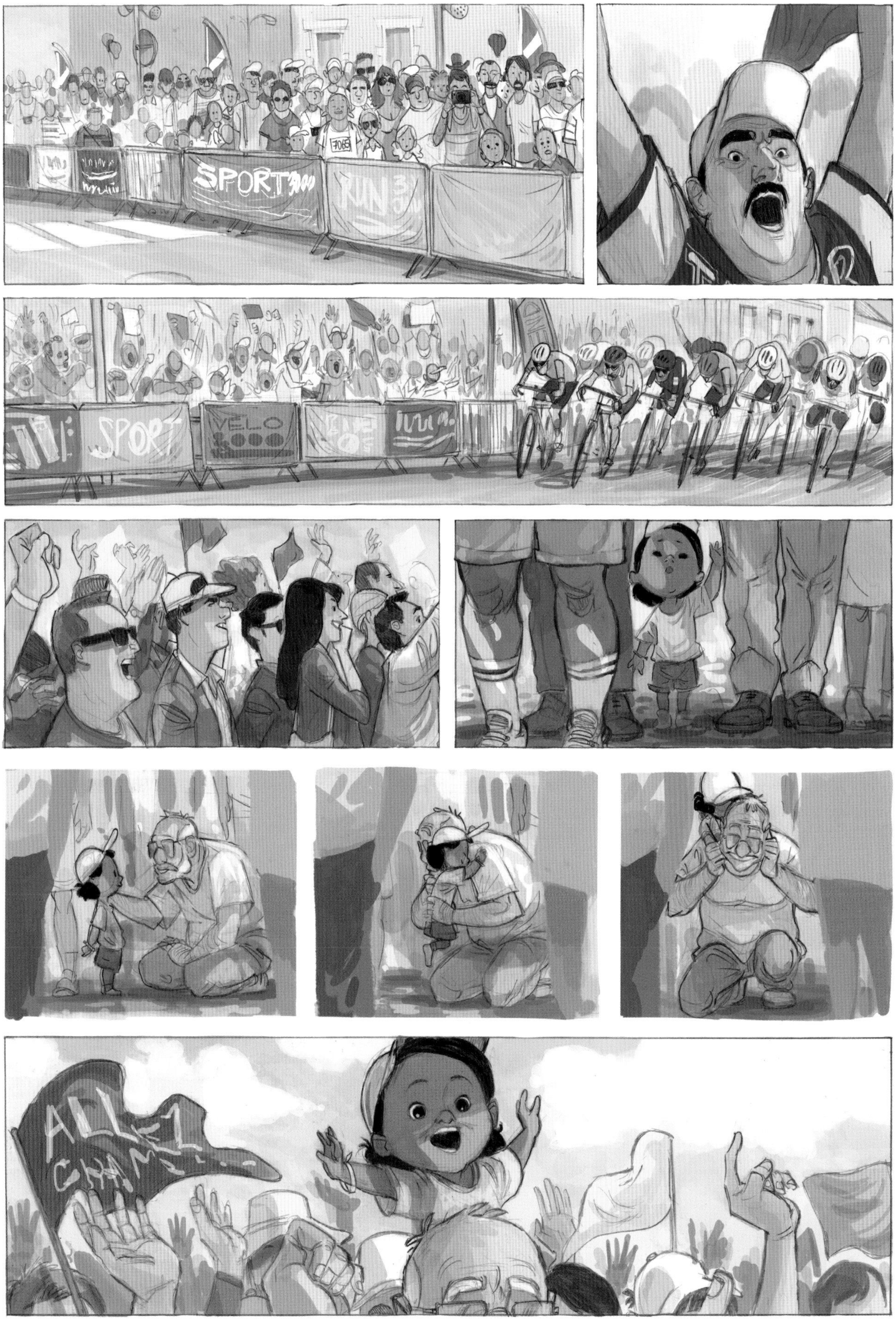
SPORT
RUN
SPORT
VELO

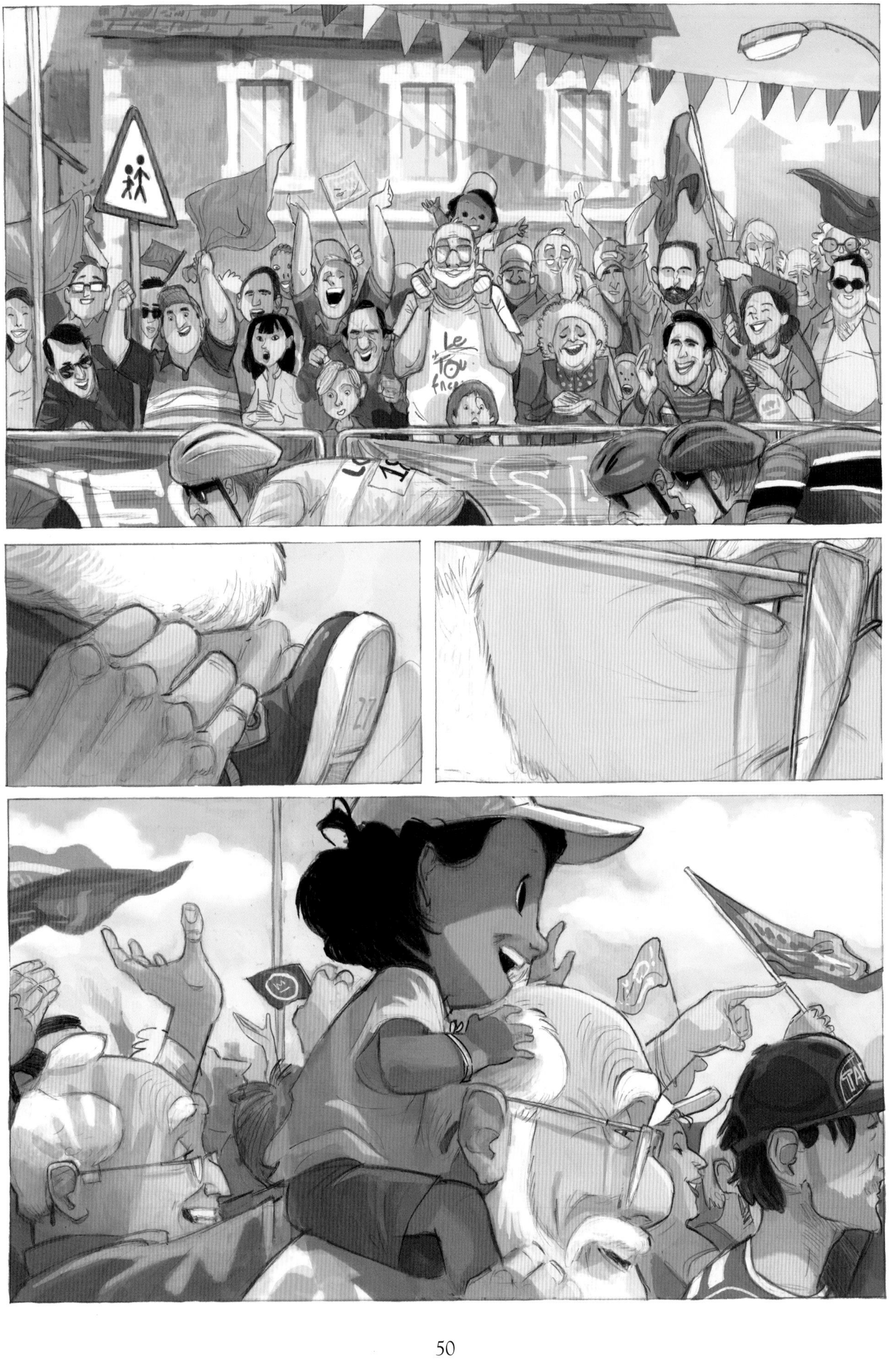

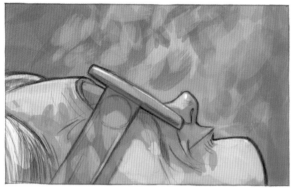

MAMiiiiii

SLOW DOWN, QINAYA!

GAMMA WISETTE!

GAMMA WISETTE!

HOW WAS THE BICYCLE RACE, DEAR?

BIKE!

ZOOM!

ZOOM!

I DROPPED OFF THE TWO SENILE DRUNKS BEFORE THEY YACKED ALL OVER.

AND WE STOPPED BY THE STORE ON THE WAY HOME...

?

WHAT? YOU'RE NOT THE ONLY ONE WHO CAN GIVE HER GIFTS!

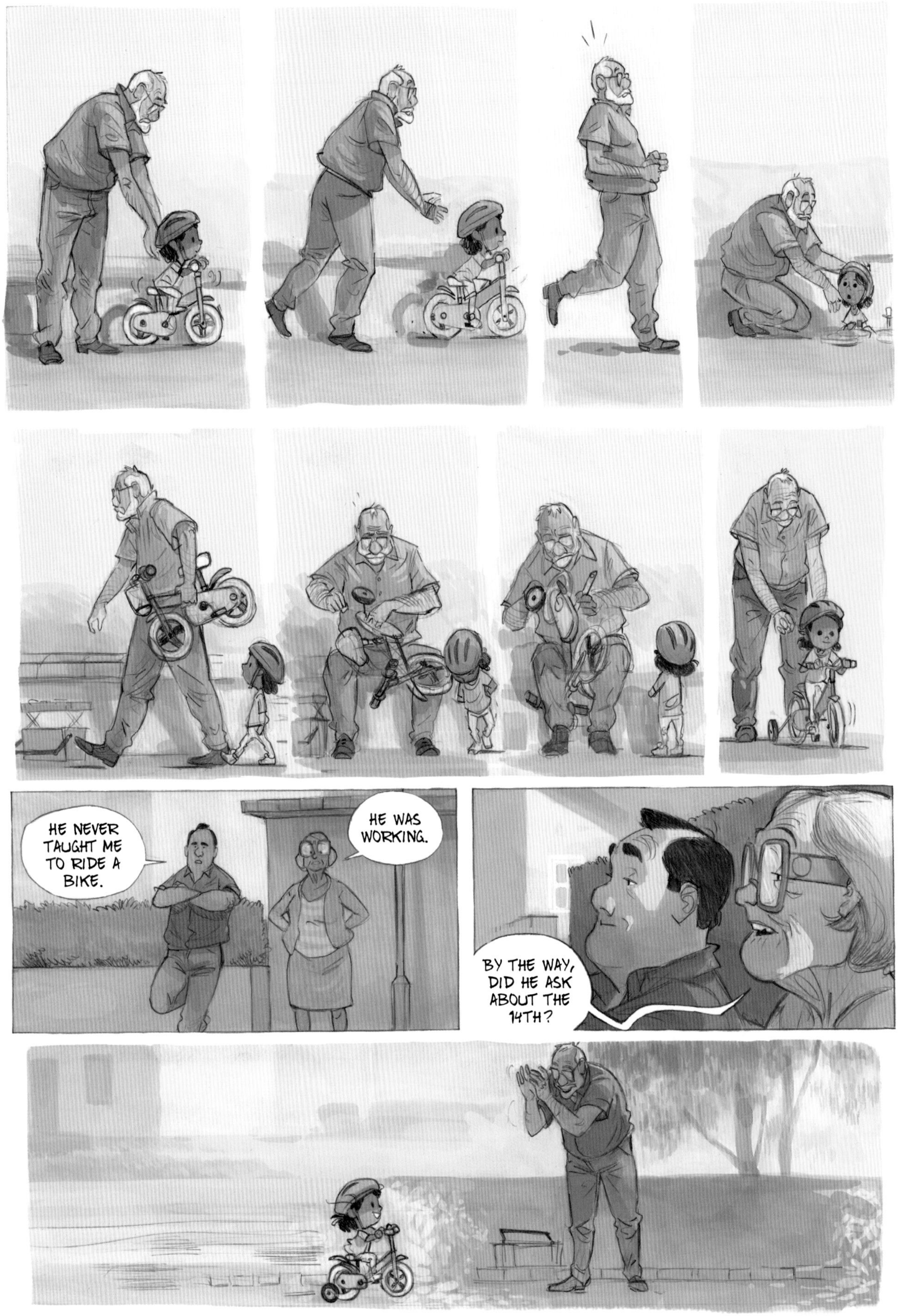
HE NEVER TAUGHT ME TO RIDE A BIKE.
HE WAS WORKING.
BY THE WAY, DID HE ASK ABOUT THE 14TH?

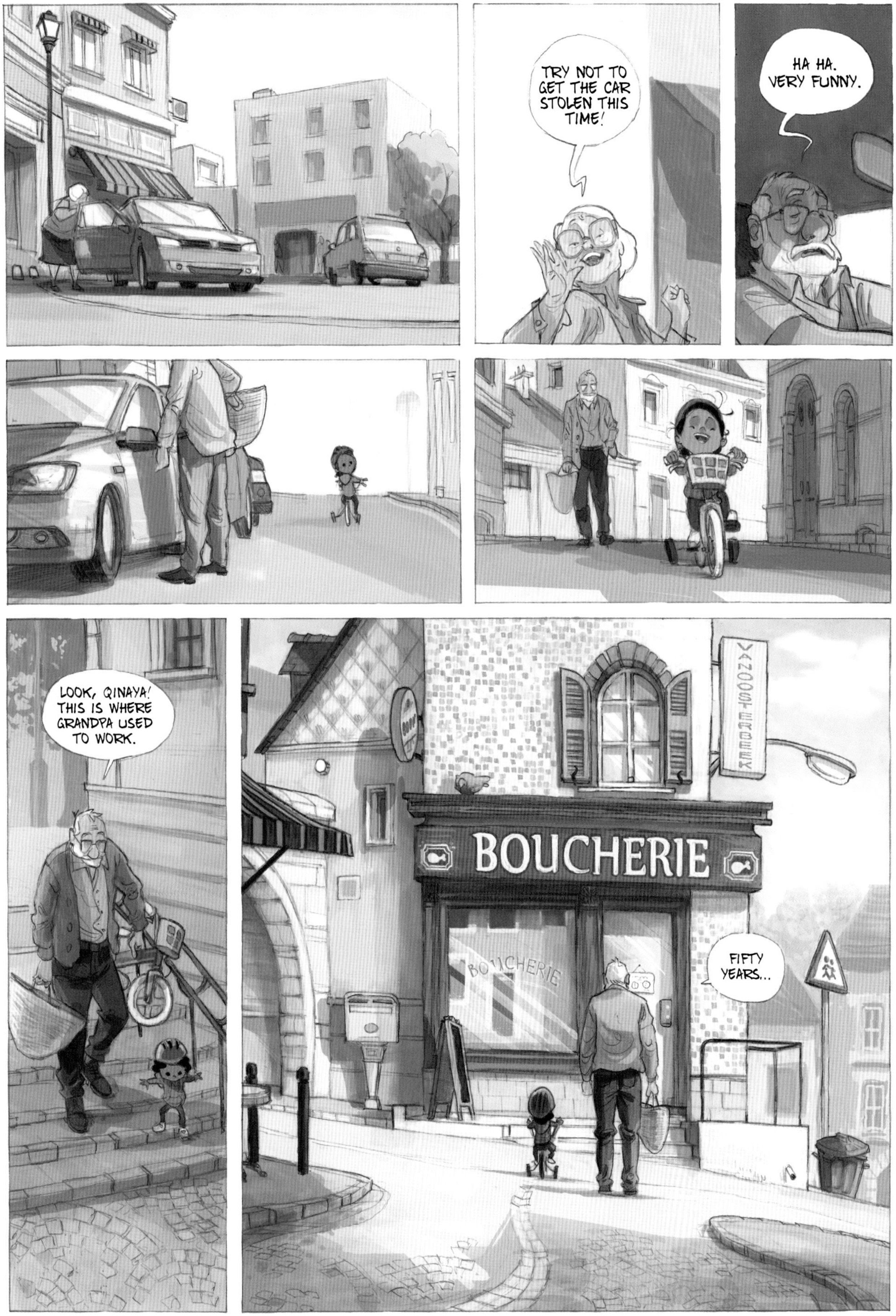
TRY NOT TO GET THE CAR STOLEN THIS TIME!
HA HA. VERY FUNNY.
LOOK, QINAYA! THIS IS WHERE GRANDPA USED TO WORK.
VANOOSTERBEEK
BOUCHERIE
BOUCHERIE
FIFTY YEARS...

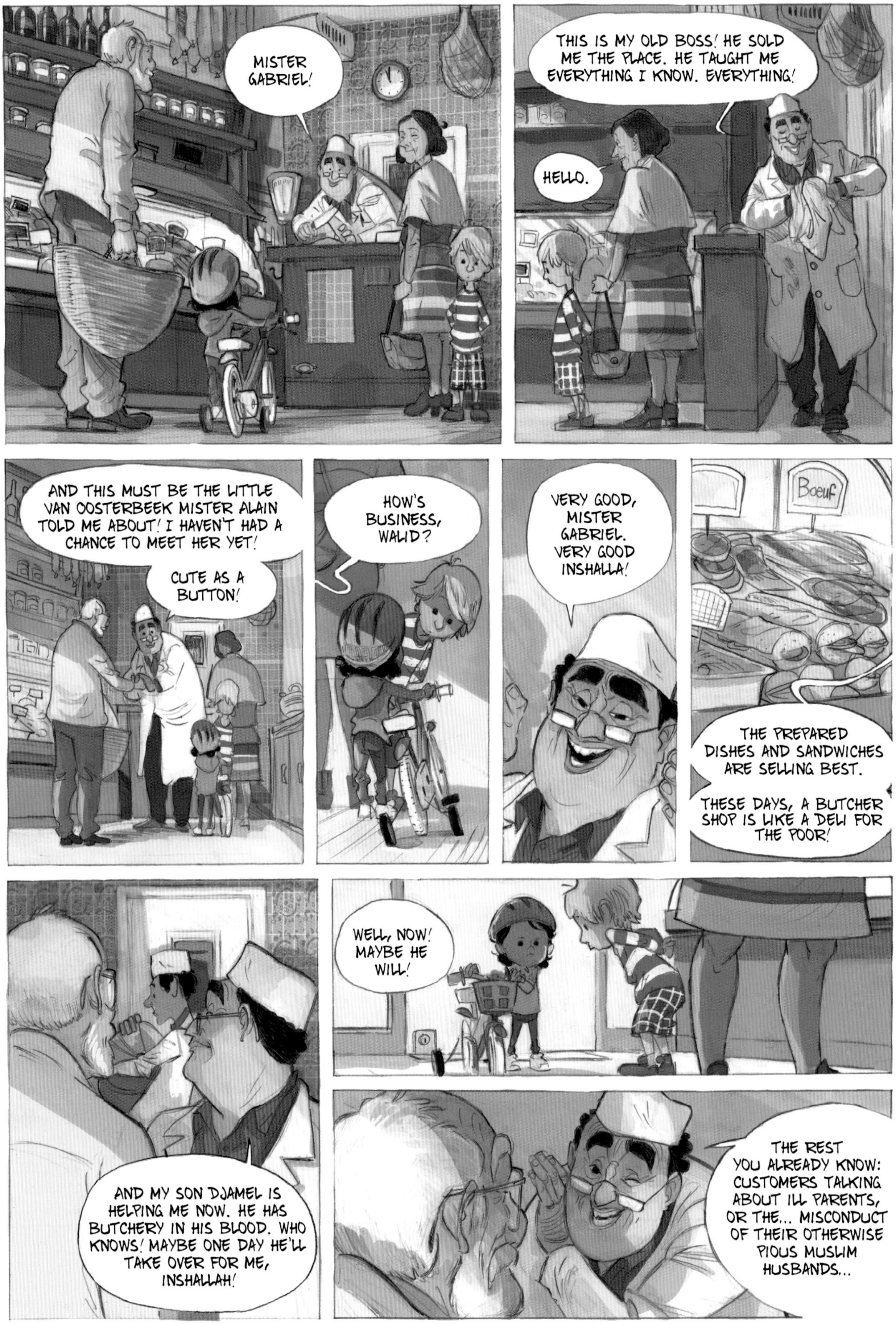
MISTER GABRIEL!
THIS IS MY OLD BOSS! HE SOLD ME THE PLACE. HE TAUGHT ME EVERYTHING I KNOW. EVERYTHING!
HELLO.
AND THIS MUST BE THE LITTLE VAN OOSTERBEEK MISTER ALAIN TOLD ME ABOUT! I HAVEN'T HAD A CHANCE TO MEET HER YET!
CUTE AS A BUTTON!
HOW'S BUSINESS, WALID?
VERY GOOD, MISTER GABRIEL. VERY GOOD INSHALLA!
Boeuf
THE PREPARED DISHES AND SANDWICHES ARE SELLING BEST.
THESE DAYS, A BUTCHER SHOP IS LIKE A DELI FOR THE POOR!
WELL, NOW! MAYBE HE WILL!
AND MY SON DJAMEL IS HELPING ME NOW. HE HAS BUTCHERY IN HIS BLOOD. WHO KNOWS! MAYBE ONE DAY HE'LL TAKE OVER FOR ME, INSHALLAH!
THE REST YOU ALREADY KNOW: CUSTOMERS TALKING ABOUT ILL PARENTS, OR THE... MISCONDUCT OF THEIR OTHERWISE PIOUS MUSLIM HUSBANDS...

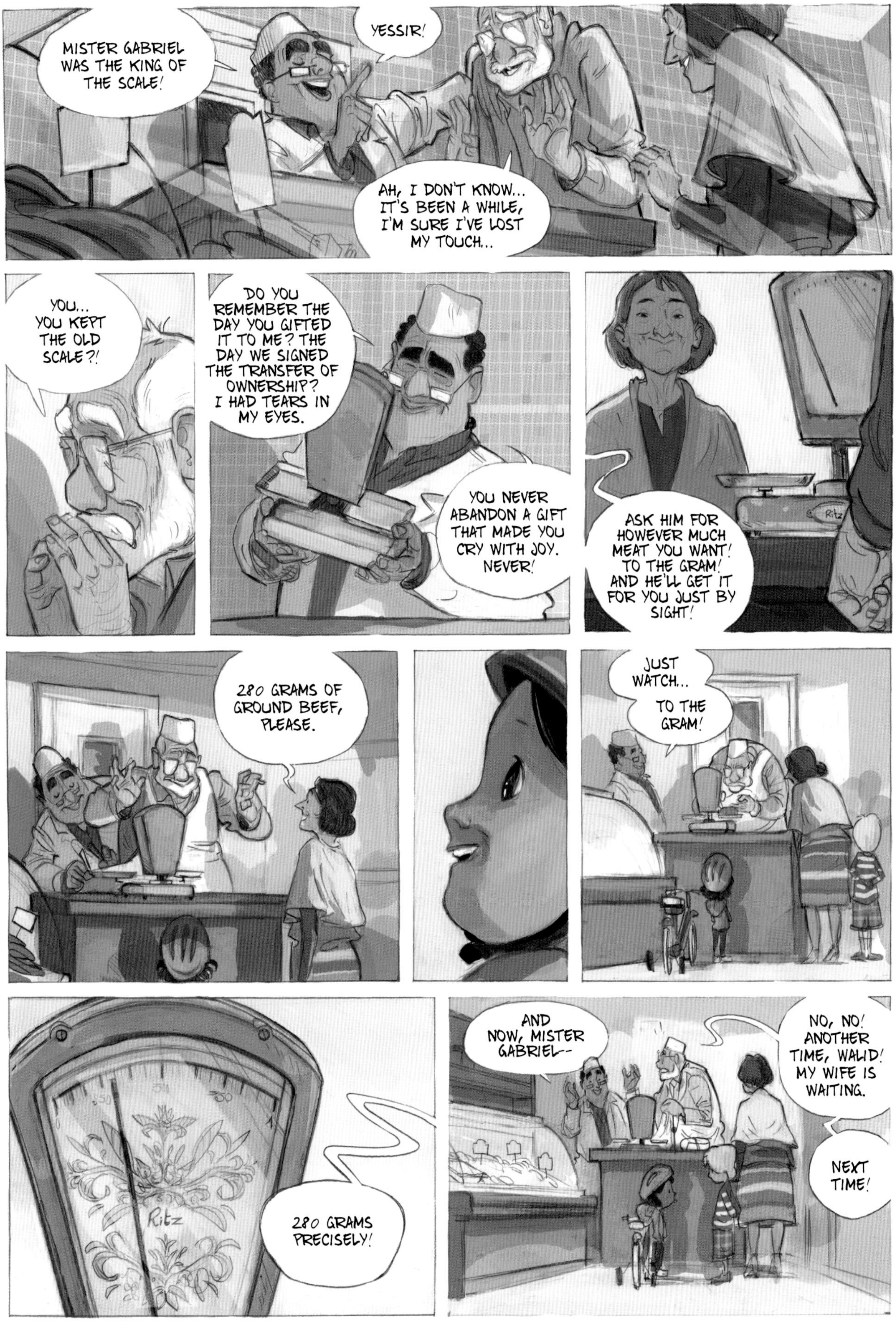
MISTER GABRIEL WAS THE KING OF THE SCALE!
YESSIR!
AH, I DON'T KNOW... IT'S BEEN A WHILE, I'M SURE I'VE LOST MY TOUCH...
YOU... YOU KEPT THE OLD SCALE?!
DO YOU REMEMBER THE DAY YOU GIFTED IT TO ME? THE DAY WE SIGNED THE TRANSFER OF OWNERSHIP? I HAD TEARS IN MY EYES.
YOU NEVER ABANDON A GIFT THAT MADE YOU CRY WITH JOY. NEVER!
ASK HIM FOR HOWEVER MUCH MEAT YOU WANT! TO THE GRAM! AND HE'LL GET IT FOR YOU JUST BY SIGHT!
280 GRAMS OF GROUND BEEF, PLEASE.
JUST WATCH...
TO THE GRAM!
Ritz
280 GRAMS PRECISELY!
AND NOW, MISTER GABRIEL--
NO, NO! ANOTHER TIME, WALID! MY WIFE IS WAITING.
NEXT TIME!

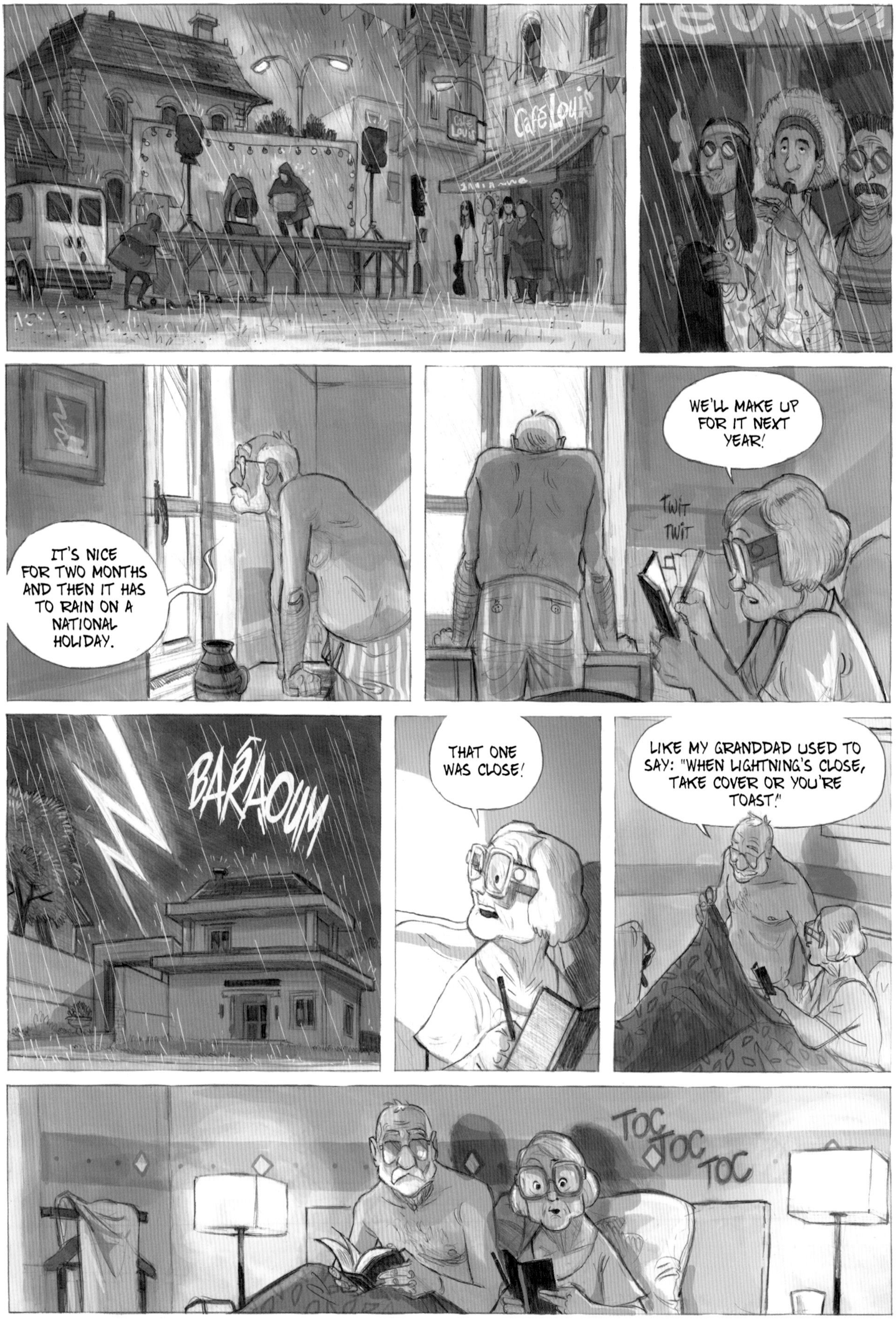
Café Louis
Café Louis
IT'S NICE FOR TWO MONTHS AND THEN IT HAS TO RAIN ON A NATIONAL HOLIDAY.
WE'LL MAKE UP FOR IT NEXT YEAR!
TWIT TWIT
BARAOUM
THAT ONE WAS CLOSE!
LIKE MY GRANDDAD USED TO SAY: "WHEN LIGHTNING'S CLOSE, TAKE COVER OR YOU'RE TOAST!"
TOC TOC TOC

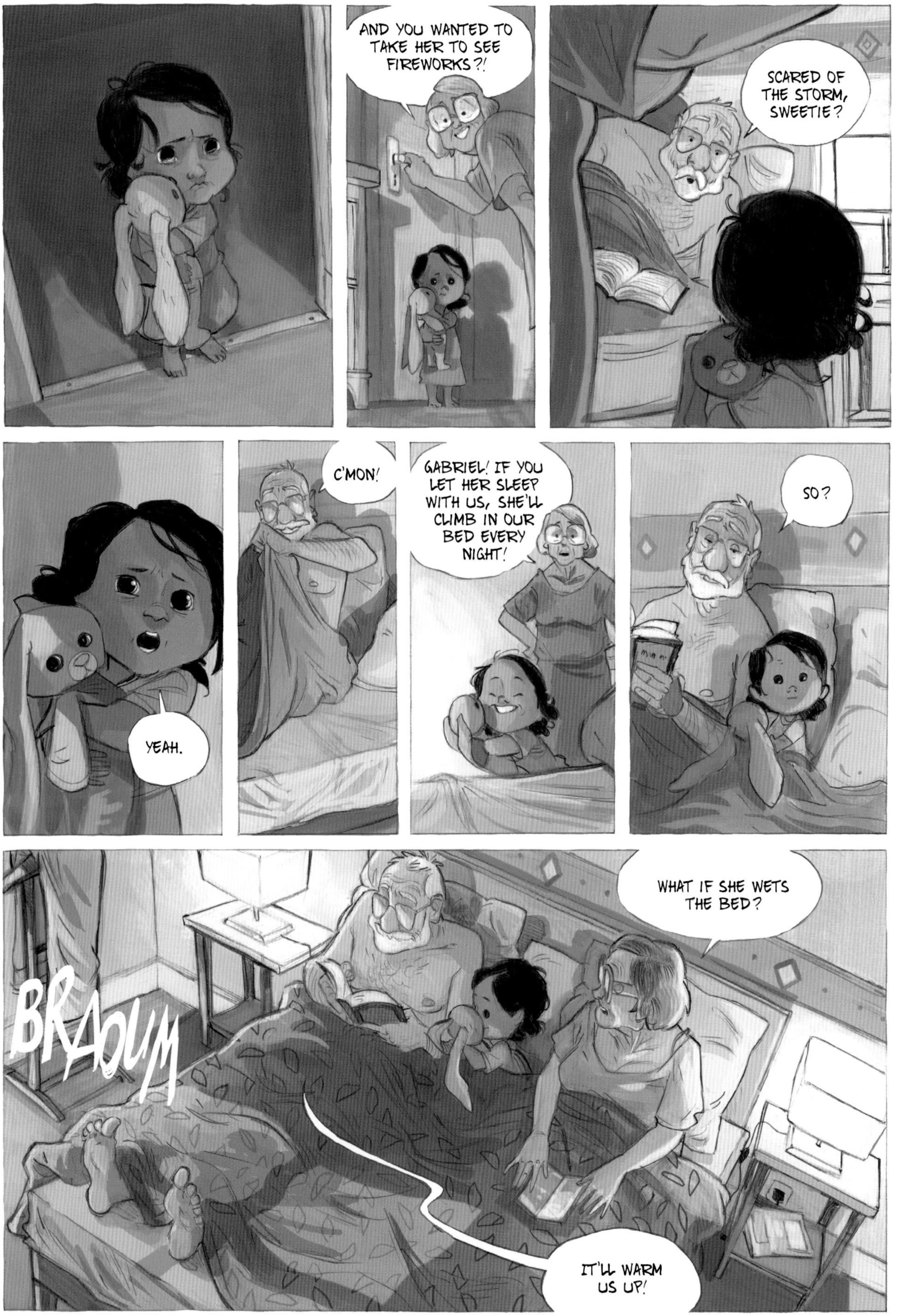
AND YOU WANTED TO TAKE HER TO SEE FIREWORKS?!
SCARED OF THE STORM, SWEETIE?
YEAH.
C'MON!
GABRIEL! IF YOU LET HER SLEEP WITH US, SHE'LL CLIMB IN OUR BED EVERY NIGHT!
SO?
WHAT IF SHE WETS THE BED?
BRAOUM
IT'LL WARM US UP!

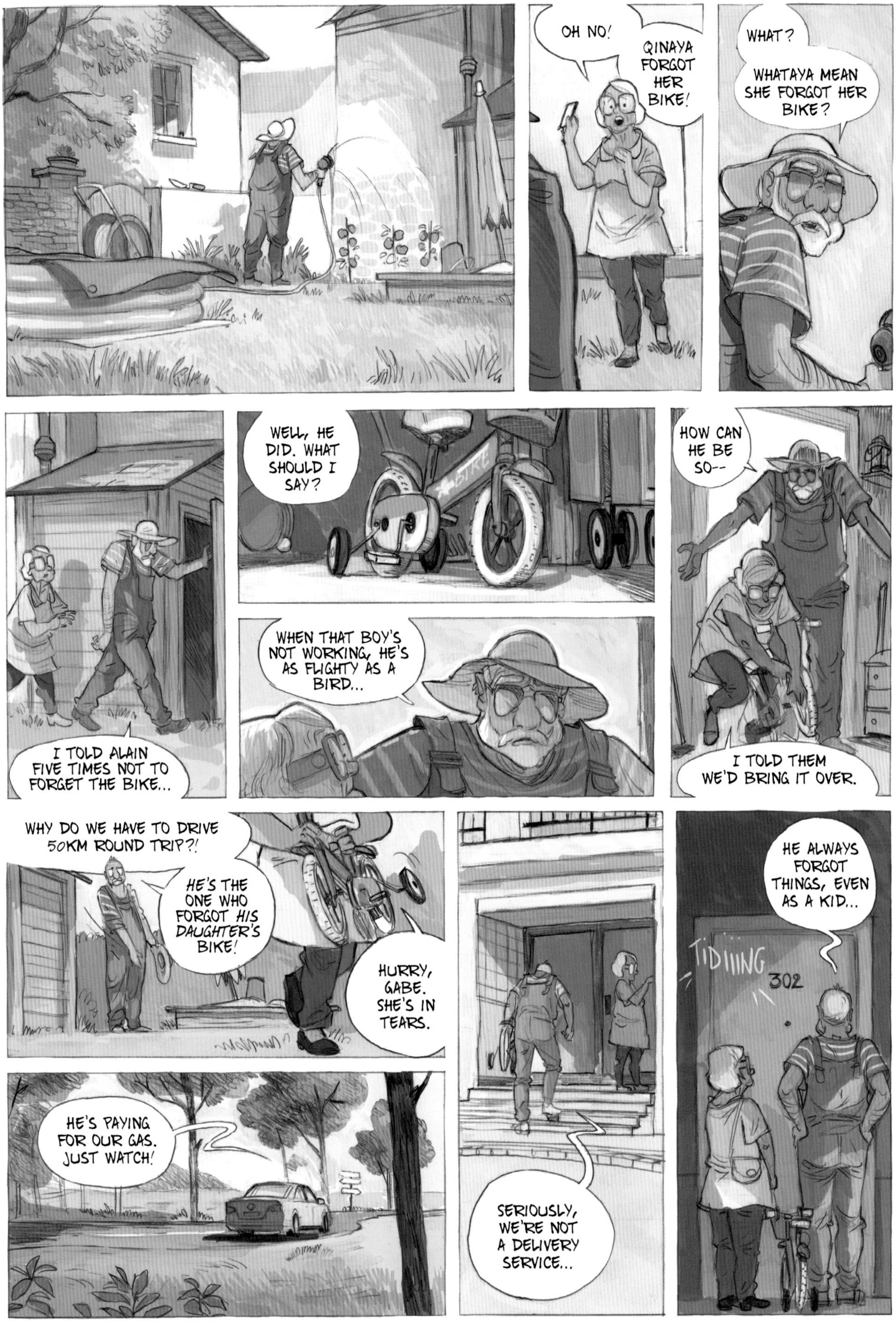
OH NO!
QINAYA FORGOT HER BIKE!
WHAT?
WHATAYA MEAN SHE FORGOT HER BIKE?
I TOLD ALAIN FIVE TIMES NOT TO FORGET THE BIKE...
WELL, HE DID. WHAT SHOULD I SAY?
WHEN THAT BOY'S NOT WORKING, HE'S AS FLIGHTY AS A BIRD...
HOW CAN HE BE SO--
I TOLD THEM WE'D BRING IT OVER.
WHY DO WE HAVE TO DRIVE 50KM ROUND TRIP?!
HE'S THE ONE WHO FORGOT HIS DAUGHTER'S BIKE!
HURRY, GABE. SHE'S IN TEARS.
HE'S PAYING FOR OUR GAS. JUST WATCH!
SERIOUSLY, WE'RE NOT A DELIVERY SERVICE...
HE ALWAYS FORGOT THINGS, EVEN AS A KID...
TIDIIING
302

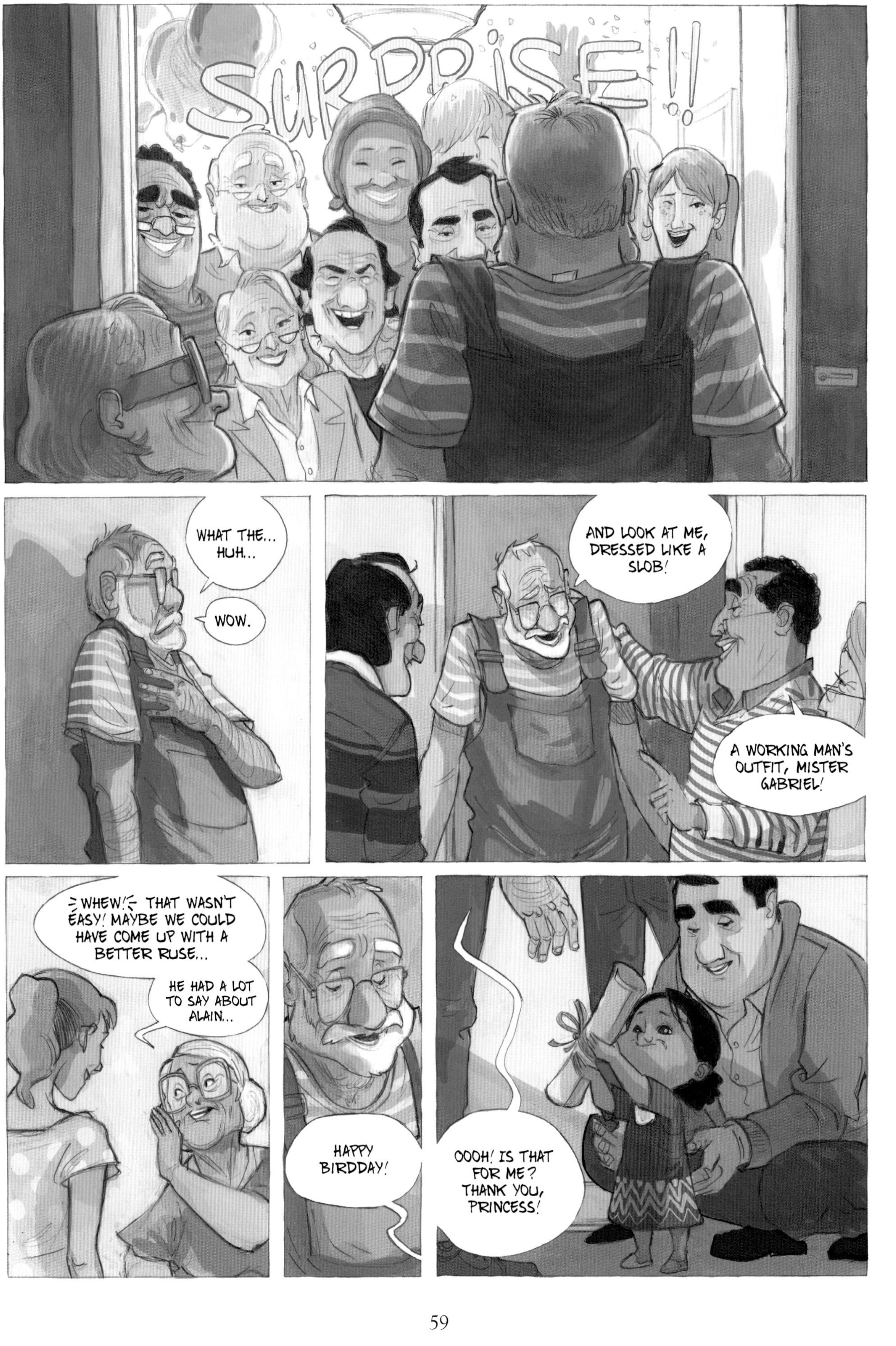
SURPRISE!!
WHAT THE... HUH...
WOW.
AND LOOK AT ME, DRESSED LIKE A SLOB!
A WORKING MAN'S OUTFIT, MISTER GABRIEL!
WHEW! THAT WASN'T EASY! MAYBE WE COULD HAVE COME UP WITH A BETTER RUSE...
HE HAD A LOT TO SAY ABOUT ALAIN...
HAPPY BIRDDAY!
OOOH! IS THAT FOR ME? THANK YOU, PRINCESS!

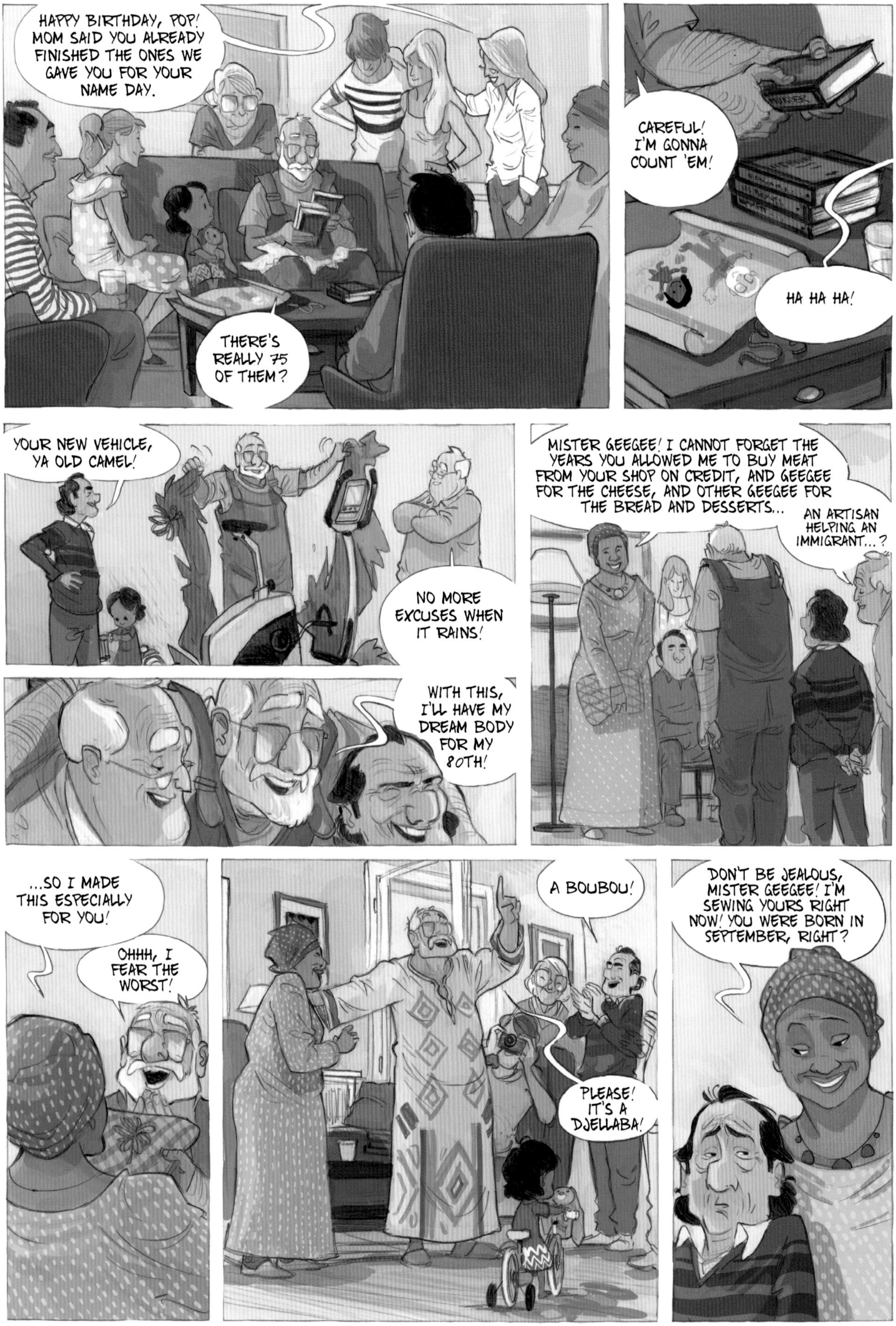
HAPPY BIRTHDAY, POP! MOM SAID YOU ALREADY FINISHED THE ONES WE GAVE YOU FOR YOUR NAME DAY.
THERE'S REALLY 75 OF THEM?
CAREFUL! I'M GONNA COUNT 'EM!
HA HA HA!
YOUR NEW VEHICLE, YA OLD CAMEL!
NO MORE EXCUSES WHEN IT RAINS!
WITH THIS, I'LL HAVE MY DREAM BODY FOR MY 80TH!
MISTER GEEGEE! I CANNOT FORGET THE YEARS YOU ALLOWED ME TO BUY MEAT FROM YOUR SHOP ON CREDIT, AND GEEGEE FOR THE CHEESE, AND OTHER GEEGEE FOR THE BREAD AND DESSERTS...
AN ARTISAN HELPING AN IMMIGRANT...?
...SO I MADE THIS ESPECIALLY FOR YOU!
OHHH, I FEAR THE WORST!
A BOUBOU!
PLEASE! IT'S A DJELLABA!
DON'T BE JEALOUS, MISTER GEEGEE! I'M SEWING YOURS RIGHT NOW! YOU WERE BORN IN SEPTEMBER, RIGHT?

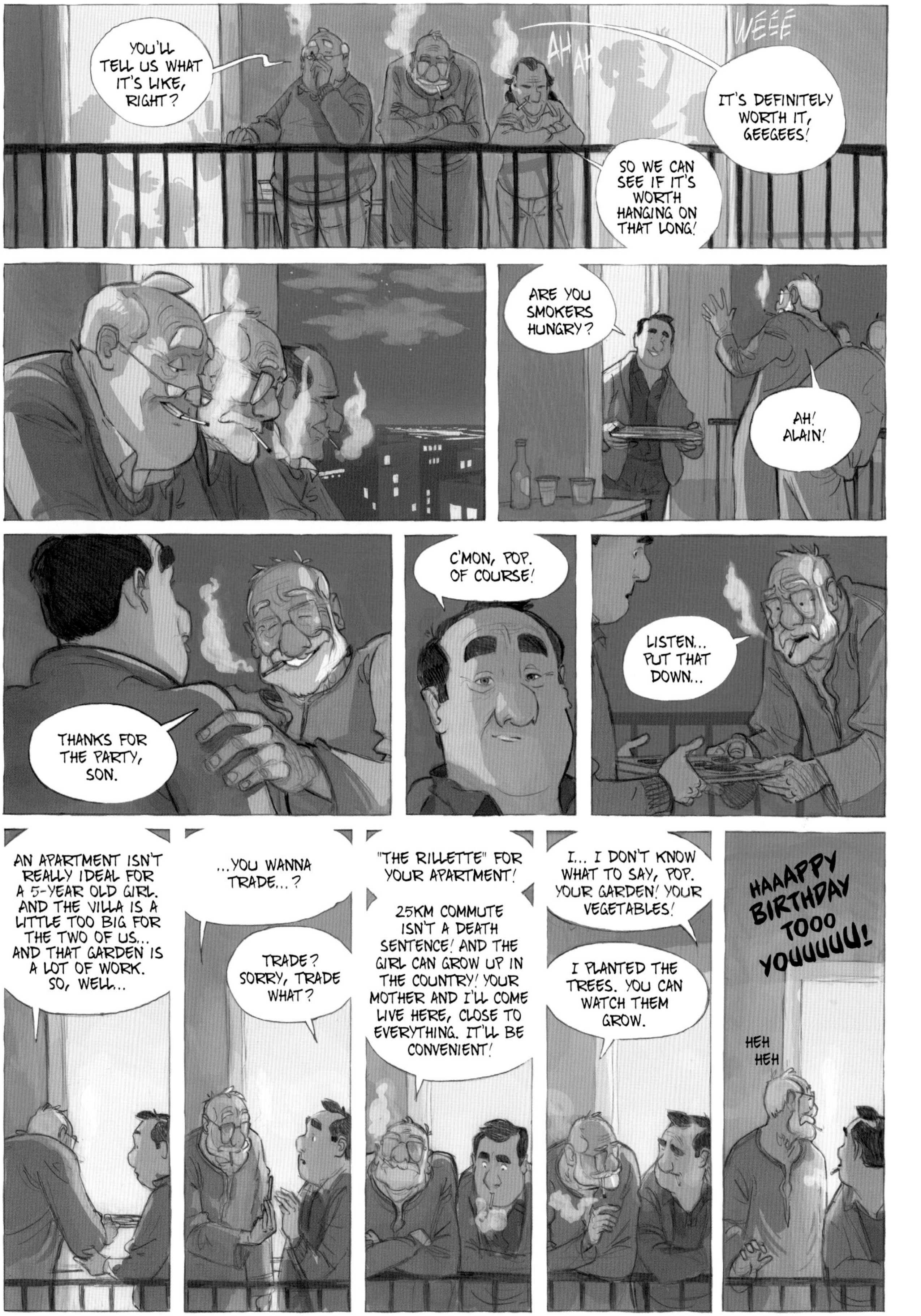
YOU'LL TELL US WHAT IT'S LIKE, RIGHT?
AH AH
WEEE
IT'S DEFINITELY WORTH IT, GEEGEES!
SO WE CAN SEE IF IT'S WORTH HANGING ON THAT LONG!
ARE YOU SMOKERS HUNGRY?
AH! ALAIN!
THANKS FOR THE PARTY, SON.
C'MON, POP. OF COURSE!
LISTEN... PUT THAT DOWN...
AN APARTMENT ISN'T REALLY IDEAL FOR A 5-YEAR OLD GIRL. AND THE VILLA IS A LITTLE TOO BIG FOR THE TWO OF US... AND THAT GARDEN IS A LOT OF WORK. SO, WELL...
...YOU WANNA TRADE...?
TRADE? SORRY, TRADE WHAT?
"THE RILLETTE" FOR YOUR APARTMENT!
25KM COMMUTE ISN'T A DEATH SENTENCE! AND THE GIRL CAN GROW UP IN THE COUNTRY! YOUR MOTHER AND I'LL COME LIVE HERE, CLOSE TO EVERYTHING. IT'LL BE CONVENIENT!
I... I DON'T KNOW WHAT TO SAY, POP. YOUR GARDEN! YOUR VEGETABLES!
I PLANTED THE TREES. YOU CAN WATCH THEM GROW.
HAAAPPY BIRTHDAY TOOO YOUUUUU!
HEH HEH

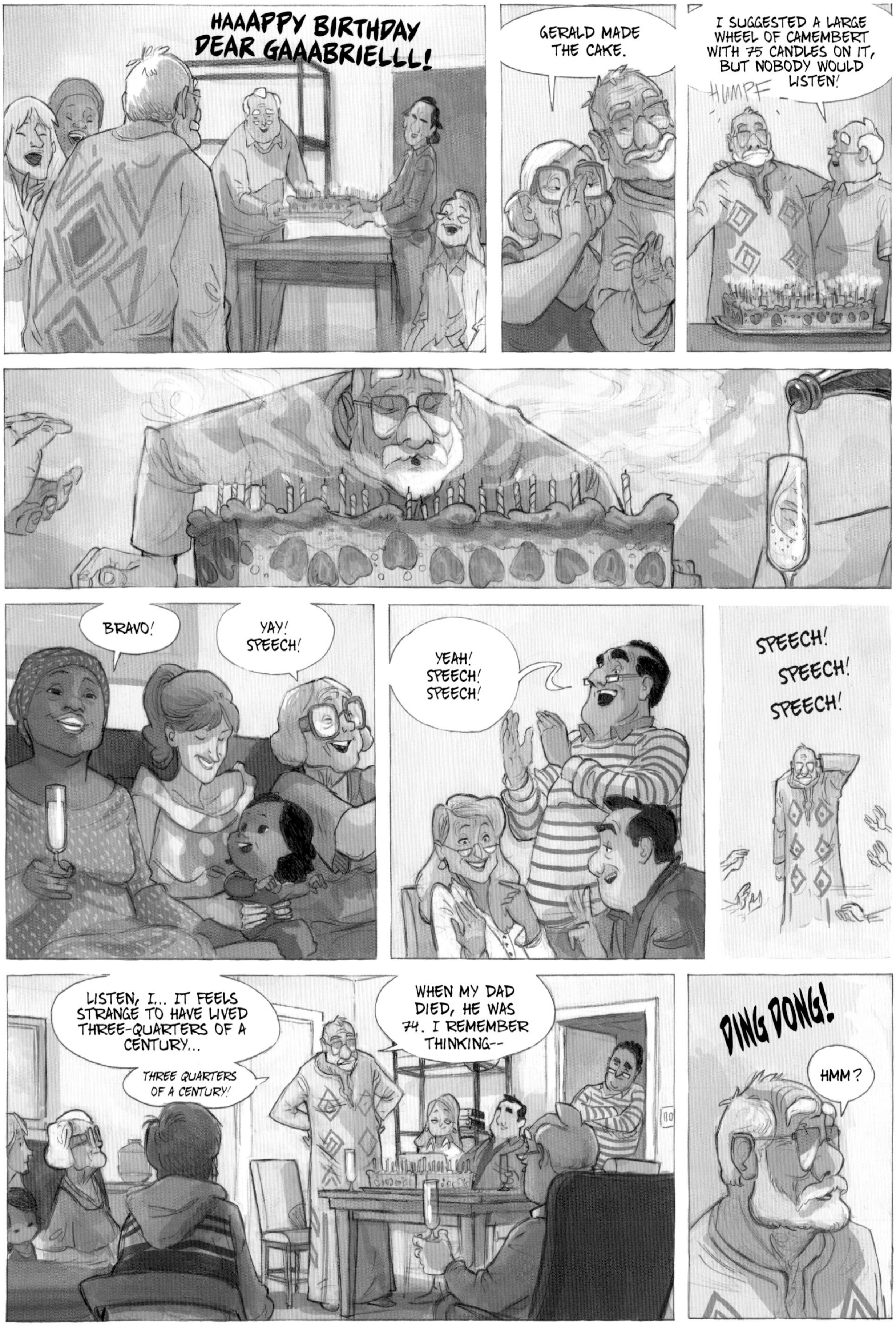
HAAAPPY BIRTHDAY DEAR GAAABRIELLL!
GERALD MADE THE CAKE.
I SUGGESTED A LARGE WHEEL OF CAMEMBERT WITH 75 CANDLES ON IT, BUT NOBODY WOULD LISTEN!
HUMPF
BRAVO!
YAY! SPEECH!
YEAH! SPEECH! SPEECH!
SPEECH! SPEECH! SPEECH!
LISTEN, I... IT FEELS STRANGE TO HAVE LIVED THREE-QUARTERS OF A CENTURY...
THREE QUARTERS OF A CENTURY!
WHEN MY DAD DIED, HE WAS 74. I REMEMBER THINKING--
DING DONG!
HMM?

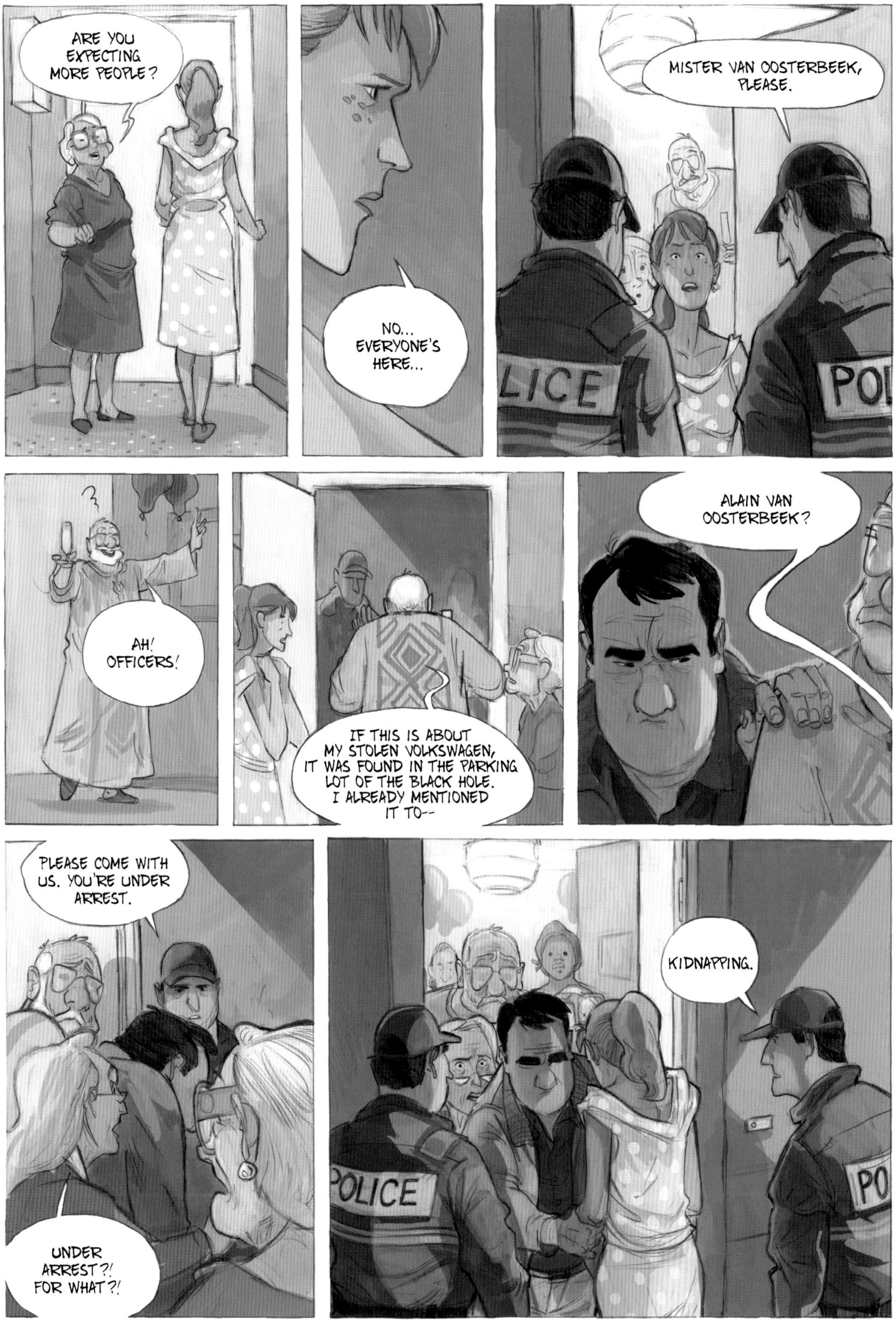
ARE YOU EXPECTING MORE PEOPLE?
NO... EVERYONE'S HERE...
MISTER VAN OOSTERBEEK, PLEASE.
LICE
POL
AH! OFFICERS!
IF THIS IS ABOUT MY STOLEN VOLKSWAGEN, IT WAS FOUND IN THE PARKING LOT OF THE BLACK HOLE. I ALREADY MENTIONED IT TO--
ALAIN VAN OOSTERBEEK?
PLEASE COME WITH US. YOU'RE UNDER ARREST.
UNDER ARREST?! FOR WHAT?!
KIDNAPPING.
POLICE
PO

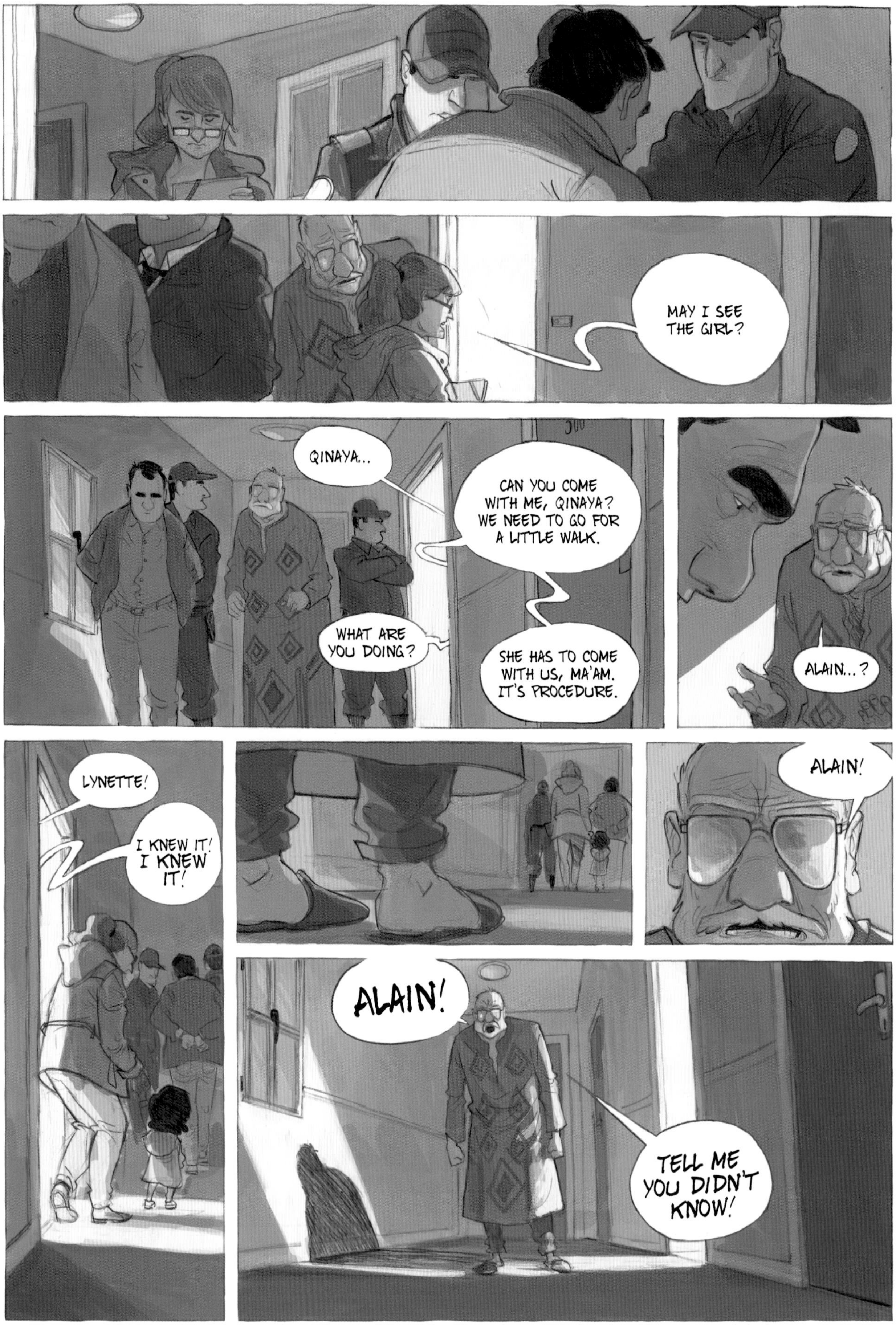
MAY I SEE THE GIRL?
QINAYA...
CAN YOU COME WITH ME, QINAYA? WE NEED TO GO FOR A LITTLE WALK.
WHAT ARE YOU DOING?
SHE HAS TO COME WITH US, MA'AM. IT'S PROCEDURE.
ALAIN...?
LYNETTE!
I KNEW IT! I KNEW IT!
ALAIN!
ALAIN!
TELL ME YOU DIDN'T KNOW!

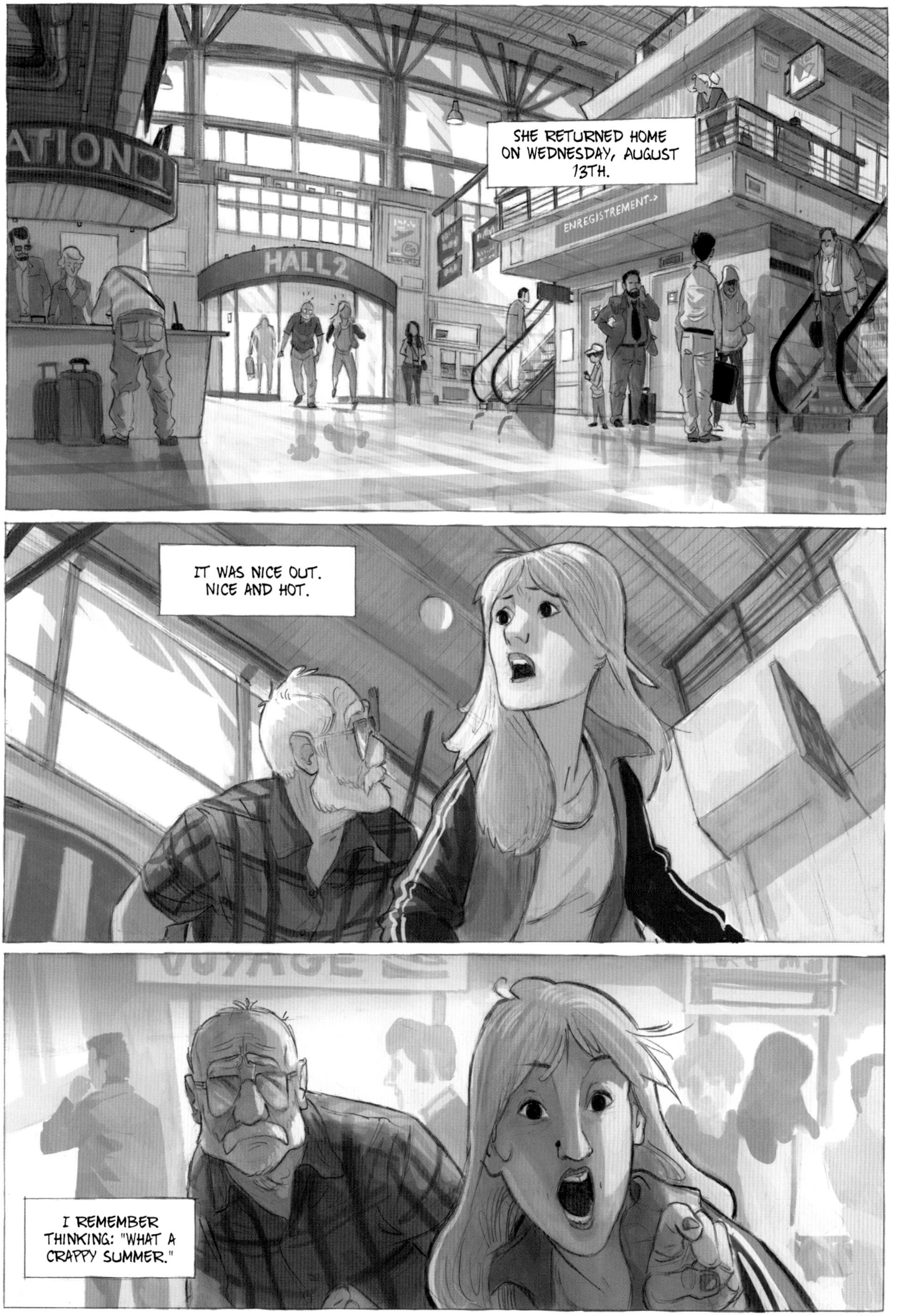
ATION
HALL2
ENREGISTREMENT->
SHE RETURNED HOME ON WEDNESDAY, AUGUST 13TH.
IT WAS NICE OUT. NICE AND HOT.
VOYAGE
I REMEMBER THINKING: "WHAT A CRAPPY SUMMER."

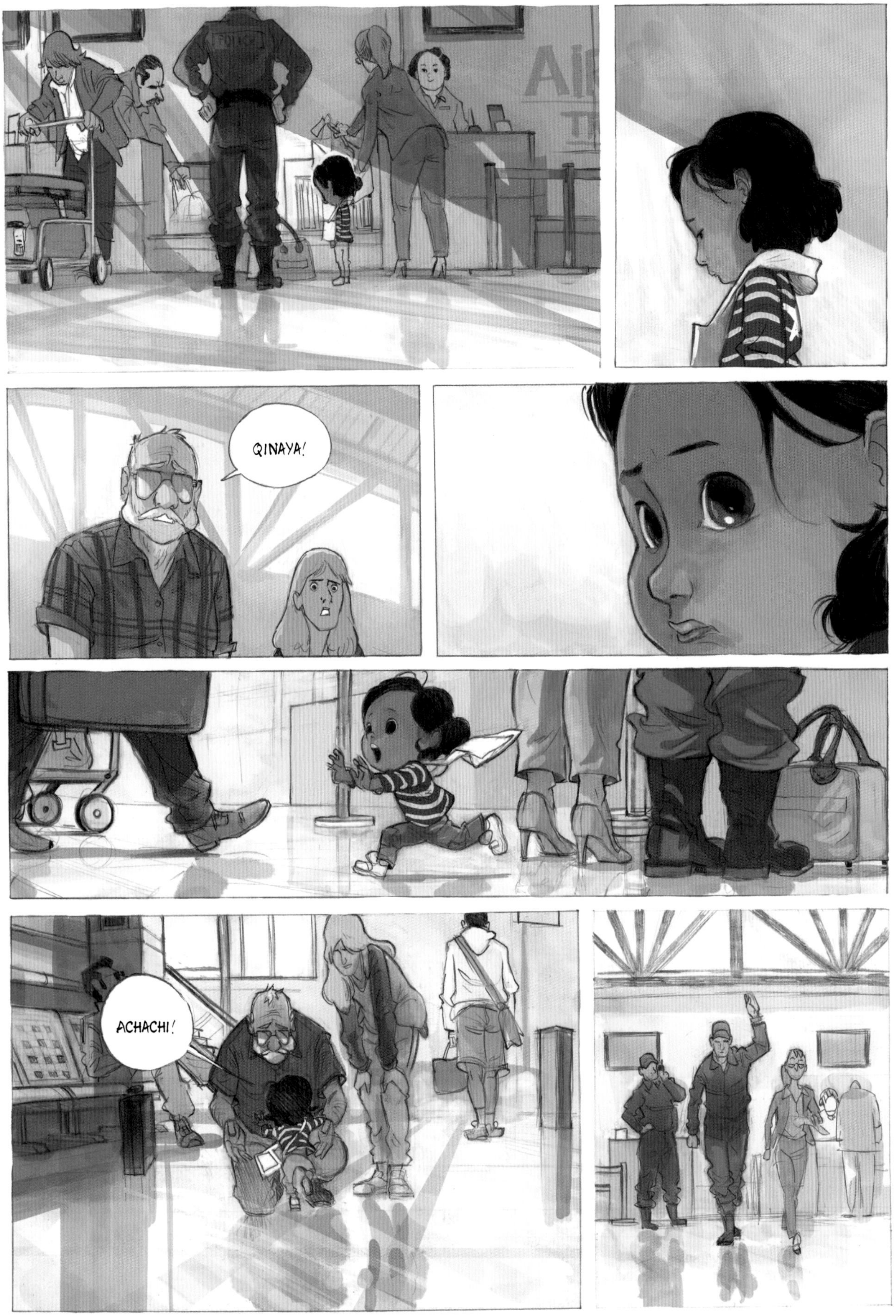

QINAYA!
ACHACHI!

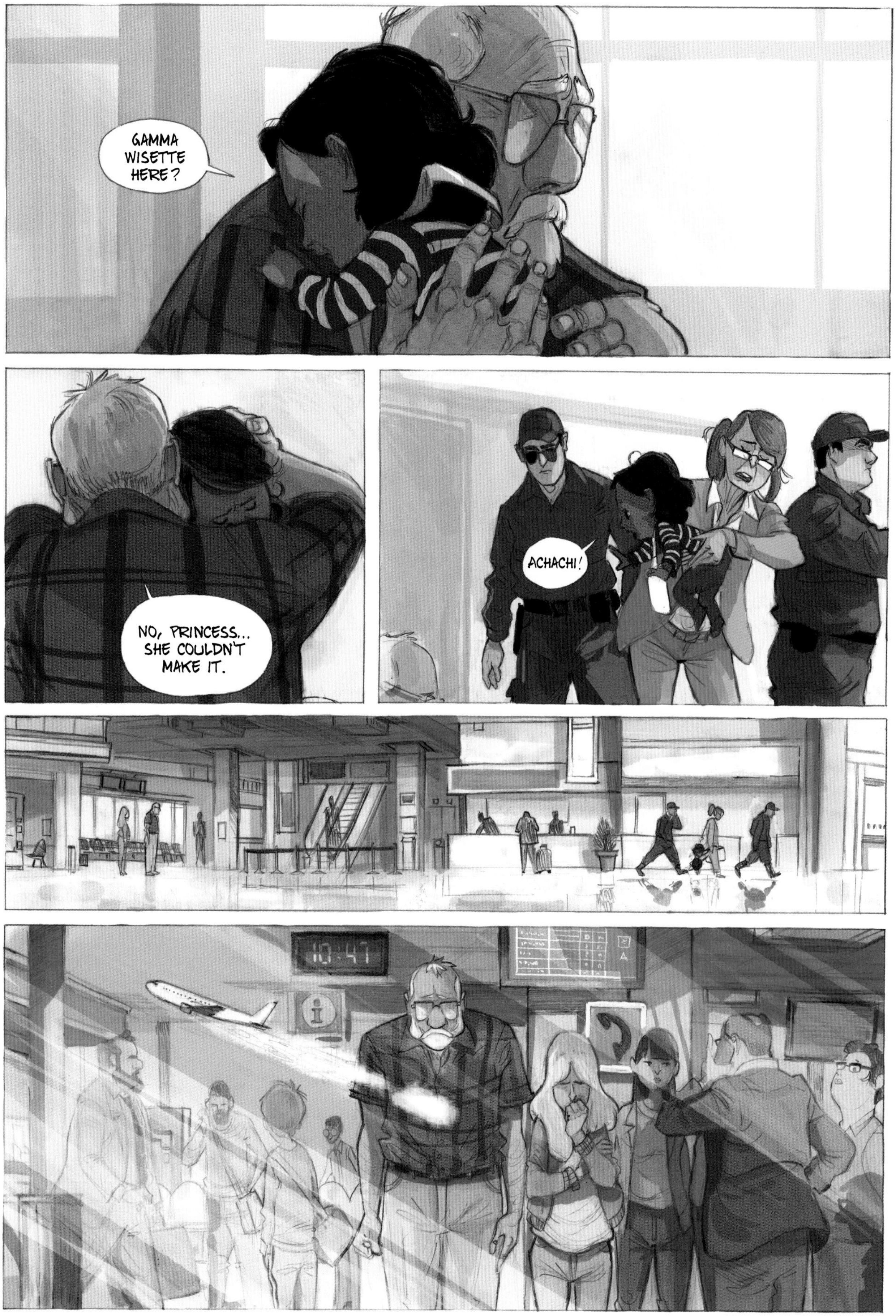
GAMMA WISETTE HERE?
NO, PRINCESS... SHE COULDN'T MAKE IT.
ACHACHI!
10:47

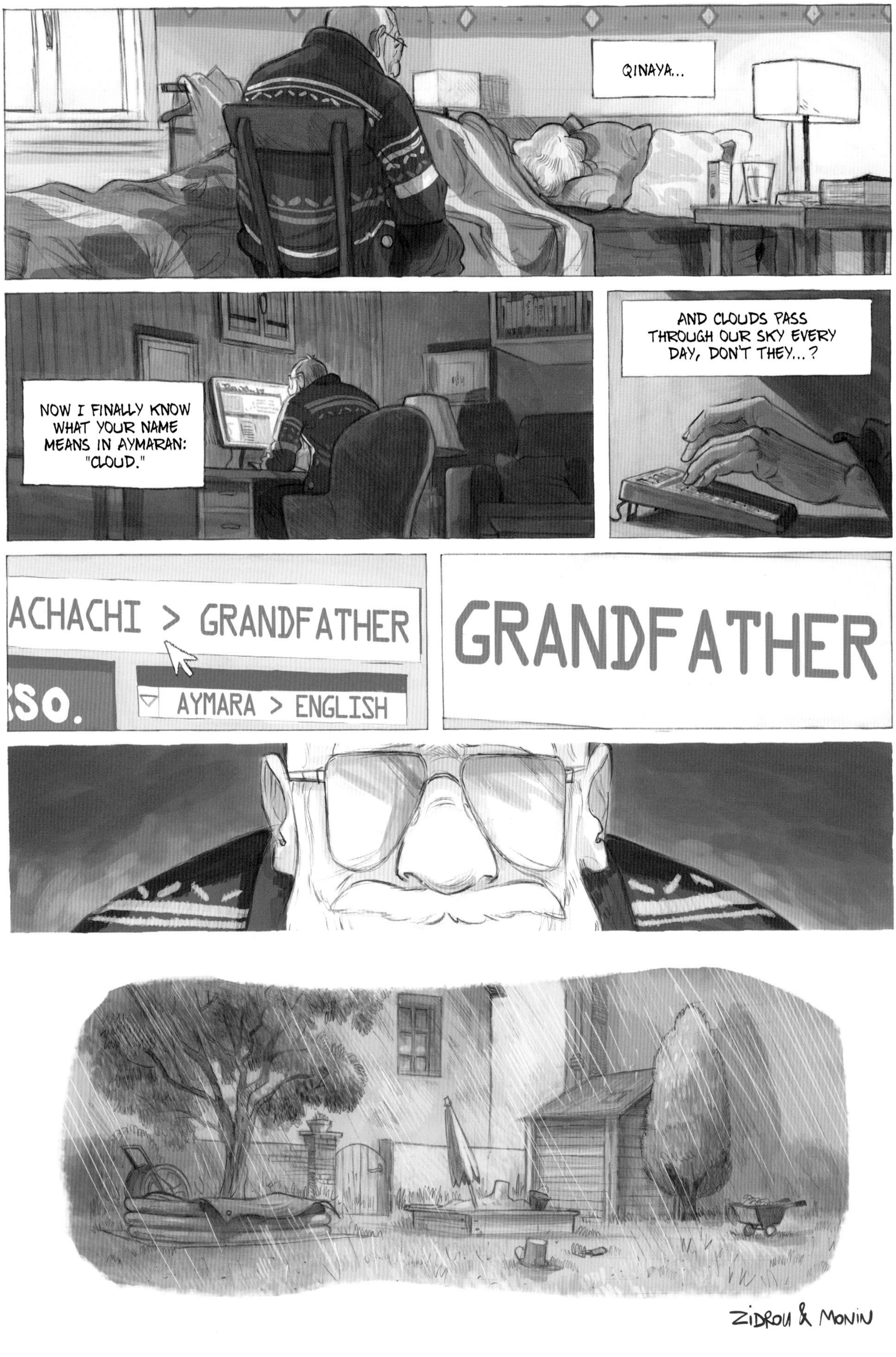
QINAYA...
NOW I FINALLY KNOW WHAT YOUR NAME MEANS IN AYMARAN: "CLOUD."
AND CLOUDS PASS THROUGH OUR SKY EVERY DAY, DON'T THEY...?
ACHACHI > GRANDFATHER
AYMARA > ENGLISH
GRANDFATHER

ZIDROU & MONIN

— LA GARÚA —

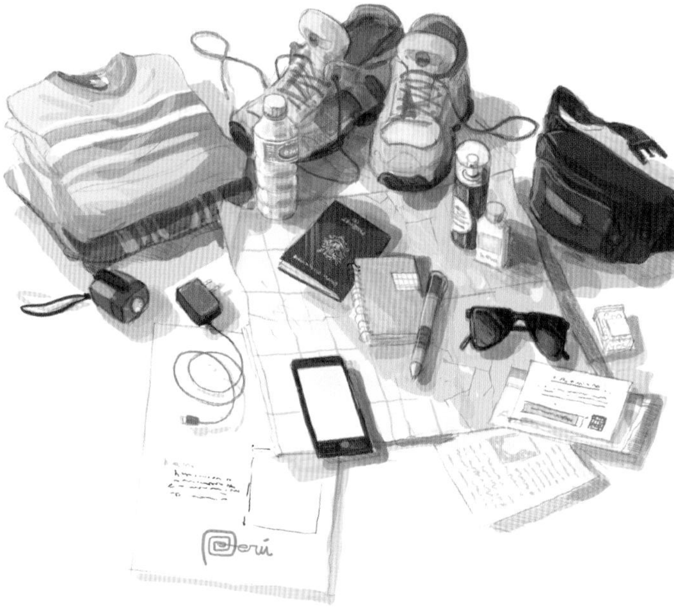
Perú

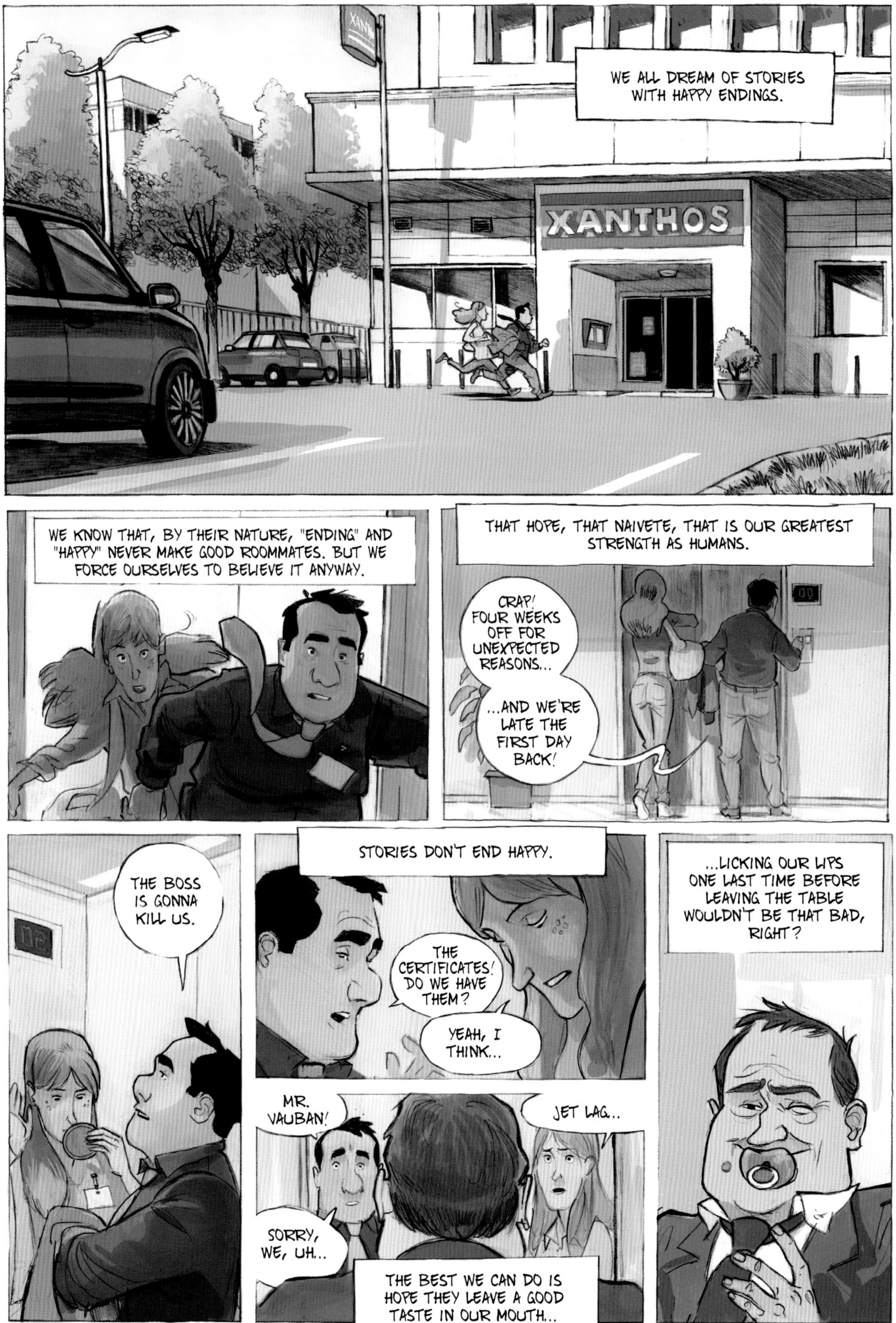
XANTHOS
WE ALL DREAM OF STORIES WITH HAPPY ENDINGS.
WE KNOW THAT, BY THEIR NATURE, "ENDING" AND "HAPPY" NEVER MAKE GOOD ROOMMATES. BUT WE FORCE OURSELVES TO BELIEVE IT ANYWAY.
THAT HOPE, THAT NAIVETE, THAT IS OUR GREATEST STRENGTH AS HUMANS.
CRAP! FOUR WEEKS OFF FOR UNEXPECTED REASONS...
...AND WE'RE LATE THE FIRST DAY BACK!
THE BOSS IS GONNA KILL US.
STORIES DON'T END HAPPY.
THE CERTIFICATES! DO WE HAVE THEM?
YEAH, I THINK...
MR. VAUBAN!
JET LAG...
SORRY, WE, UH...
THE BEST WE CAN DO IS HOPE THEY LEAVE A GOOD TASTE IN OUR MOUTH...
...LICKING OUR LIPS ONE LAST TIME BEFORE LEAVING THE TABLE WOULDN'T BE THAT BAD, RIGHT?

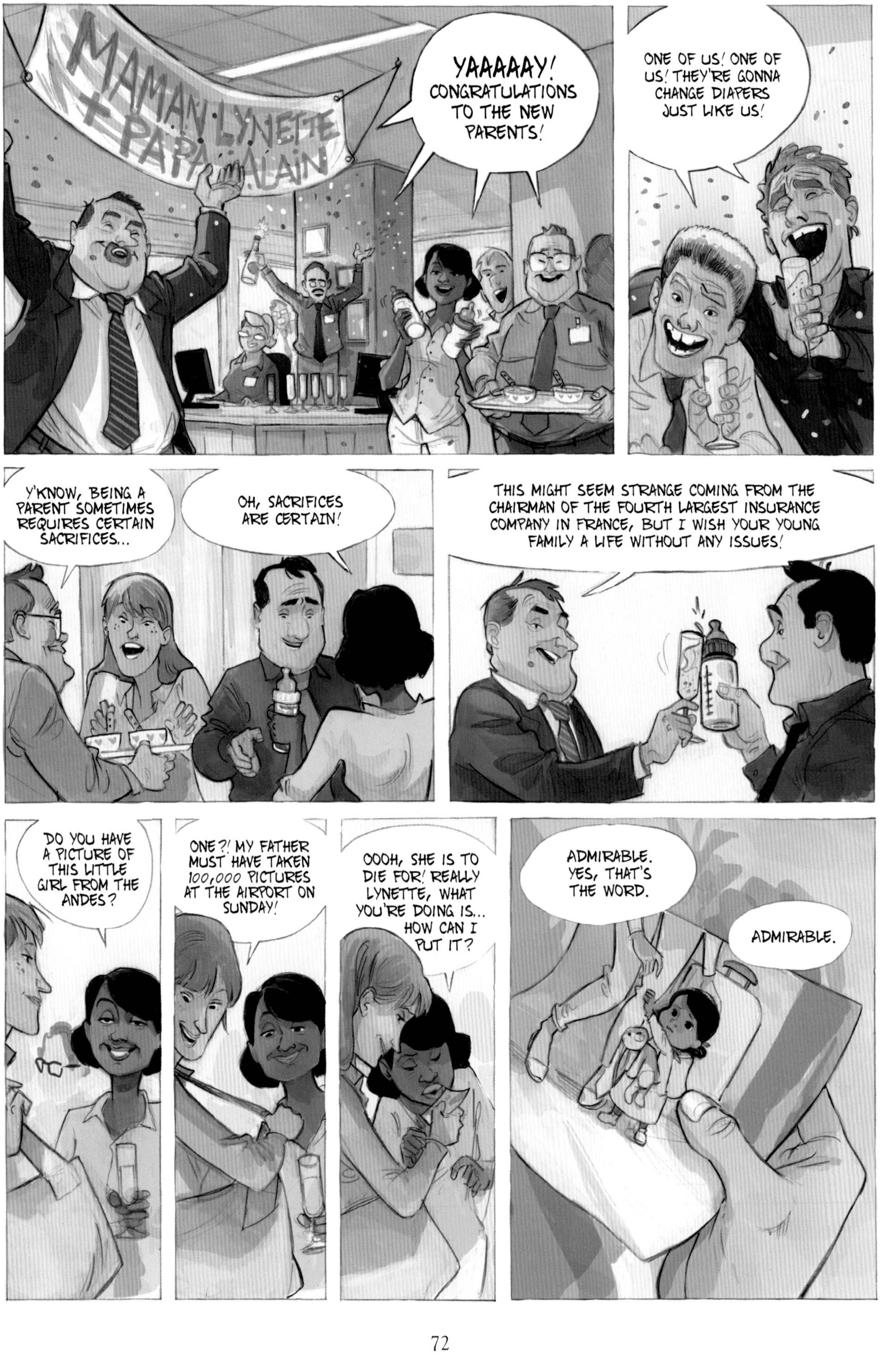
MAMAN LYNETTE + PAPA ALAIN
YAAAAAY! CONGRATULATIONS TO THE NEW PARENTS!
ONE OF US! ONE OF US! THEY'RE GONNA CHANGE DIAPERS JUST LIKE US!
Y'KNOW, BEING A PARENT SOMETIMES REQUIRES CERTAIN SACRIFICES...
OH, SACRIFICES ARE CERTAIN!
THIS MIGHT SEEM STRANGE COMING FROM THE CHAIRMAN OF THE FOURTH LARGEST INSURANCE COMPANY IN FRANCE, BUT I WISH YOUR YOUNG FAMILY A LIFE WITHOUT ANY ISSUES!
DO YOU HAVE A PICTURE OF THIS LITTLE GIRL FROM THE ANDES?
ONE?! MY FATHER MUST HAVE TAKEN 100,000 PICTURES AT THE AIRPORT ON SUNDAY!
OOOH, SHE IS TO DIE FOR! REALLY LYNETTE, WHAT YOU'RE DOING IS... HOW CAN I PUT IT?
ADMIRABLE. YES, THAT'S THE WORD.
ADMIRABLE.

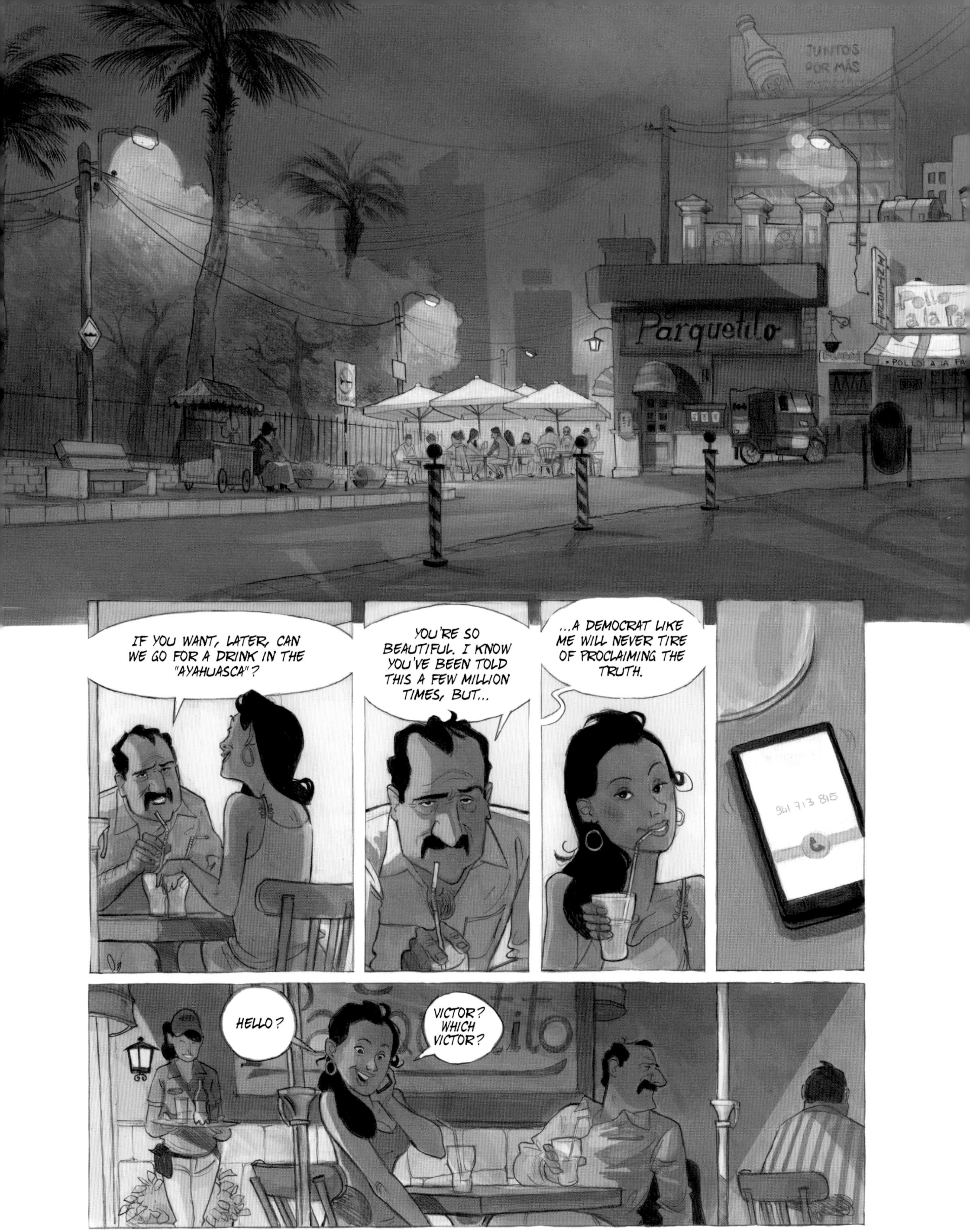
JUNTOS POR MÁS
Parquetito
Pollo a la Pa
POLLO A LA PA
IF YOU WANT, LATER, CAN WE GO FOR A DRINK IN THE "AYAHUASCA"?
YOU'RE SO BEAUTIFUL. I KNOW YOU'VE BEEN TOLD THIS A FEW MILLION TIMES, BUT...
...A DEMOCRAT LIKE ME WILL NEVER TIRE OF PROCLAIMING THE TRUTH.
941 713 815
HELLO?
VICTOR? WHICH VICTOR?

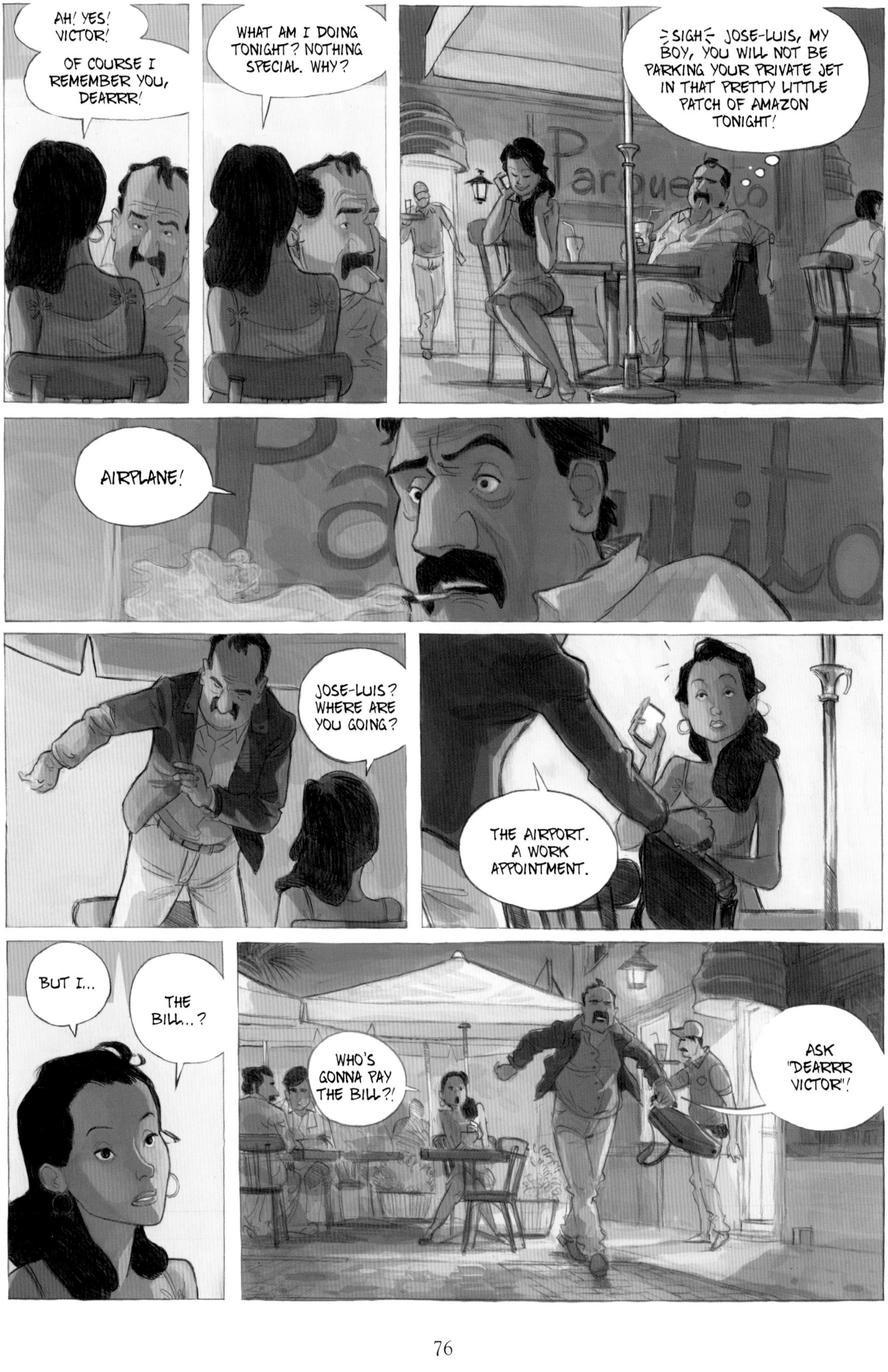
AH! YES! VICTOR!
OF COURSE I REMEMBER YOU, DEARRR!
WHAT AM I DOING TONIGHT? NOTHING SPECIAL. WHY?
Parquecito
=SIGH= JOSE-LUIS, MY BOY, YOU WILL NOT BE PARKING YOUR PRIVATE JET IN THAT PRETTY LITTLE PATCH OF AMAZON TONIGHT!
AIRPLANE!
JOSE-LUIS? WHERE ARE YOU GOING?
THE AIRPORT. A WORK APPOINTMENT.
BUT I...
THE BILL...?
WHO'S GONNA PAY THE BILL?!
ASK "DEARRR VICTOR"!

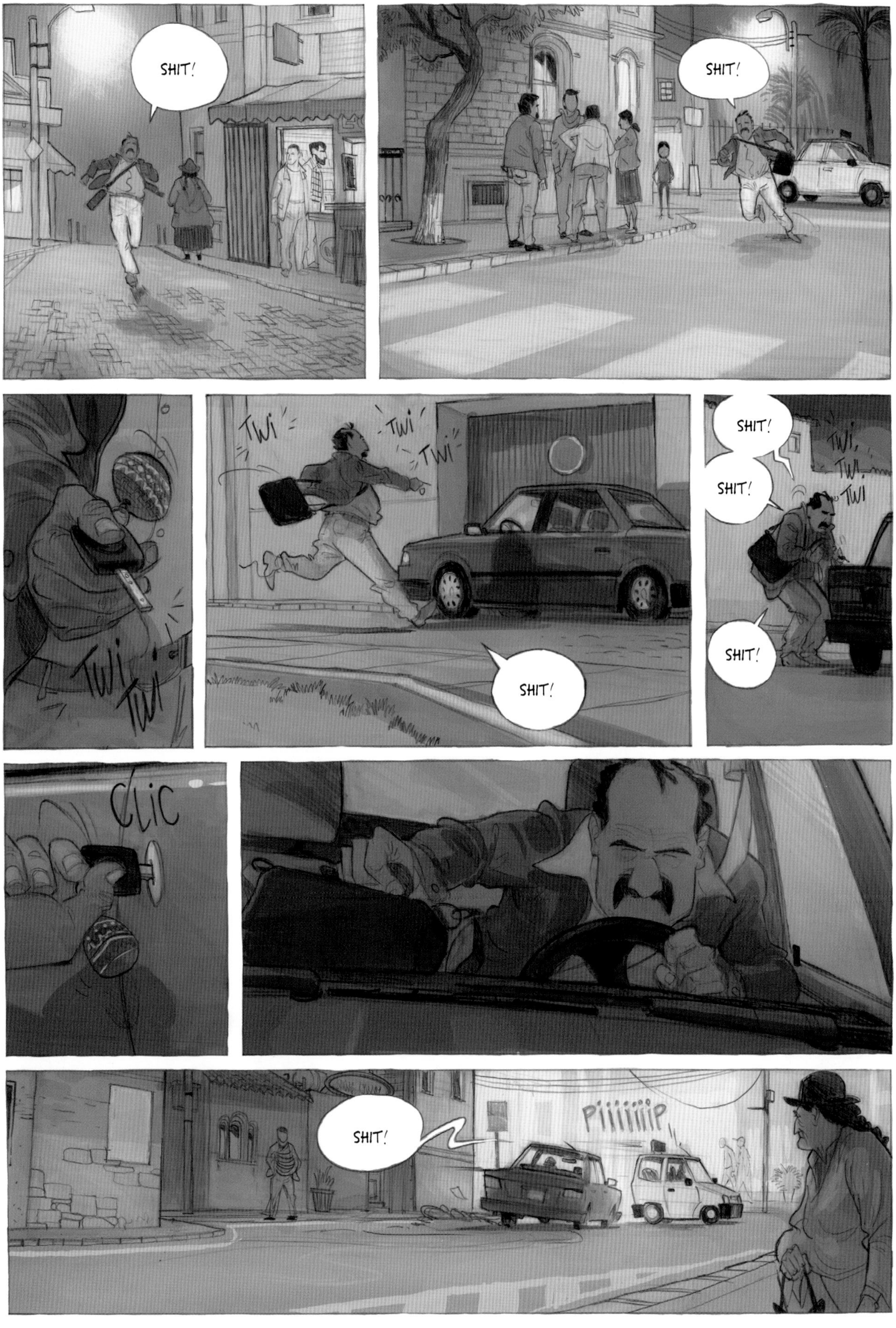
SHIT!
SHIT!
TWI
TWI
TWI
TWI
TWI
TWI
SHIT!
SHIT!
SHIT!
TWI
TWI
TWI
SHIT!
CLIC
SHIT!
PIIIIIIIP

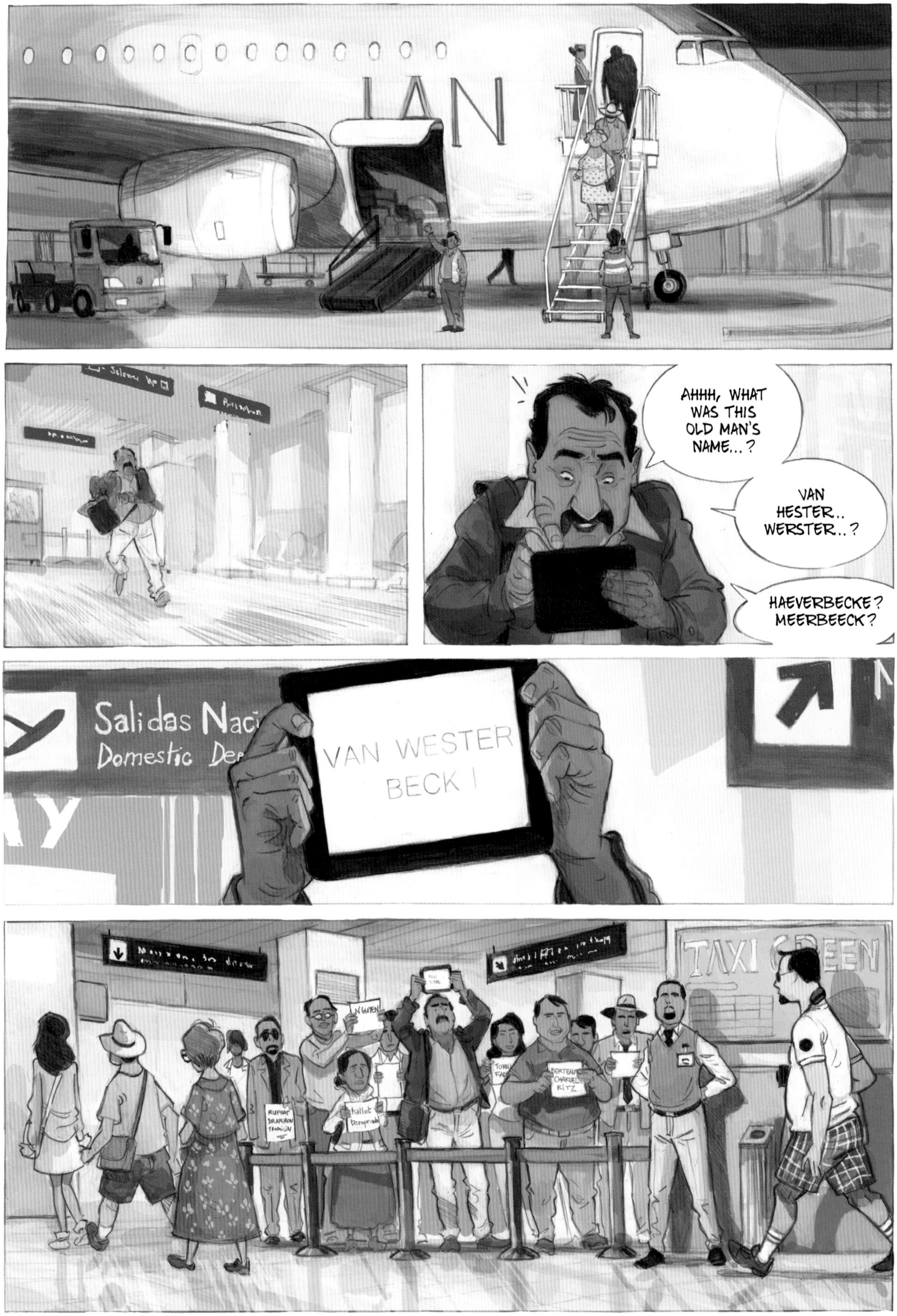
LAN
AHHH, WHAT WAS THIS OLD MAN'S NAME...?
VAN HESTER.. WERSTER..?
HAEVERBECKE? MEERBEECK?
Salidas Naci
Domestic De
VAN WESTER BECK !
TAXI GREEN
N'GUYEN

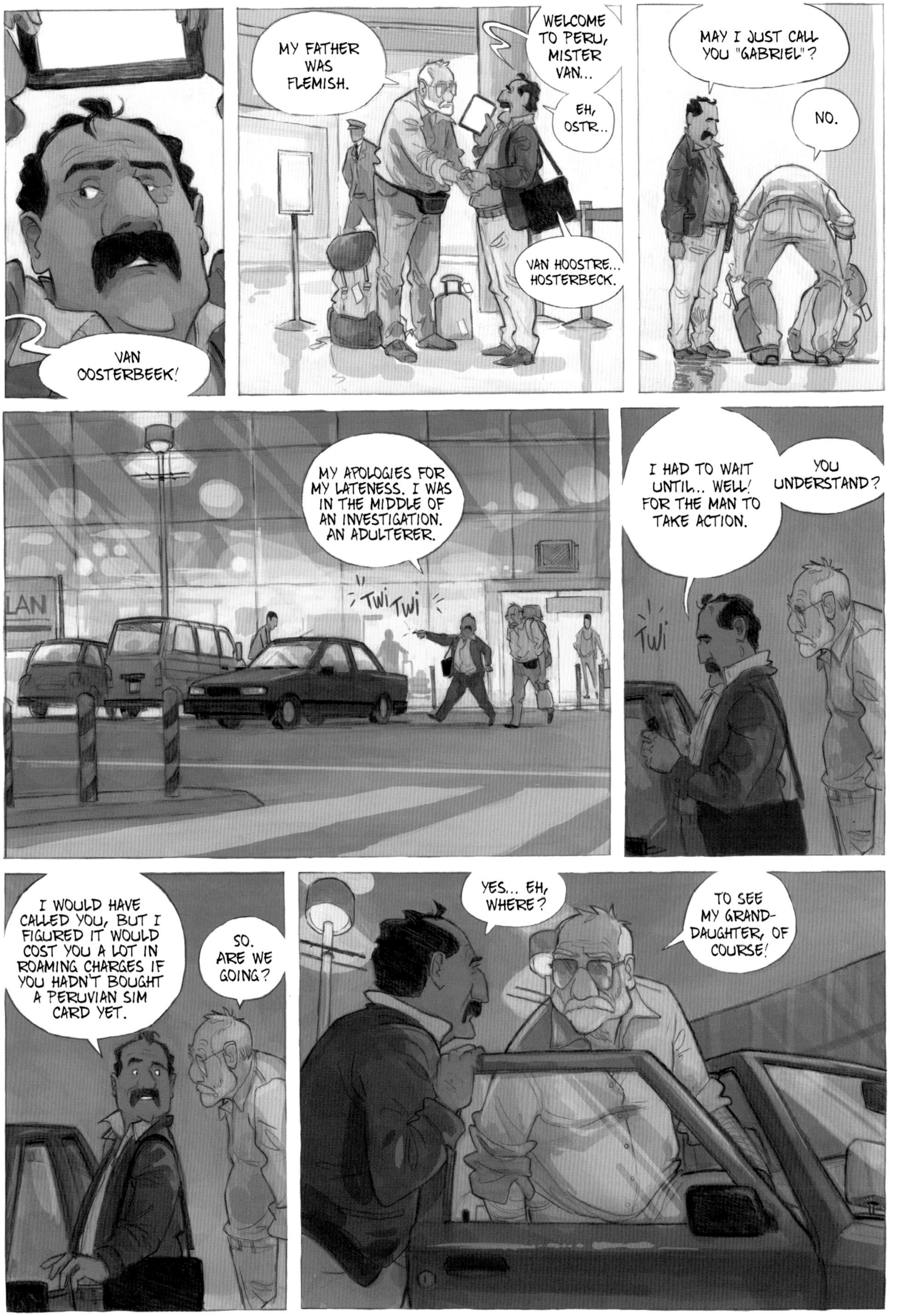
VAN OOSTERBEEK!
WELCOME TO PERU, MISTER VAN...
EH, OSTR..
VAN HOOSTRE... HOSTERBECK.
MY FATHER WAS FLEMISH.
MAY I JUST CALL YOU "GABRIEL"?
NO.
LAN
MY APOLOGIES FOR MY LATENESS. I WAS IN THE MIDDLE OF AN INVESTIGATION. AN ADULTERER.
TWI TWI
I HAD TO WAIT UNTIL... WELL! FOR THE MAN TO TAKE ACTION.
YOU UNDERSTAND?
TWI
I WOULD HAVE CALLED YOU, BUT I FIGURED IT WOULD COST YOU A LOT IN ROAMING CHARGES IF YOU HADN'T BOUGHT A PERUVIAN SIM CARD YET.
SO. ARE WE GOING?
YES... EH, WHERE?
TO SEE MY GRAND-DAUGHTER, OF COURSE!

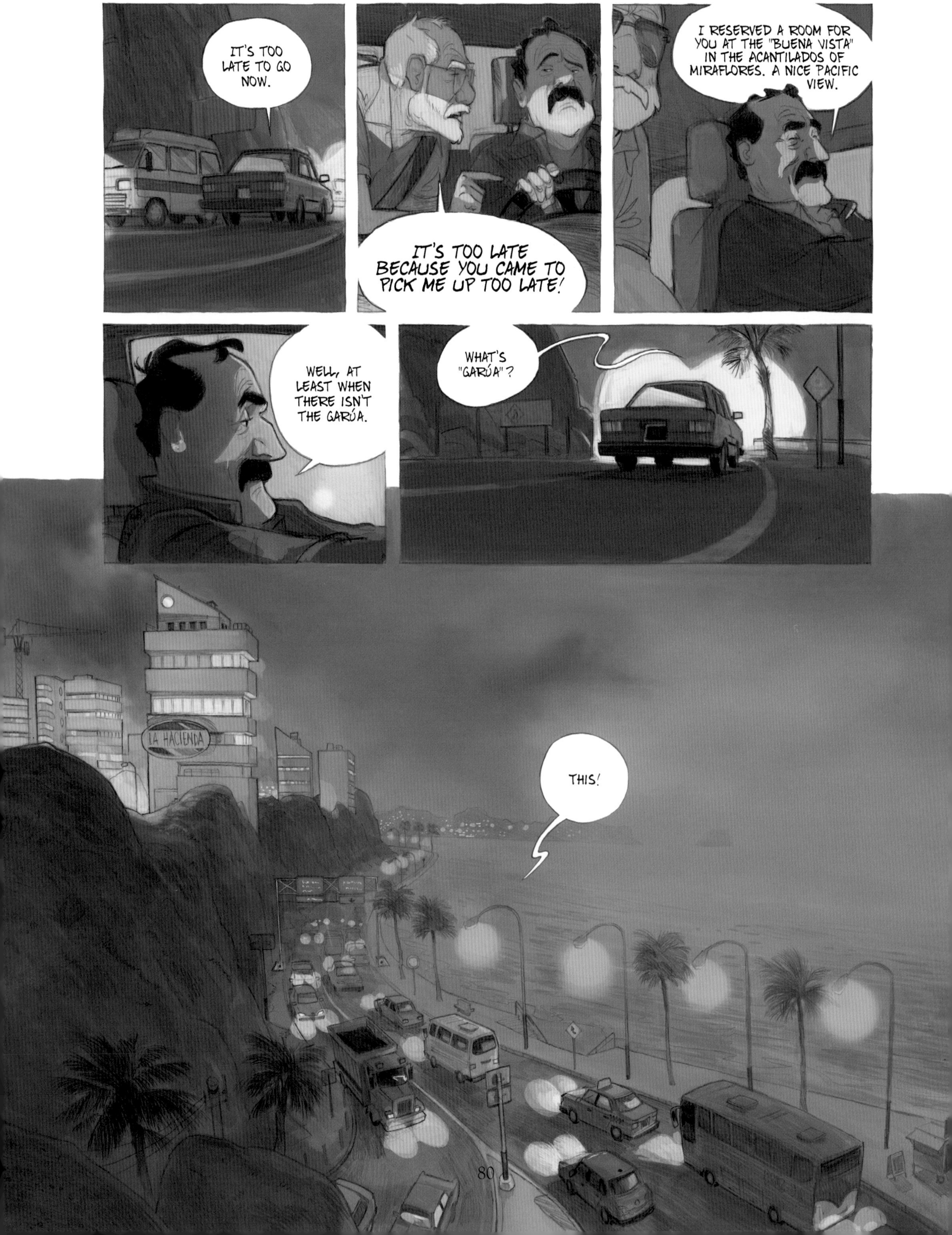

IT'S TOO LATE TO GO NOW.
IT'S TOO LATE BECAUSE YOU CAME TO PICK ME UP TOO LATE!
I RESERVED A ROOM FOR YOU AT THE "BUENA VISTA" IN THE ACANTILADOS OF MIRAFLORES. A NICE PACIFIC VIEW.
WELL, AT LEAST WHEN THERE ISN'T THE GARÚA.
WHAT'S "GARÚA"?
LA HACIENDA
THIS!

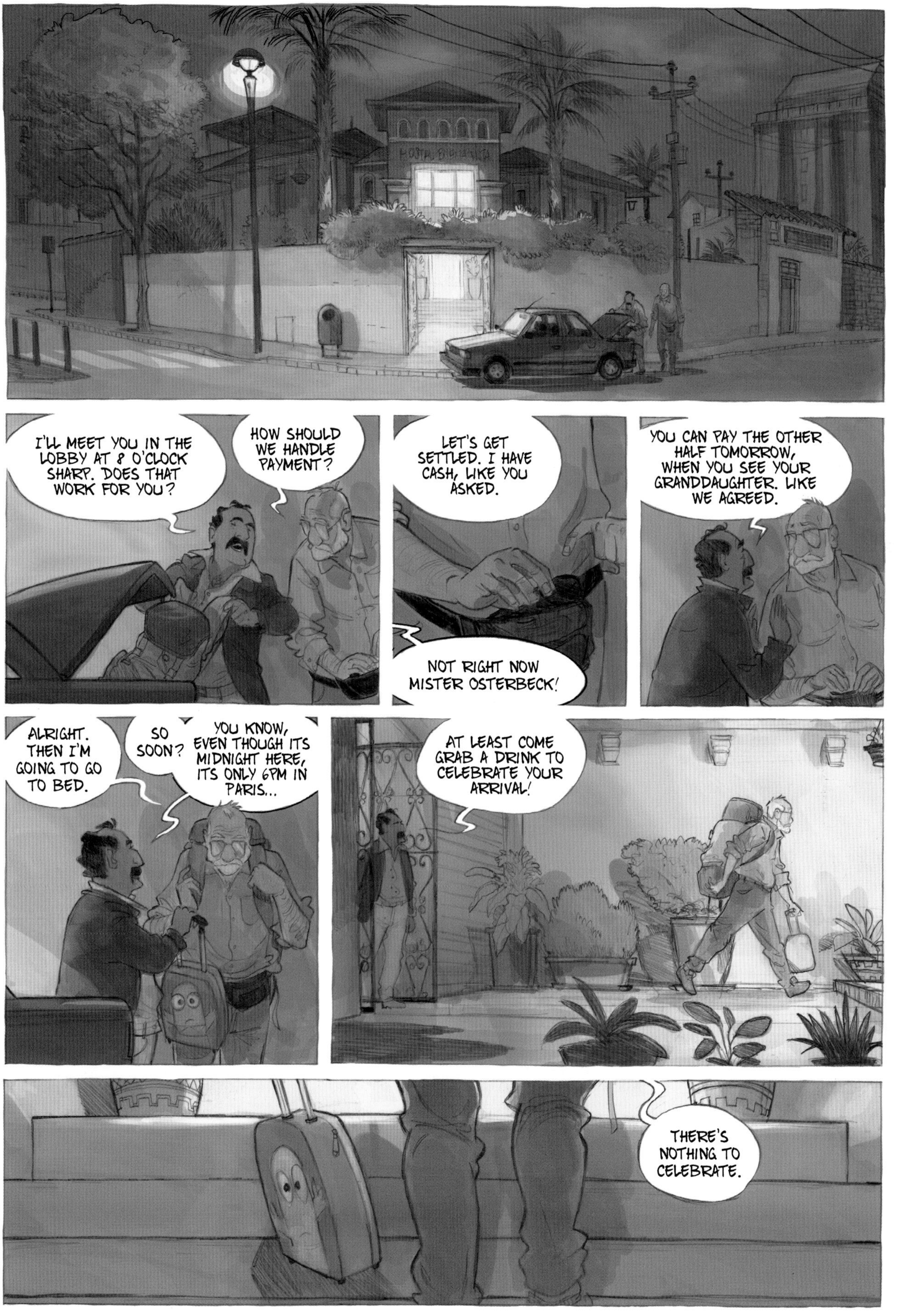
I'LL MEET YOU IN THE LOBBY AT 8 O'CLOCK SHARP. DOES THAT WORK FOR YOU?
HOW SHOULD WE HANDLE PAYMENT?
LET'S GET SETTLED. I HAVE CASH, LIKE YOU ASKED.
NOT RIGHT NOW MISTER OSTERBECK!
YOU CAN PAY THE OTHER HALF TOMORROW, WHEN YOU SEE YOUR GRANDDAUGHTER. LIKE WE AGREED.
ALRIGHT. THEN I'M GOING TO GO TO BED.
SO SOON?
YOU KNOW, EVEN THOUGH ITS MIDNIGHT HERE, ITS ONLY 6PM IN PARIS...
AT LEAST COME GRAB A DRINK TO CELEBRATE YOUR ARRIVAL!
THERE'S NOTHING TO CELEBRATE.

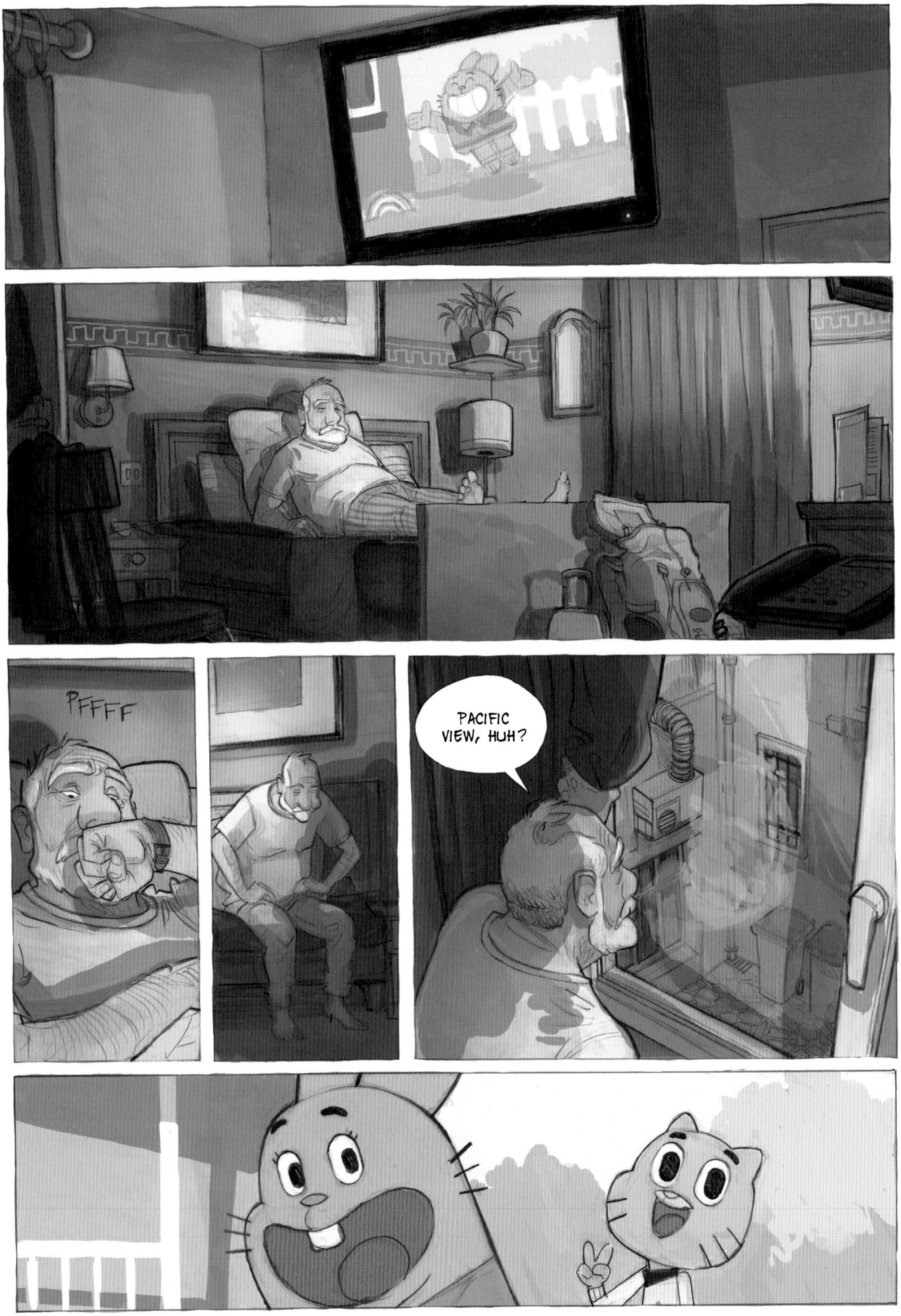
PFFFF
PACIFIC VIEW, HUH?

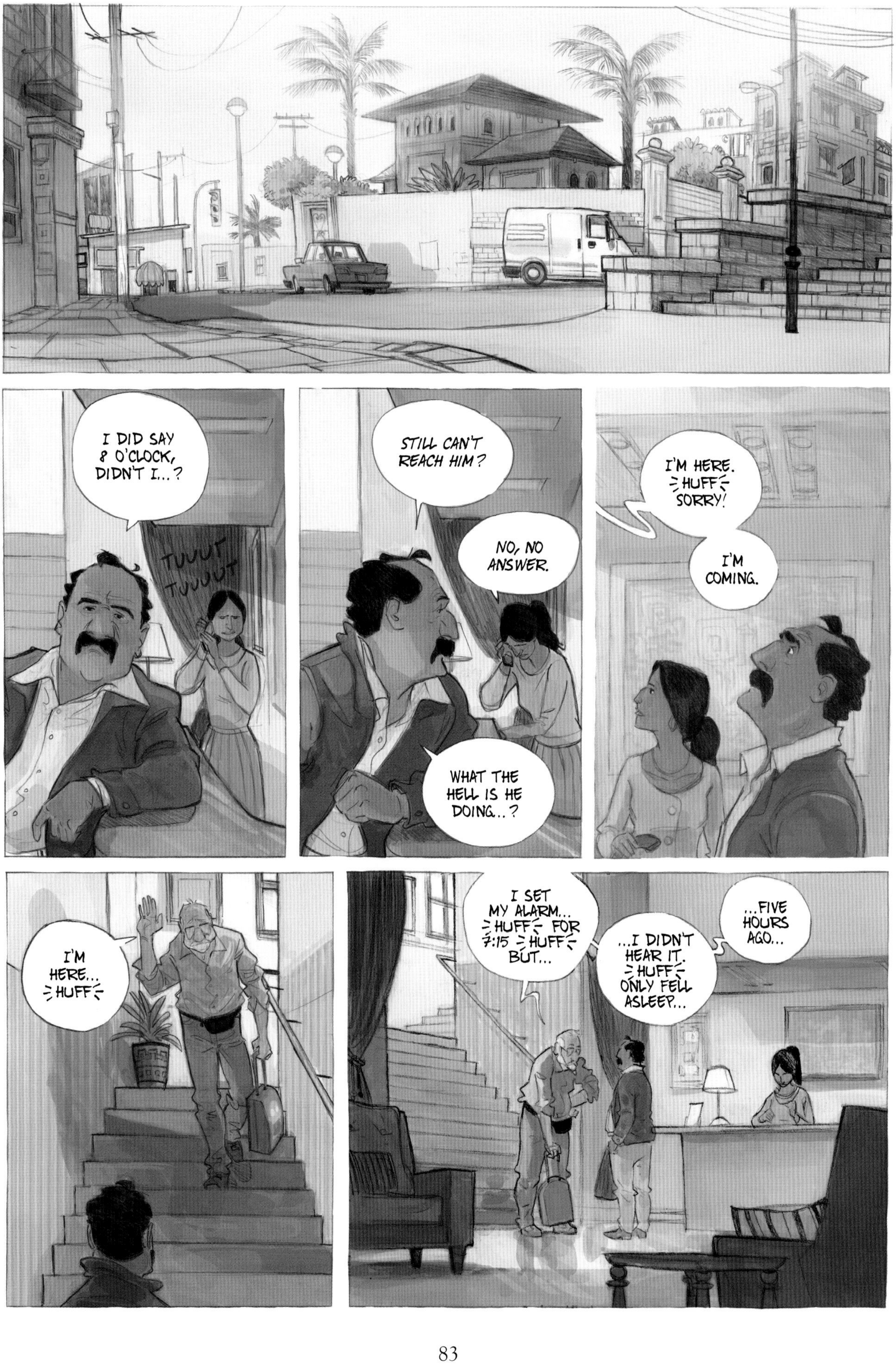

I DID SAY 8 O'CLOCK, DIDN'T I...?
TUUUT TUUUUT
STILL CAN'T REACH HIM?
NO, NO ANSWER.
WHAT THE HELL IS HE DOING...?
I'M HERE. HUFF SORRY!
I'M COMING.
I'M HERE... HUFF
I SET MY ALARM... HUFF FOR 7:15 HUFF BUT...
...I DIDN'T HEAR IT. HUFF ONLY FELL ASLEEP...
...FIVE HOURS AGO...

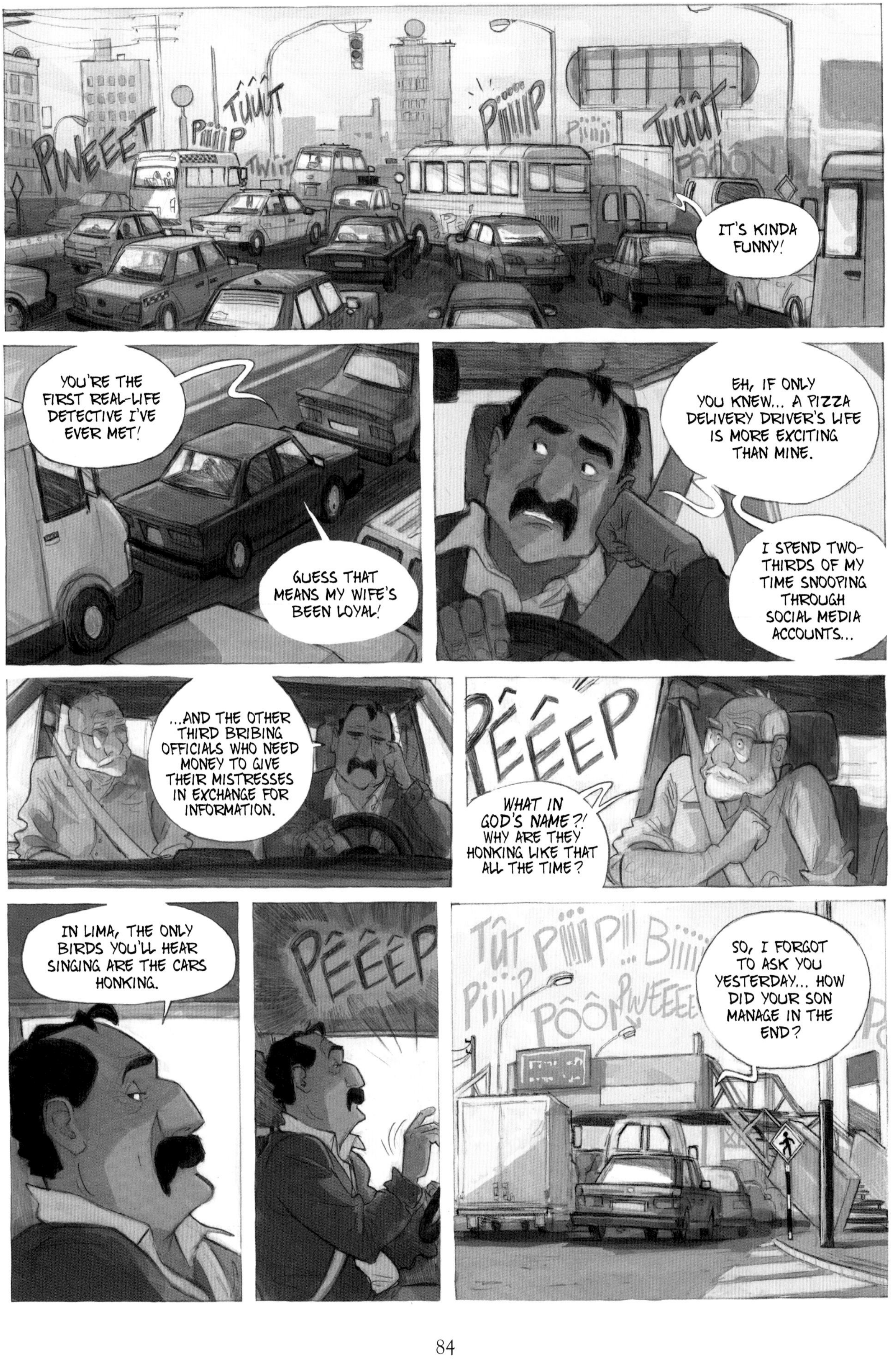
PWEEET
TÛÛÛT
PÎÎÎP
TÛÛÛT
PÔÔÔN
IT'S KINDA FUNNY!
YOU'RE THE FIRST REAL-LIFE DETECTIVE I'VE EVER MET!
GUESS THAT MEANS MY WIFE'S BEEN LOYAL!
EH, IF ONLY YOU KNEW... A PIZZA DELIVERY DRIVER'S LIFE IS MORE EXCITING THAN MINE.
I SPEND TWO-THIRDS OF MY TIME SNOOPING THROUGH SOCIAL MEDIA ACCOUNTS...
...AND THE OTHER THIRD BRIBING OFFICIALS WHO NEED MONEY TO GIVE THEIR MISTRESSES IN EXCHANGE FOR INFORMATION.
PÊÊÊP
WHAT IN GOD'S NAME?! WHY ARE THEY HONKING LIKE THAT ALL THE TIME?
IN LIMA, THE ONLY BIRDS YOU'LL HEAR SINGING ARE THE CARS HONKING.
PÊÊÊP
TÛT
PÔÔN
SO, I FORGOT TO ASK YOU YESTERDAY... HOW DID YOUR SON MANAGE IN THE END?

HE GOT SADDLED WITH THREE YEARS.

HE TOOK THE FULL RAP HIMSELF TO SAVE HIS WIFE, LYNETTE.

THE JUDGE TOOK INTO ACCOUNT "THE PROFOUND DESPAIR OF A WOMAN UNABLE TO GIVE LIFE..."

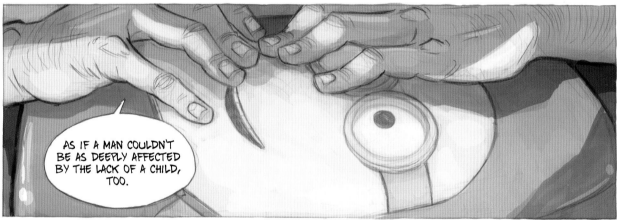

AS IF A MAN COULDN'T BE AS DEEPLY AFFECTED BY THE LACK OF A CHILD, TOO.

LYNETTE WENT BACK TO ENGLAND, AND THEY STARTED DIVORCE PROCEEDINGS.

...OUR "GENTLEMAN" IS DETAINED IN CARQUEFOU NOW.

WHAT A MESS! THEY WANTED TO START A FAMILY, AND NOW THEY'VE DESTROYED ONE!

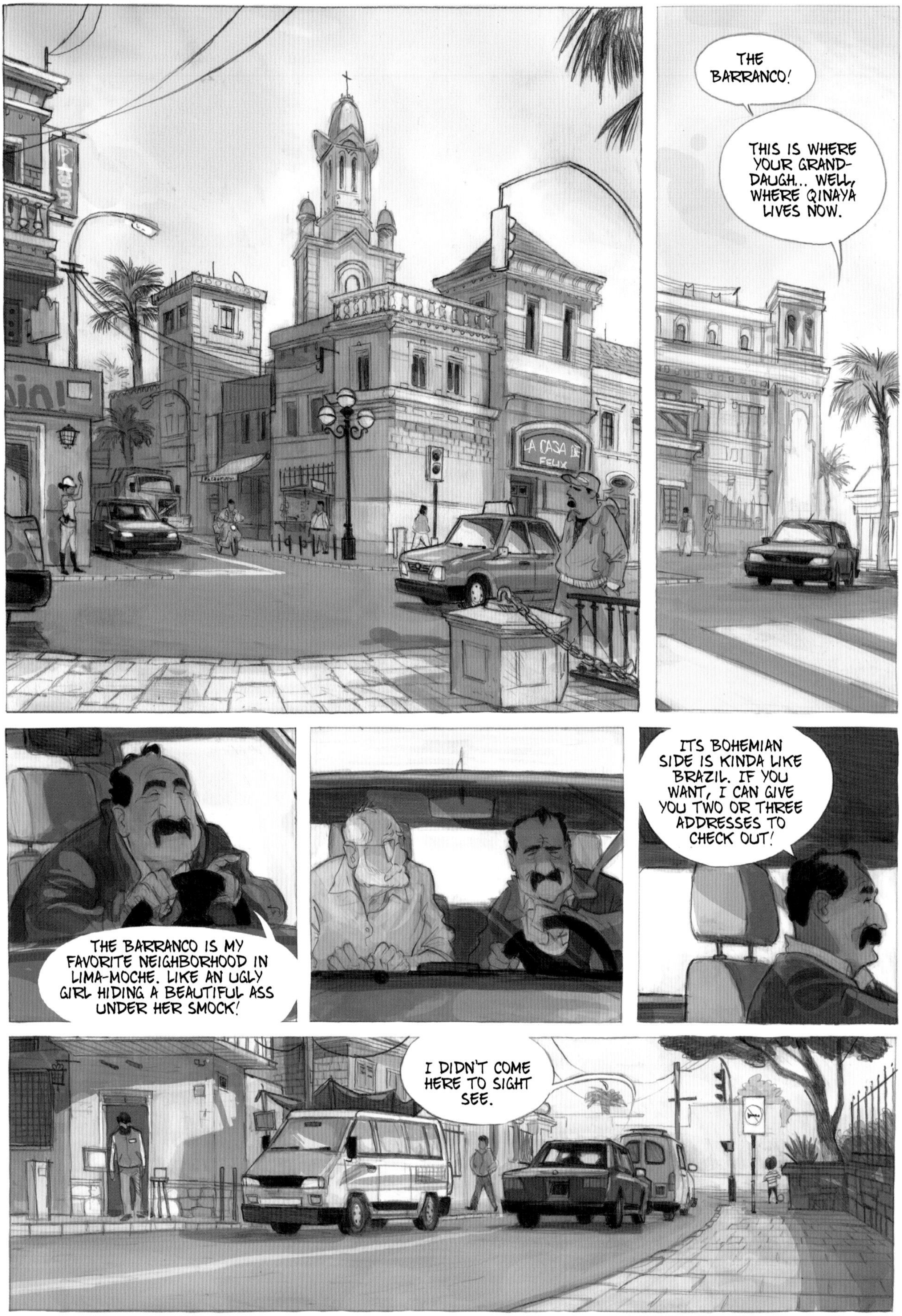
LA CASA DE FELIX
THE BARRANCO!
THIS IS WHERE YOUR GRAND-DAUGH... WELL, WHERE QINAYA LIVES NOW.
THE BARRANCO IS MY FAVORITE NEIGHBORHOOD IN LIMA-MOCHE. LIKE AN UGLY GIRL HIDING A BEAUTIFUL ASS UNDER HER SMOCK!
ITS BOHEMIAN SIDE IS KINDA LIKE BRAZIL. IF YOU WANT, I CAN GIVE YOU TWO OR THREE ADDRESSES TO CHECK OUT!
I DIDN'T COME HERE TO SIGHT SEE.

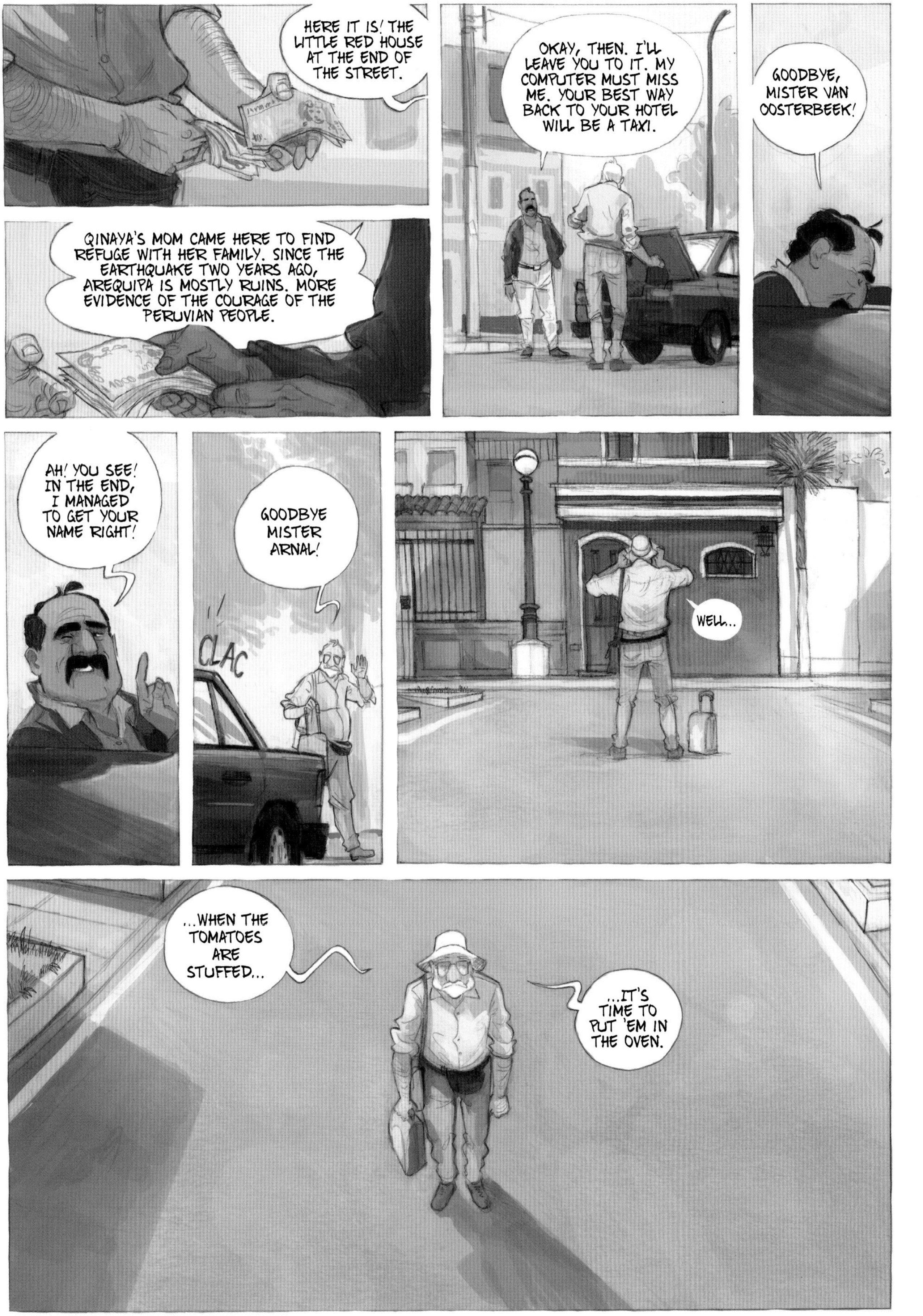
HERE IT IS! THE LITTLE RED HOUSE AT THE END OF THE STREET.
QINAYA'S MOM CAME HERE TO FIND REFUGE WITH HER FAMILY. SINCE THE EARTHQUAKE TWO YEARS AGO, AREQUIPA IS MOSTLY RUINS. MORE EVIDENCE OF THE COURAGE OF THE PERUVIAN PEOPLE.
OKAY, THEN. I'LL LEAVE YOU TO IT. MY COMPUTER MUST MISS ME. YOUR BEST WAY BACK TO YOUR HOTEL WILL BE A TAXI.
GOODBYE, MISTER VAN OOSTERBEEK!
AH! YOU SEE! IN THE END, I MANAGED TO GET YOUR NAME RIGHT!
GOODBYE MISTER ARNAL!
CLAC
WELL...
...WHEN THE TOMATOES ARE STUFFED...
...IT'S TIME TO PUT 'EM IN THE OVEN.

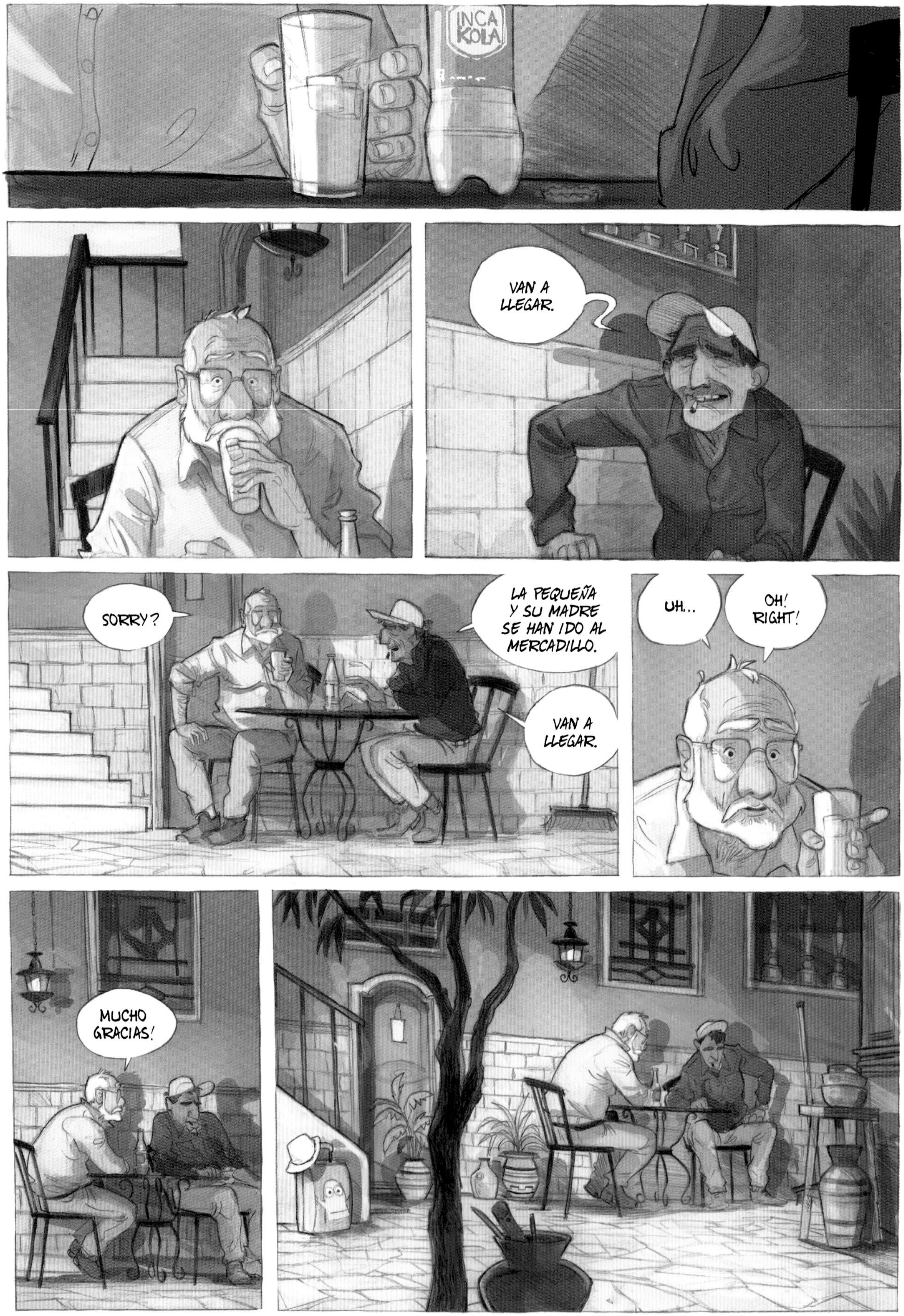
INCA KOLA
VAN A LLEGAR.
SORRY?
LA PEQUEÑA Y SU MADRE SE HAN IDO AL MERCADILLO.
VAN A LLEGAR.
UH...
OH! RIGHT!
MUCHO GRACIAS!

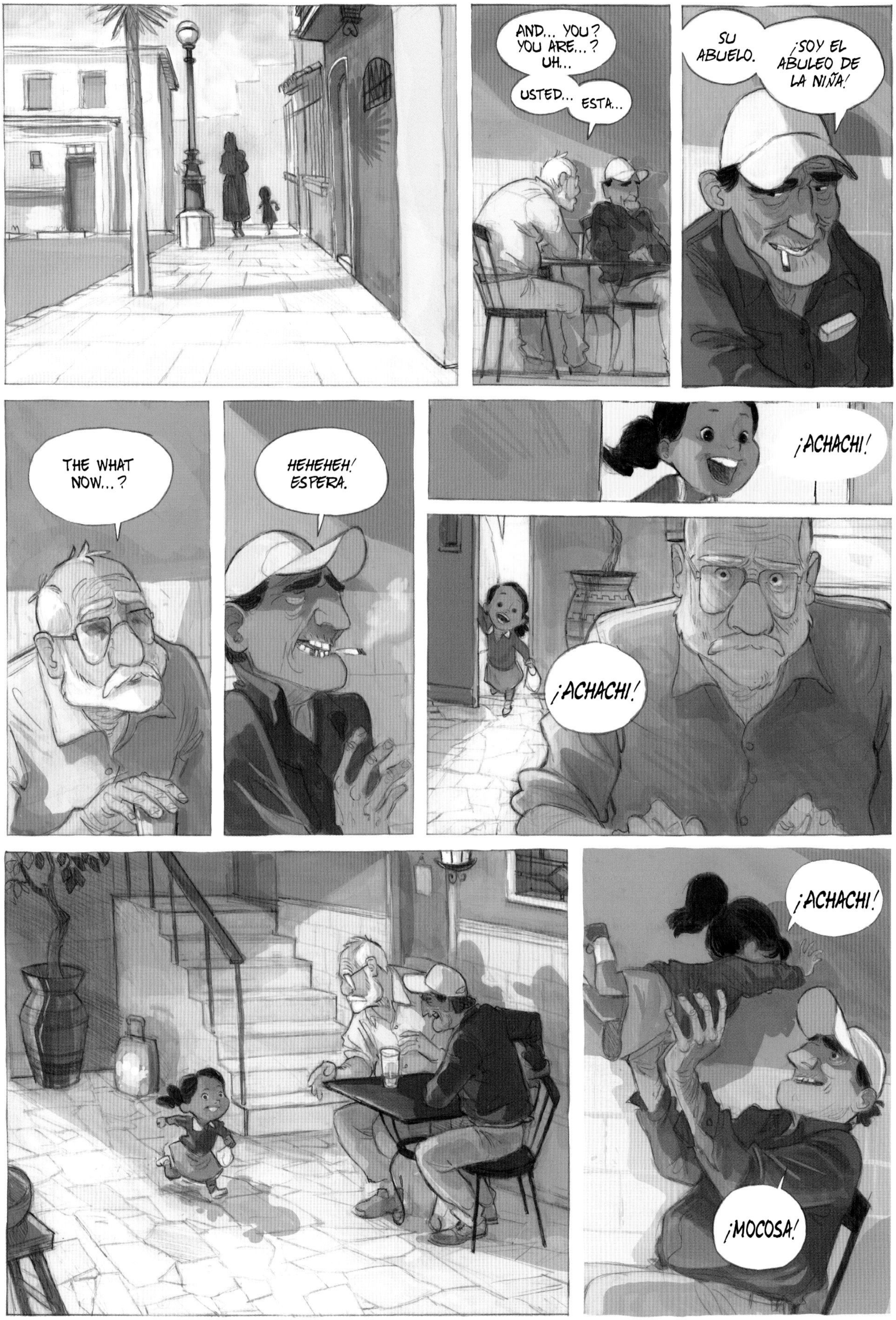
AND... YOU? YOU ARE...? UH...
USTED... ESTA...
SU ABUELO.
¡SOY EL ABULEO DE LA NIÑA!
THE WHAT NOW...?
HEHEHEH! ESPERA.
¡ACHACHI!
¡ACHACHI!
¡ACHACHI!
¡MOCOSA!

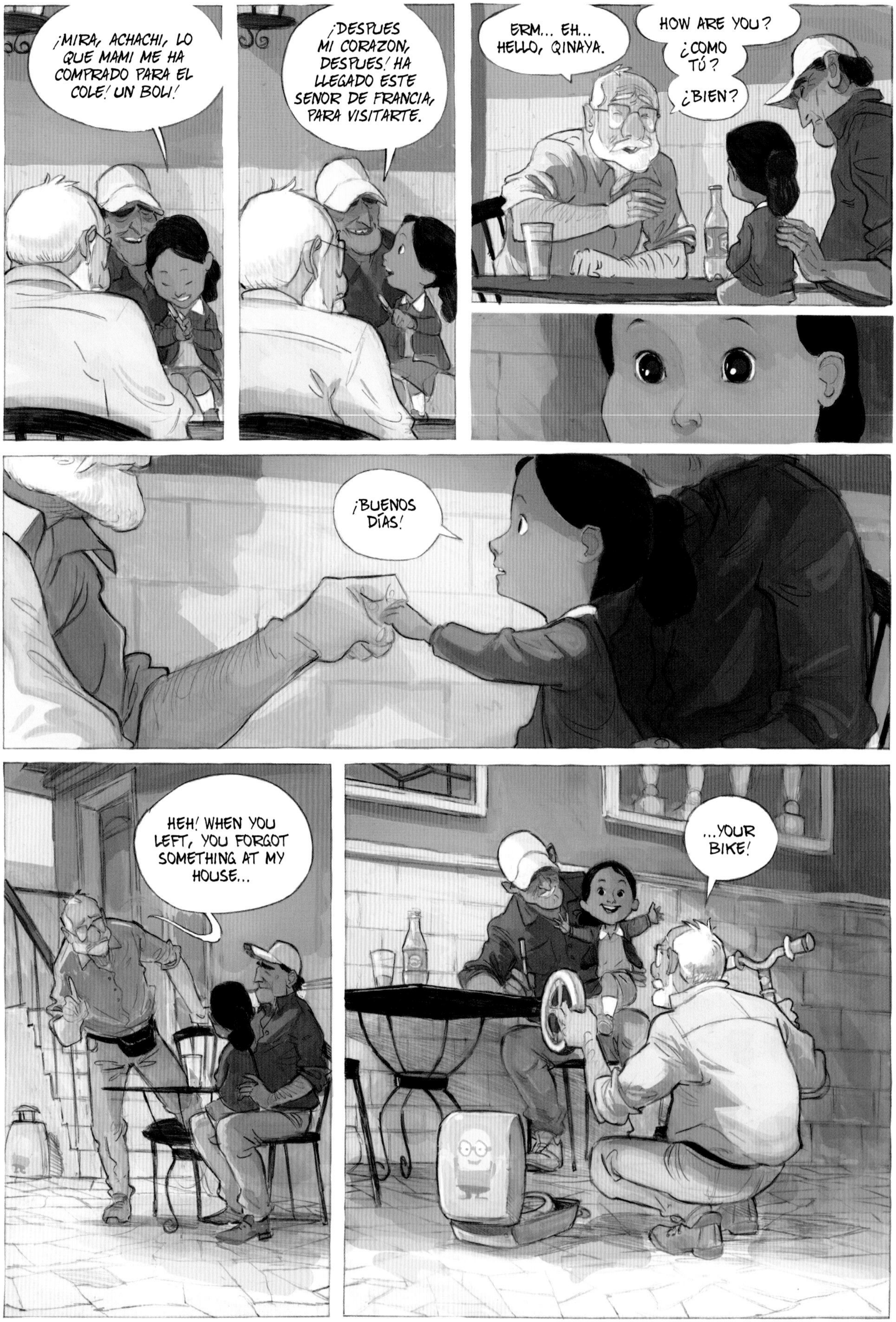
¡MIRA, ACHACHI, LO QUE MAMI ME HA COMPRADO PARA EL COLE! UN BOLI!
¡DESPUES MI CORAZON, DESPUES! HA LLEGADO ESTE SENOR DE FRANCIA, PARA VISITARTE.
ERM... EH... HELLO, QINAYA.
HOW ARE YOU?
¿COMO TÚ?
¿BIEN?
¡BUENOS DÍAS!
HEH! WHEN YOU LEFT, YOU FORGOT SOMETHING AT MY HOUSE...
...YOUR BIKE!

HERE! I'LL REBUILD IT FOR YOU!

IT STILL WORKS GREAT, YOU'LL SEE!

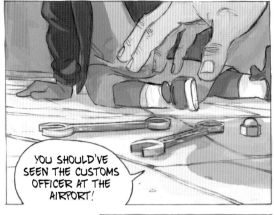

YOU SHOULD'VE SEEN THE CUSTOMS OFFICER AT THE AIRPORT!

I THINK HE THOUGHT I WAS PLANNING ON CLIMBING THE ANDES WITH IT, OR SOMETHING LIKE THAT! HEH HEH...

I HOPE YOU HAVEN'T FORGOTTEN HOW TO RIDE A BIKE...

THERE!

HMM...

I GUESS I NEED TO RAISE THE SEAT A LITTLE BIT...

91

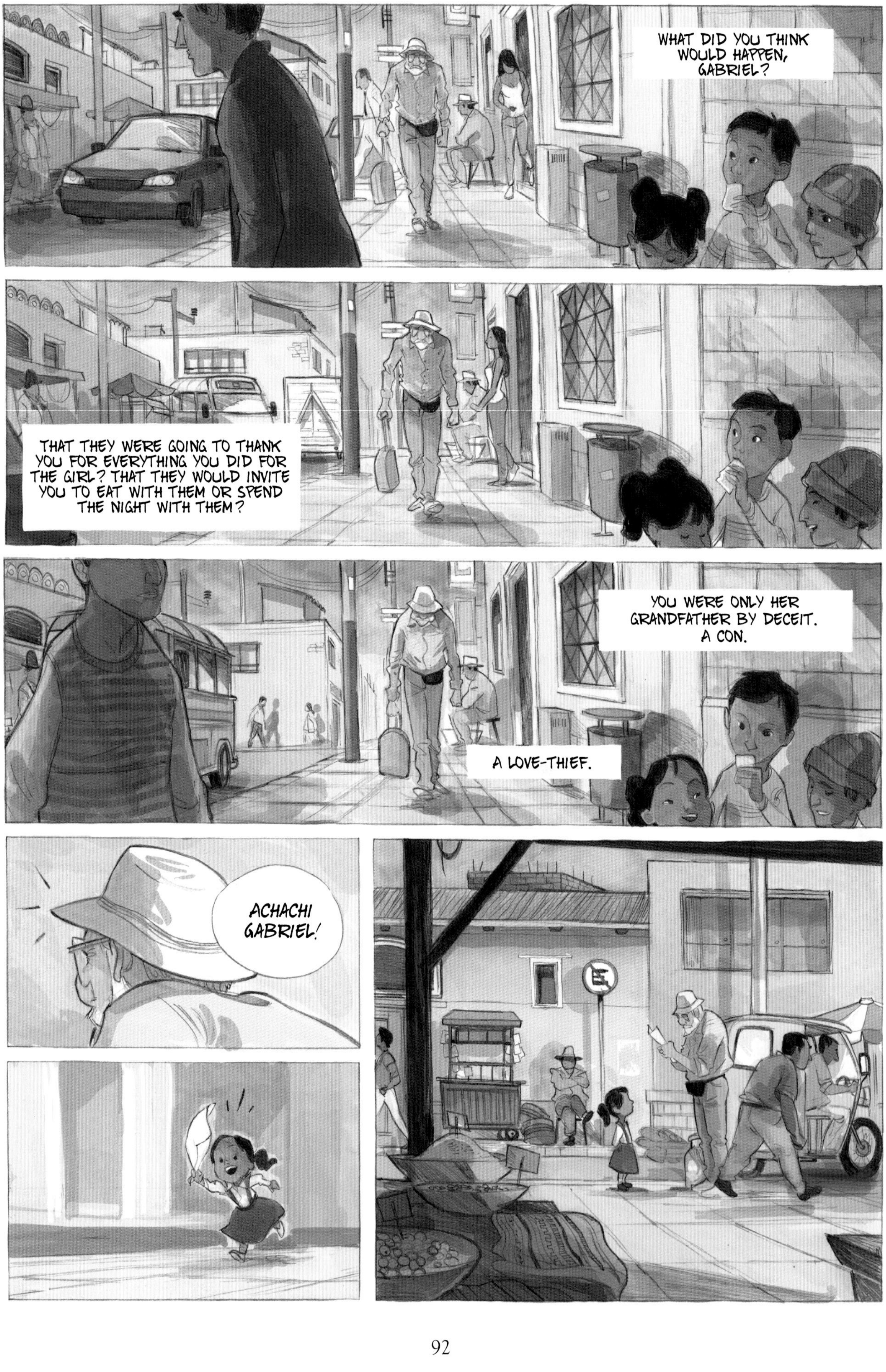
WHAT DID YOU THINK WOULD HAPPEN, GABRIEL?
THAT THEY WERE GOING TO THANK YOU FOR EVERYTHING YOU DID FOR THE GIRL? THAT THEY WOULD INVITE YOU TO EAT WITH THEM OR SPEND THE NIGHT WITH THEM?
YOU WERE ONLY HER GRANDFATHER BY DECEIT. A CON.
A LOVE-THIEF.
ACHACHI GABRIEL!

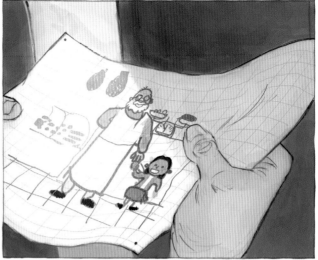

YOUR DRAWING IS VERY NICE, QINAYA! BONITO! MUCHO BONITO! I...

HERE! TAKE THE SUITCASE! IT'S FOR YOU.

THAT WAY...

IF YOU EVER..

MAYBE SOMEDAY...

...GOODBYE, LITTLE CLOUD.

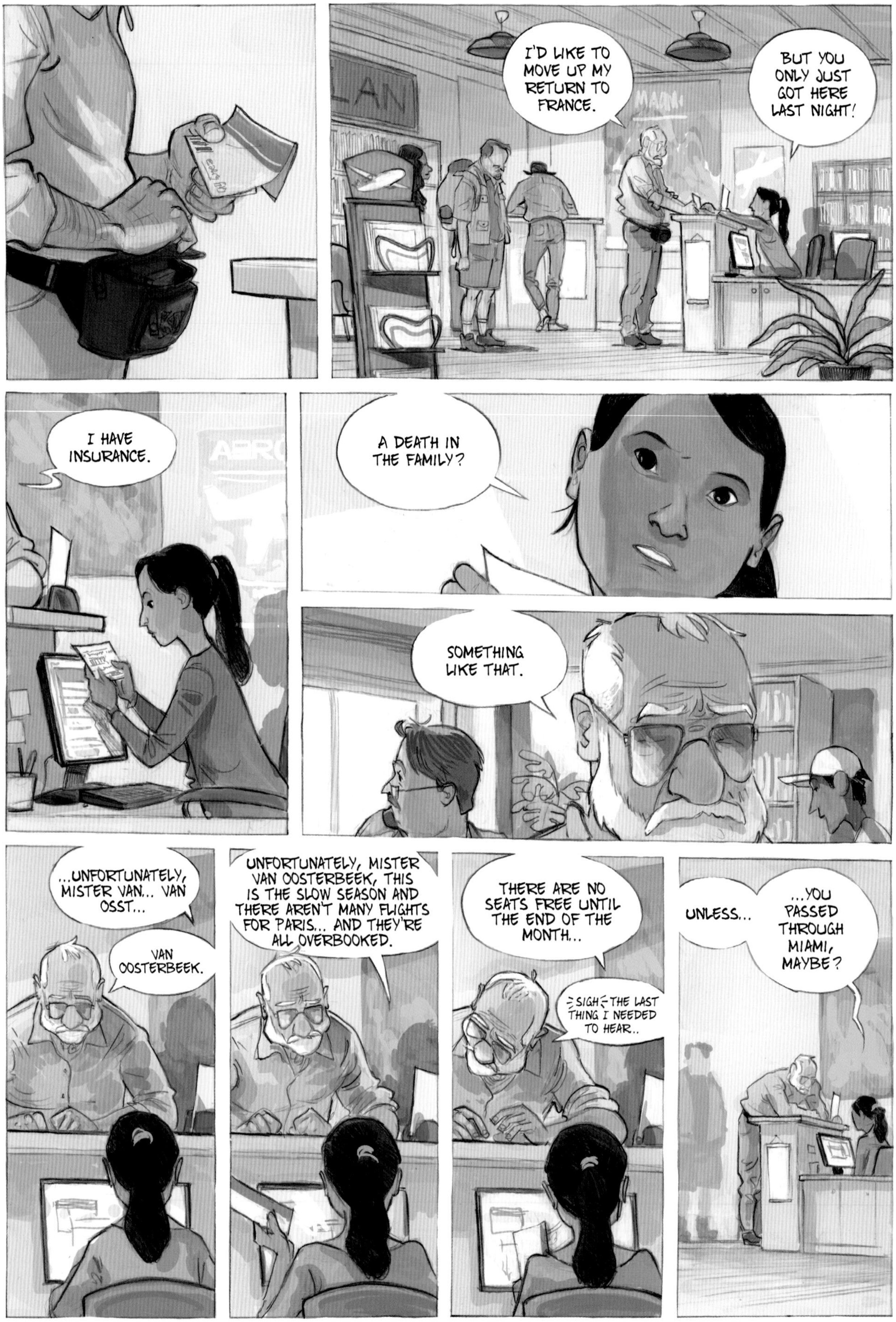
I'D LIKE TO MOVE UP MY RETURN TO FRANCE.
BUT YOU ONLY JUST GOT HERE LAST NIGHT!
I HAVE INSURANCE.
A DEATH IN THE FAMILY?
SOMETHING LIKE THAT.
...UNFORTUNATELY, MISTER VAN... VAN OSST...
VAN OOSTERBEEK.
UNFORTUNATELY, MISTER VAN OOSTERBEEK, THIS IS THE SLOW SEASON AND THERE AREN'T MANY FLIGHTS FOR PARIS... AND THEY'RE ALL OVERBOOKED.
THERE ARE NO SEATS FREE UNTIL THE END OF THE MONTH...
SIGH THE LAST THING I NEEDED TO HEAR..
UNLESS...
...YOU PASSED THROUGH MIAMI, MAYBE?

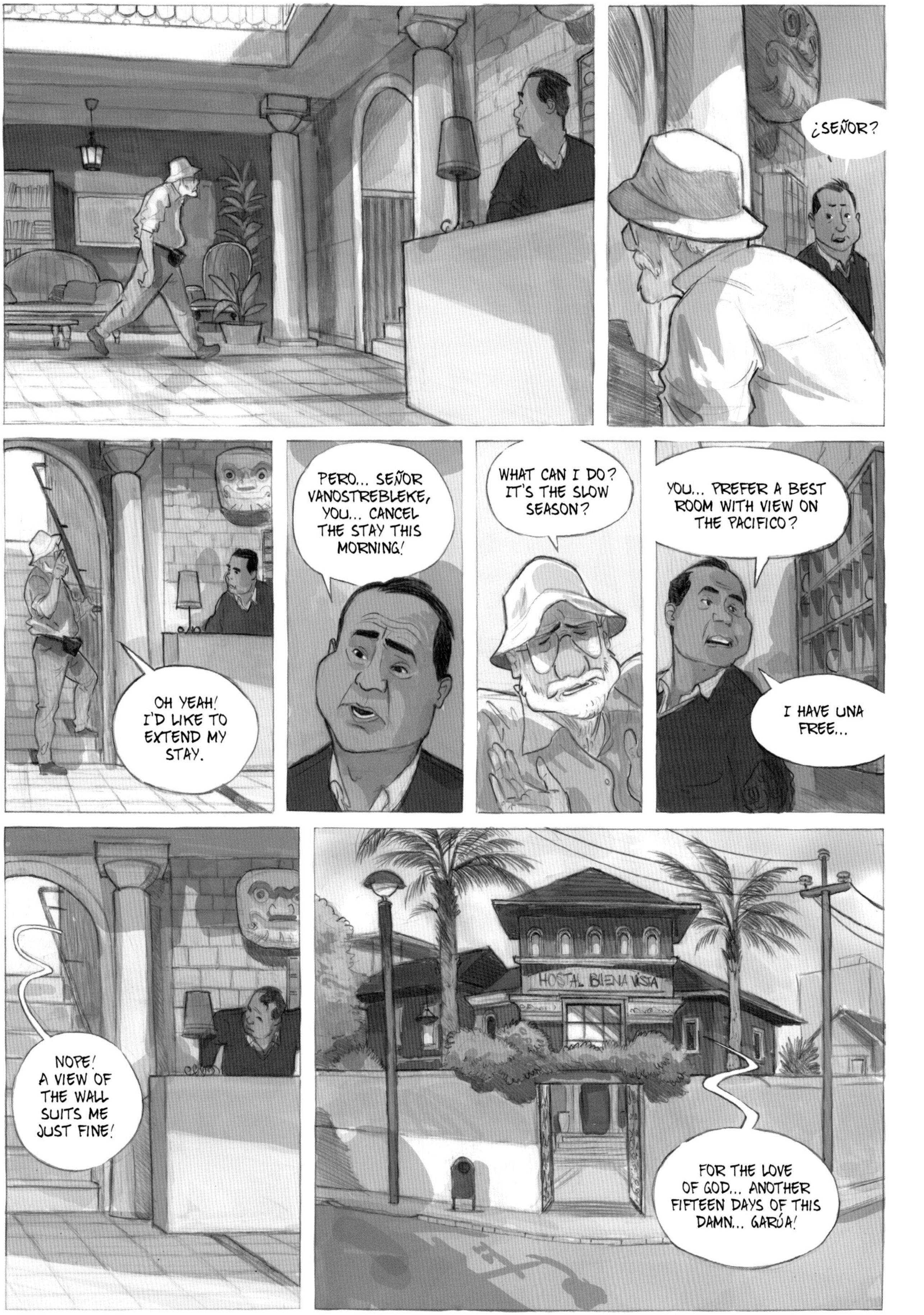
¿SEÑOR?
OH YEAH! I'D LIKE TO EXTEND MY STAY.
PERO... SEÑOR VANOSTREBLEKE, YOU... CANCEL THE STAY THIS MORNING!
WHAT CAN I DO? IT'S THE SLOW SEASON?
YOU... PREFER A BEST ROOM WITH VIEW ON THE PACIFICO?
I HAVE UNA FREE...
NOPE! A VIEW OF THE WALL SUITS ME JUST FINE!
HOSTAL BUENA VISTA
FOR THE LOVE OF GOD... ANOTHER FIFTEEN DAYS OF THIS DAMN... GARÚA!

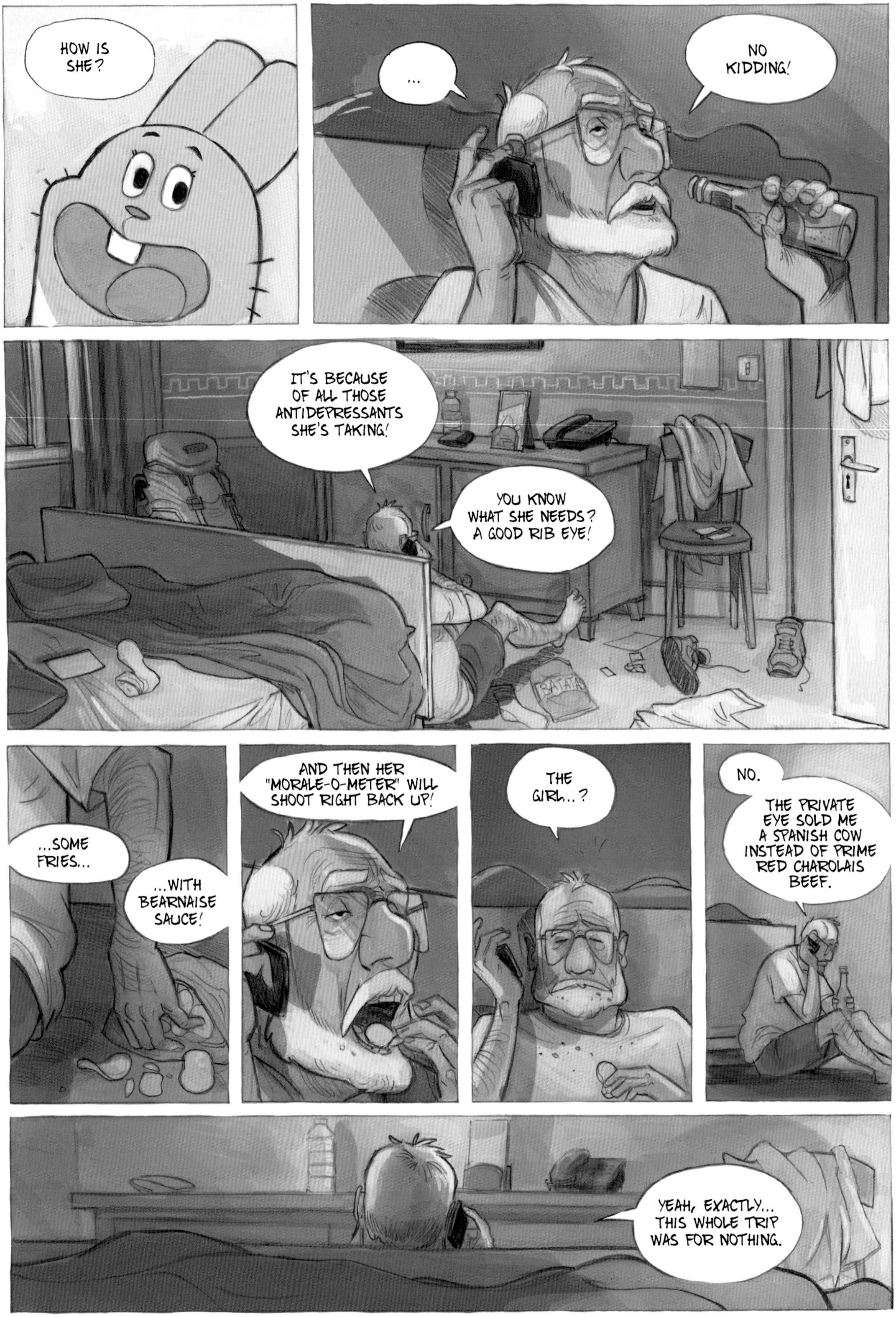
HOW IS SHE?
...
NO KIDDING!
IT'S BECAUSE OF ALL THOSE ANTIDEPRESSANTS SHE'S TAKING!
YOU KNOW WHAT SHE NEEDS? A GOOD RIB EYE!
BATATA
...SOME FRIES...
...WITH BEARNAISE SAUCE!
AND THEN HER "MORALE-O-METER" WILL SHOOT RIGHT BACK UP!
THE GIRL...?
NO.
THE PRIVATE EYE SOLD ME A SPANISH COW INSTEAD OF PRIME RED CHAROLAIS BEEF.
YEAH, EXACTLY... THIS WHOLE TRIP WAS FOR NOTHING.

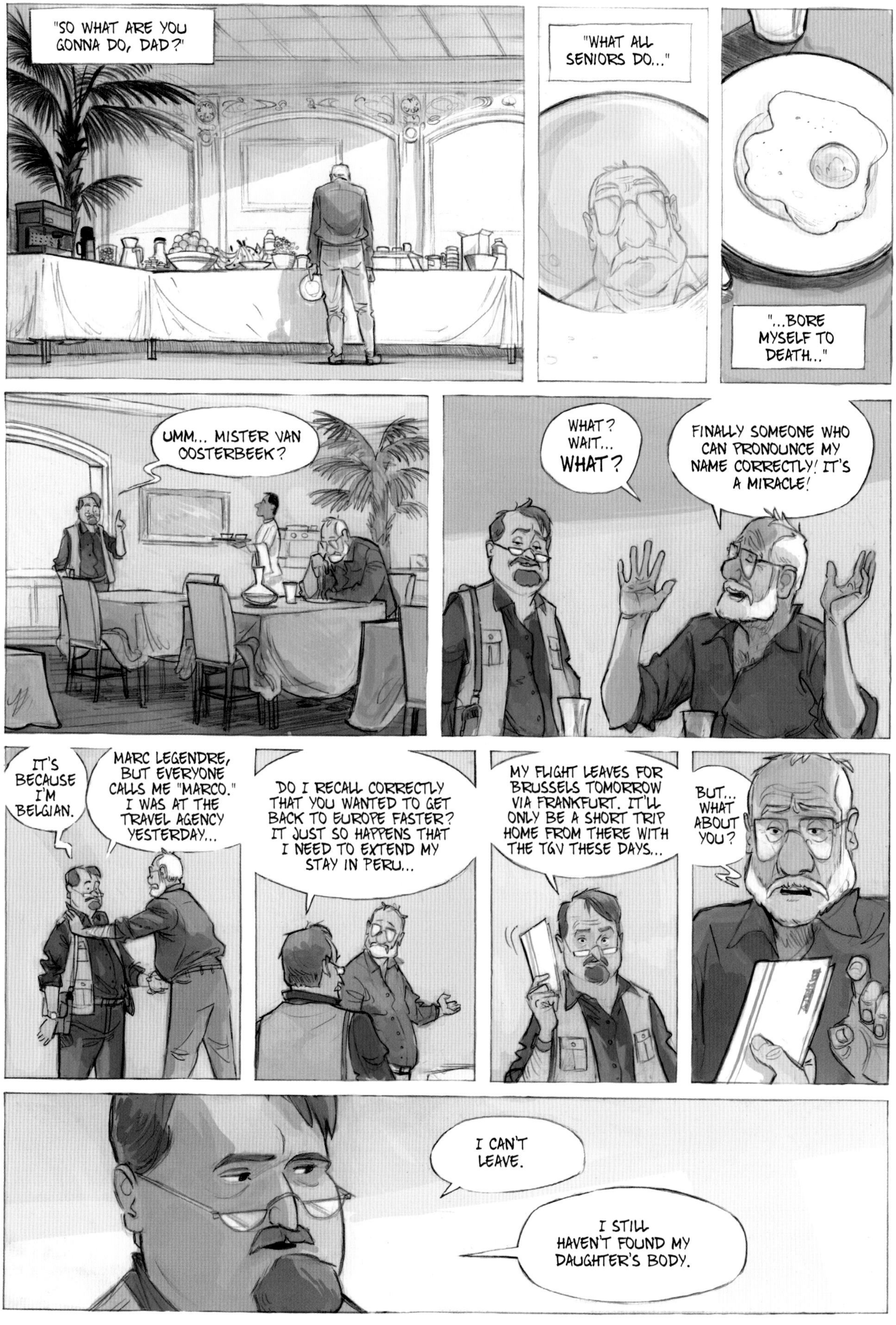
"SO WHAT ARE YOU GONNA DO, DAD?"
"WHAT ALL SENIORS DO..."
"...BORE MYSELF TO DEATH..."
UMM... MISTER VAN OOSTERBEEK?
WHAT? WAIT... WHAT?
FINALLY SOMEONE WHO CAN PRONOUNCE MY NAME CORRECTLY! IT'S A MIRACLE!
IT'S BECAUSE I'M BELGIAN.
MARC LEGENDRE, BUT EVERYONE CALLS ME "MARCO." I WAS AT THE TRAVEL AGENCY YESTERDAY...
DO I RECALL CORRECTLY THAT YOU WANTED TO GET BACK TO EUROPE FASTER? IT JUST SO HAPPENS THAT I NEED TO EXTEND MY STAY IN PERU...
MY FLIGHT LEAVES FOR BRUSSELS TOMORROW VIA FRANKFURT. IT'LL ONLY BE A SHORT TRIP HOME FROM THERE WITH THE TGV THESE DAYS...
BUT... WHAT ABOUT YOU?
I CAN'T LEAVE.
I STILL HAVEN'T FOUND MY DAUGHTER'S BODY.

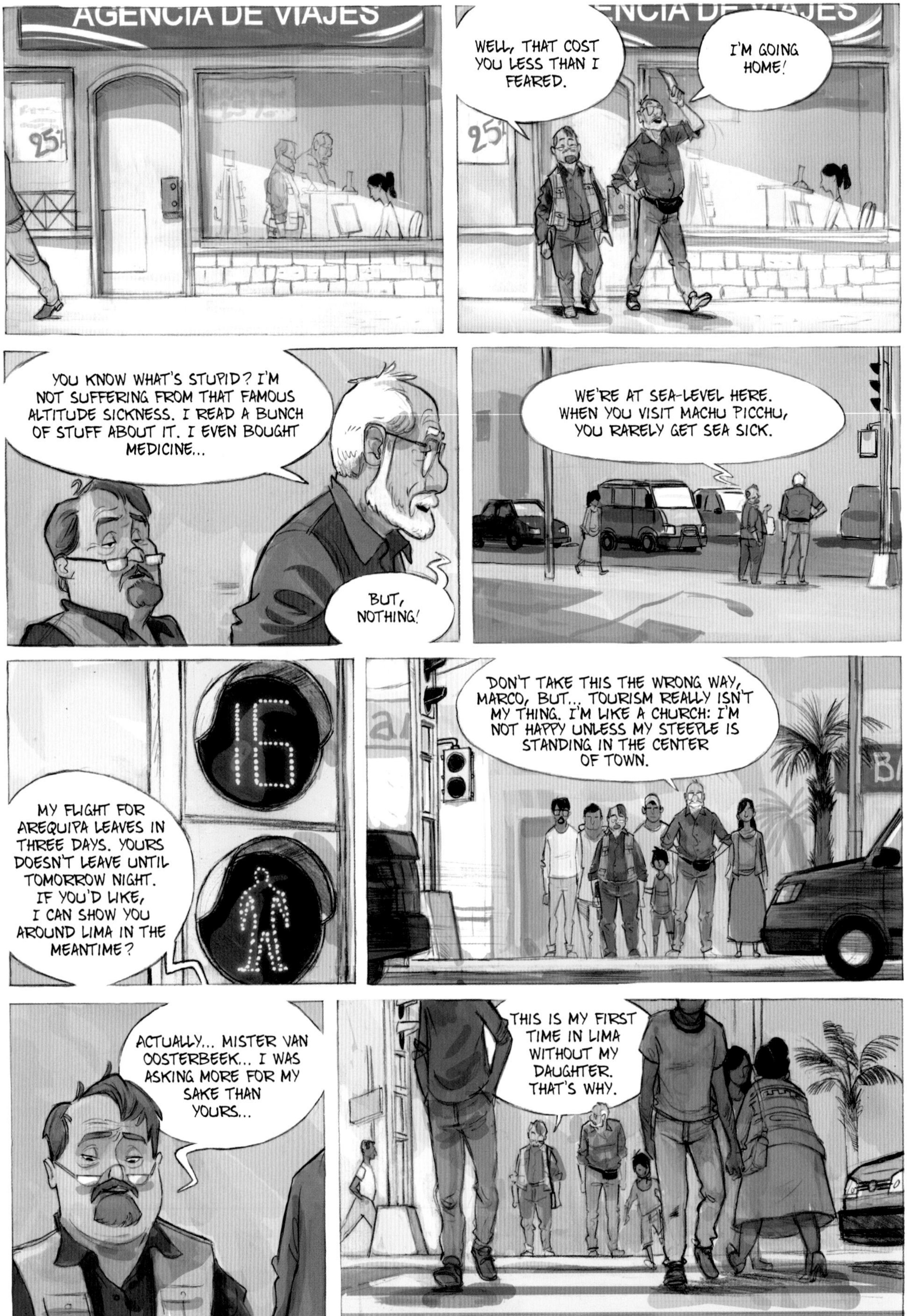
AGENCIA DE VIAJES
25%
WELL, THAT COST YOU LESS THAN I FEARED.
I'M GOING HOME!
YOU KNOW WHAT'S STUPID? I'M NOT SUFFERING FROM THAT FAMOUS ALTITUDE SICKNESS. I READ A BUNCH OF STUFF ABOUT IT. I EVEN BOUGHT MEDICINE...
BUT, NOTHING!
WE'RE AT SEA-LEVEL HERE. WHEN YOU VISIT MACHU PICCHU, YOU RARELY GET SEA SICK.
16
MY FLIGHT FOR AREQUIPA LEAVES IN THREE DAYS. YOURS DOESN'T LEAVE UNTIL TOMORROW NIGHT. IF YOU'D LIKE, I CAN SHOW YOU AROUND LIMA IN THE MEANTIME?
DON'T TAKE THIS THE WRONG WAY, MARCO, BUT... TOURISM REALLY ISN'T MY THING. I'M LIKE A CHURCH: I'M NOT HAPPY UNLESS MY STEEPLE IS STANDING IN THE CENTER OF TOWN.
ACTUALLY... MISTER VAN OOSTERBEEK... I WAS ASKING MORE FOR MY SAKE THAN YOURS...
THIS IS MY FIRST TIME IN LIMA WITHOUT MY DAUGHTER. THAT'S WHY.

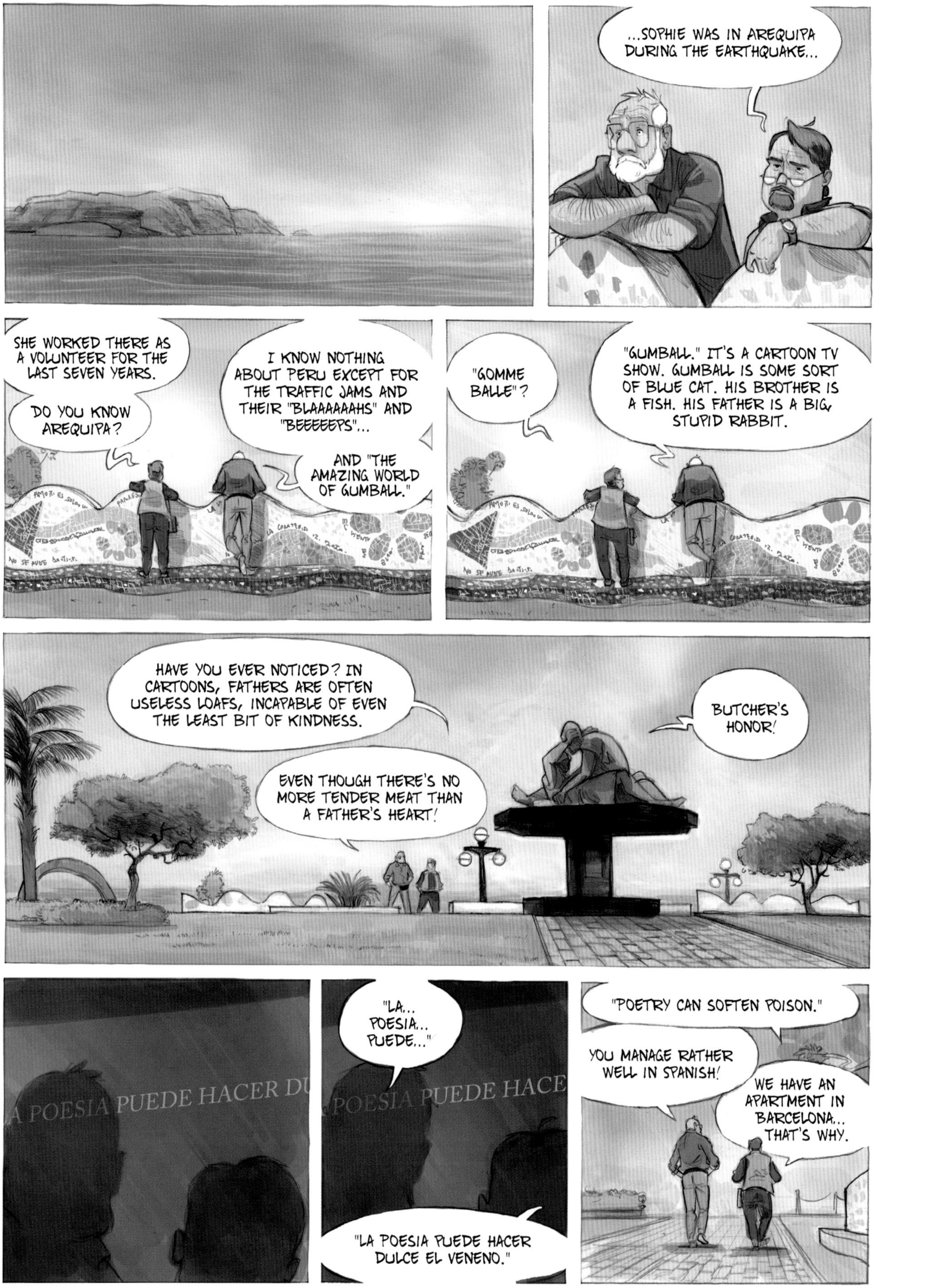
...SOPHIE WAS IN AREQUIPA DURING THE EARTHQUAKE...
SHE WORKED THERE AS A VOLUNTEER FOR THE LAST SEVEN YEARS.
DO YOU KNOW AREQUIPA?
I KNOW NOTHING ABOUT PERU EXCEPT FOR THE TRAFFIC JAMS AND THEIR "BLAAAAAAHS" AND "BEEEEEPS"...
AND "THE AMAZING WORLD OF GUMBALL."
"GOMME BALLE"?
"GUMBALL." IT'S A CARTOON TV SHOW. GUMBALL IS SOME SORT OF BLUE CAT. HIS BROTHER IS A FISH. HIS FATHER IS A BIG STUPID RABBIT.
HAVE YOU EVER NOTICED? IN CARTOONS, FATHERS ARE OFTEN USELESS LOAFS, INCAPABLE OF EVEN THE LEAST BIT OF KINDNESS.
EVEN THOUGH THERE'S NO MORE TENDER MEAT THAN A FATHER'S HEART!
BUTCHER'S HONOR!
LA POESIA PUEDE HACER DU
"LA... POESIA... PUEDE..."
POESIA PUEDE HACE
"LA POESIA PUEDE HACER DULCE EL VENENO."
"POETRY CAN SOFTEN POISON."
YOU MANAGE RATHER WELL IN SPANISH!
WE HAVE AN APARTMENT IN BARCELONA... THAT'S WHY.

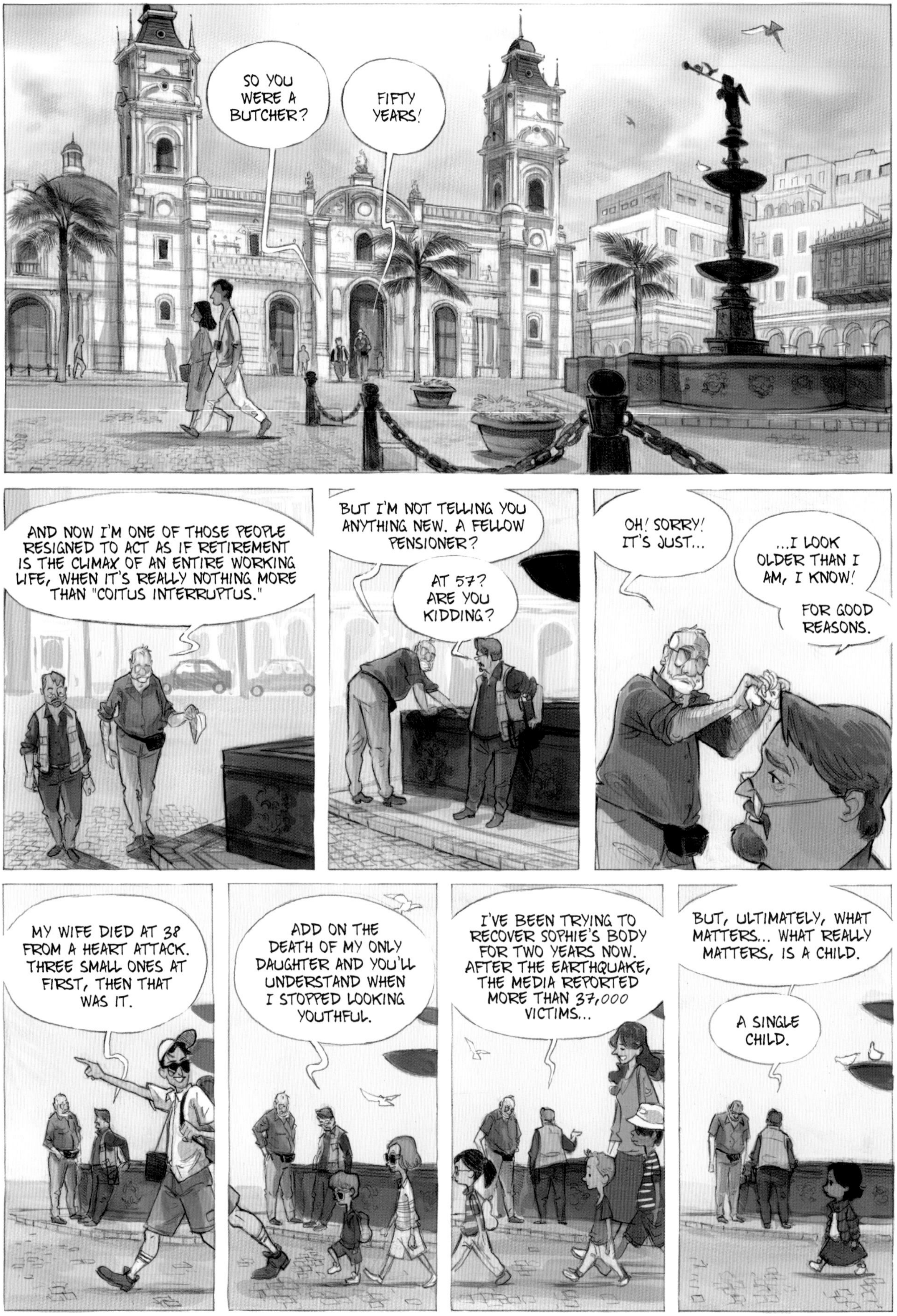

SO YOU WERE A BUTCHER?
FIFTY YEARS!
AND NOW I'M ONE OF THOSE PEOPLE RESIGNED TO ACT AS IF RETIREMENT IS THE CLIMAX OF AN ENTIRE WORKING LIFE, WHEN IT'S REALLY NOTHING MORE THAN "COITUS INTERRUPTUS."
BUT I'M NOT TELLING YOU ANYTHING NEW. A FELLOW PENSIONER?
AT 57? ARE YOU KIDDING?
OH! SORRY! IT'S JUST...
...I LOOK OLDER THAN I AM, I KNOW!
FOR GOOD REASONS.
MY WIFE DIED AT 38 FROM A HEART ATTACK. THREE SMALL ONES AT FIRST, THEN THAT WAS IT.
ADD ON THE DEATH OF MY ONLY DAUGHTER AND YOU'LL UNDERSTAND WHEN I STOPPED LOOKING YOUTHFUL.
I'VE BEEN TRYING TO RECOVER SOPHIE'S BODY FOR TWO YEARS NOW. AFTER THE EARTHQUAKE, THE MEDIA REPORTED MORE THAN 37,000 VICTIMS...
BUT, ULTIMATELY, WHAT MATTERS... WHAT REALLY MATTERS, IS A CHILD.
A SINGLE CHILD.

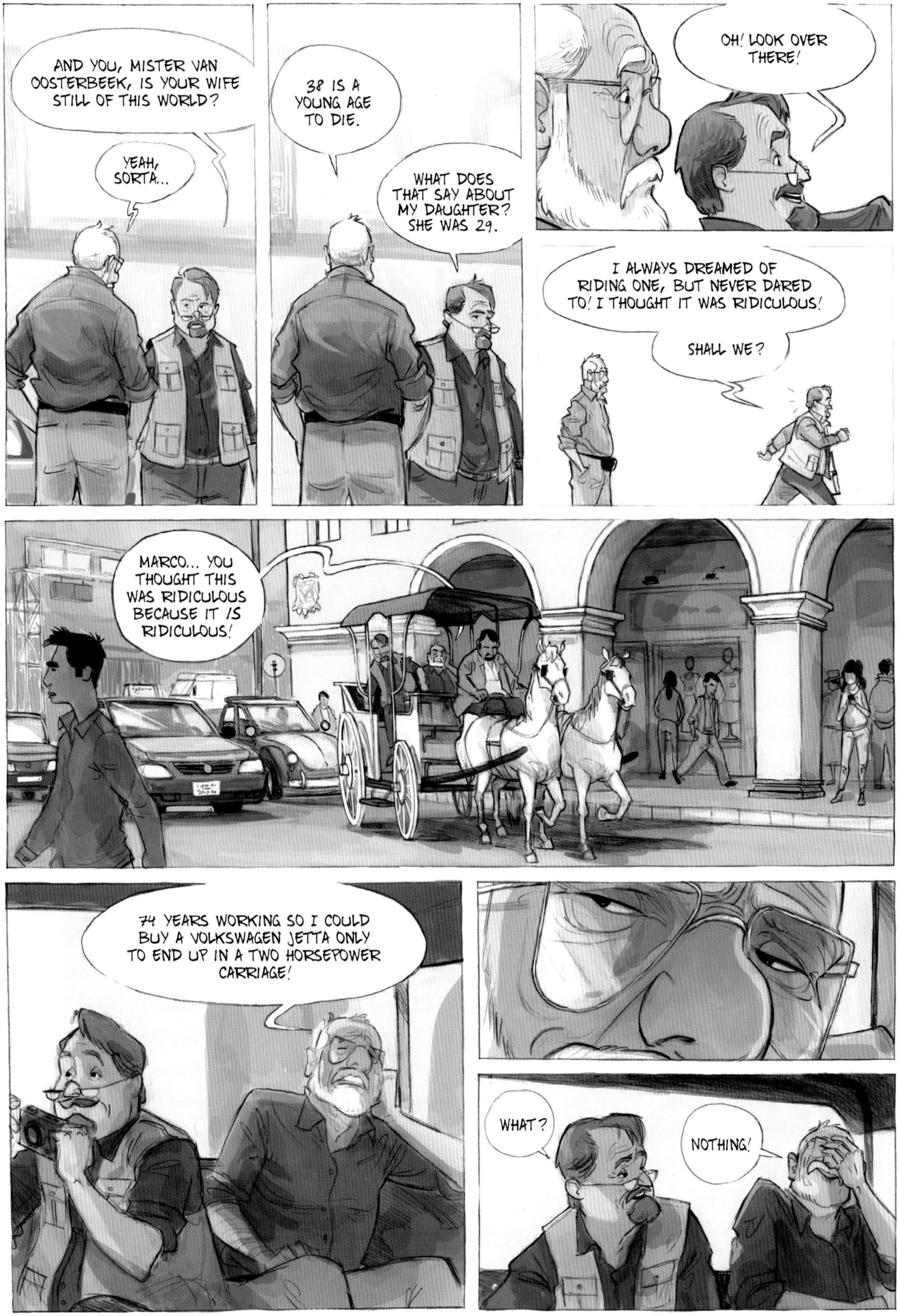
AND YOU, MISTER VAN OOSTERBEEK, IS YOUR WIFE STILL OF THIS WORLD?
YEAH, SORTA...
38 IS A YOUNG AGE TO DIE.
WHAT DOES THAT SAY ABOUT MY DAUGHTER? SHE WAS 29.
OH! LOOK OVER THERE!
I ALWAYS DREAMED OF RIDING ONE, BUT NEVER DARED TO! I THOUGHT IT WAS RIDICULOUS!
SHALL WE?
MARCO... YOU THOUGHT THIS WAS RIDICULOUS BECAUSE IT IS RIDICULOUS!
74 YEARS WORKING SO I COULD BUY A VOLKSWAGEN JETTA ONLY TO END UP IN A TWO HORSEPOWER CARRIAGE!
WHAT?
NOTHING!

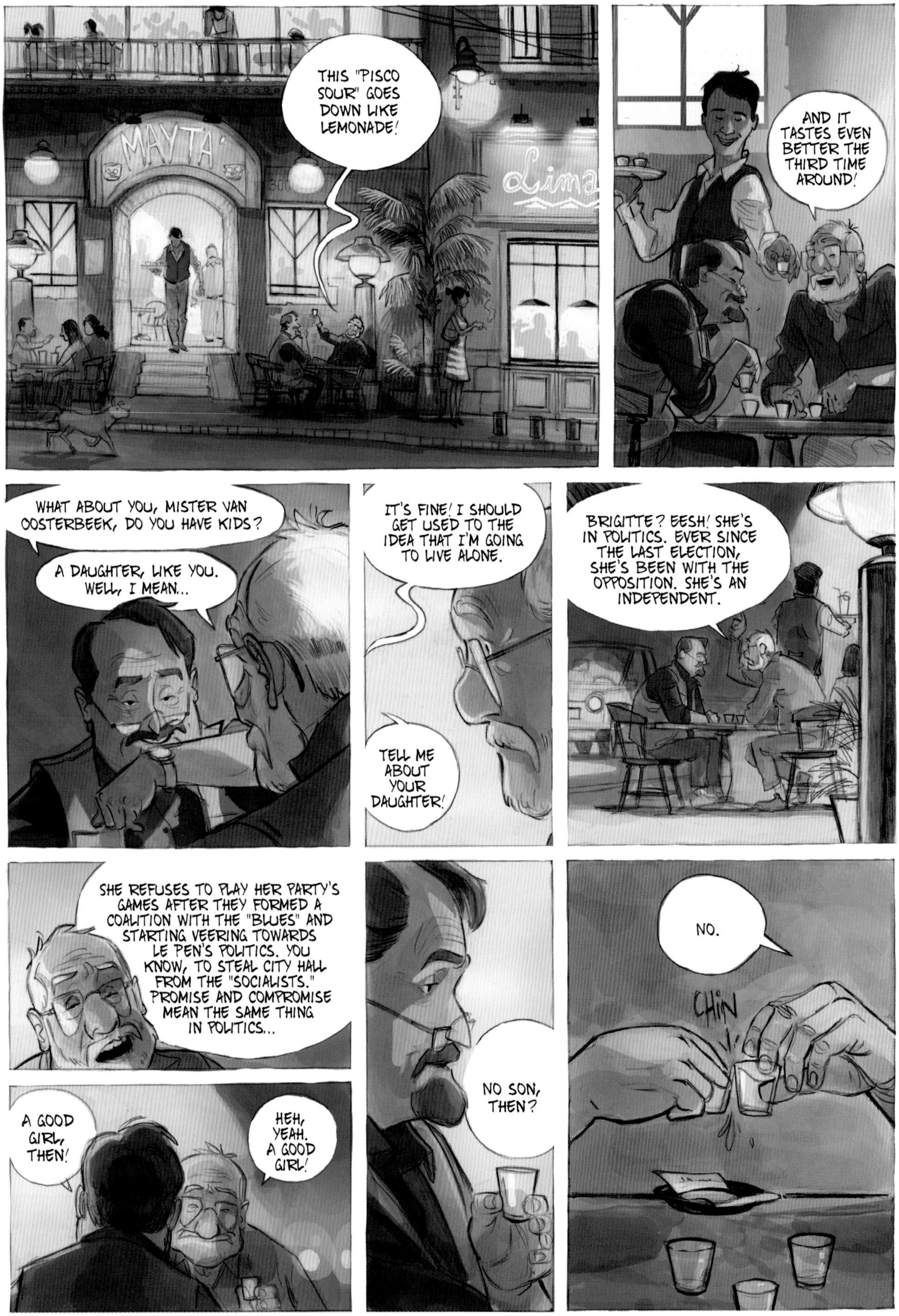

THIS "PISCO SOUR" GOES DOWN LIKE LEMONADE!
MAYTA'
Lima
AND IT TASTES EVEN BETTER THE THIRD TIME AROUND!
WHAT ABOUT YOU, MISTER VAN OOSTERBEEK, DO YOU HAVE KIDS?
A DAUGHTER, LIKE YOU. WELL, I MEAN...
IT'S FINE! I SHOULD GET USED TO THE IDEA THAT I'M GOING TO LIVE ALONE.
TELL ME ABOUT YOUR DAUGHTER!
BRIGITTE? EESH! SHE'S IN POLITICS. EVER SINCE THE LAST ELECTION, SHE'S BEEN WITH THE OPPOSITION. SHE'S AN INDEPENDENT.
SHE REFUSES TO PLAY HER PARTY'S GAMES AFTER THEY FORMED A COALITION WITH THE "BLUES" AND STARTING VEERING TOWARDS LE PEN'S POLITICS. YOU KNOW, TO STEAL CITY HALL FROM THE "SOCIALISTS." PROMISE AND COMPROMISE MEAN THE SAME THING IN POLITICS...
A GOOD GIRL, THEN!
HEH, YEAH. A GOOD GIRL!
NO SON, THEN?
NO.
CHIN

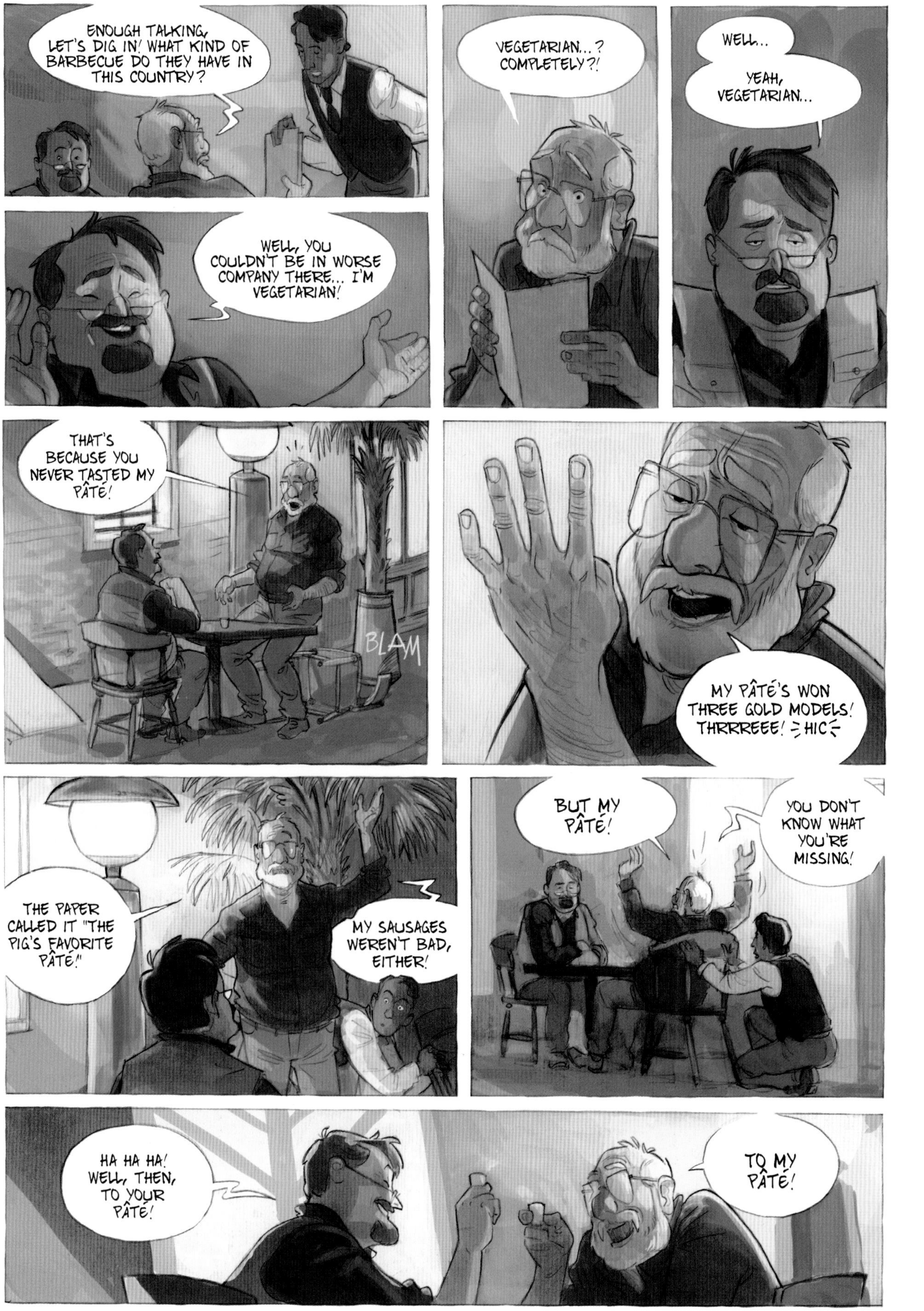
ENOUGH TALKING, LET'S DIG IN! WHAT KIND OF BARBECUE DO THEY HAVE IN THIS COUNTRY?
VEGETARIAN...? COMPLETELY?!
WELL...
YEAH, VEGETARIAN...
WELL, YOU COULDN'T BE IN WORSE COMPANY THERE... I'M VEGETARIAN!
THAT'S BECAUSE YOU NEVER TASTED MY PÂTÉ!
BLAM
MY PÂTÉ'S WON THREE GOLD MODELS! THRRREEE! HIC
THE PAPER CALLED IT "THE PIG'S FAVORITE PÂTÉ!"
MY SAUSAGES WEREN'T BAD, EITHER!
BUT MY PÂTÉ!
YOU DON'T KNOW WHAT YOU'RE MISSING!
HA HA HA! WELL, THEN, TO YOUR PÂTÉ!
TO MY PÂTÉ!

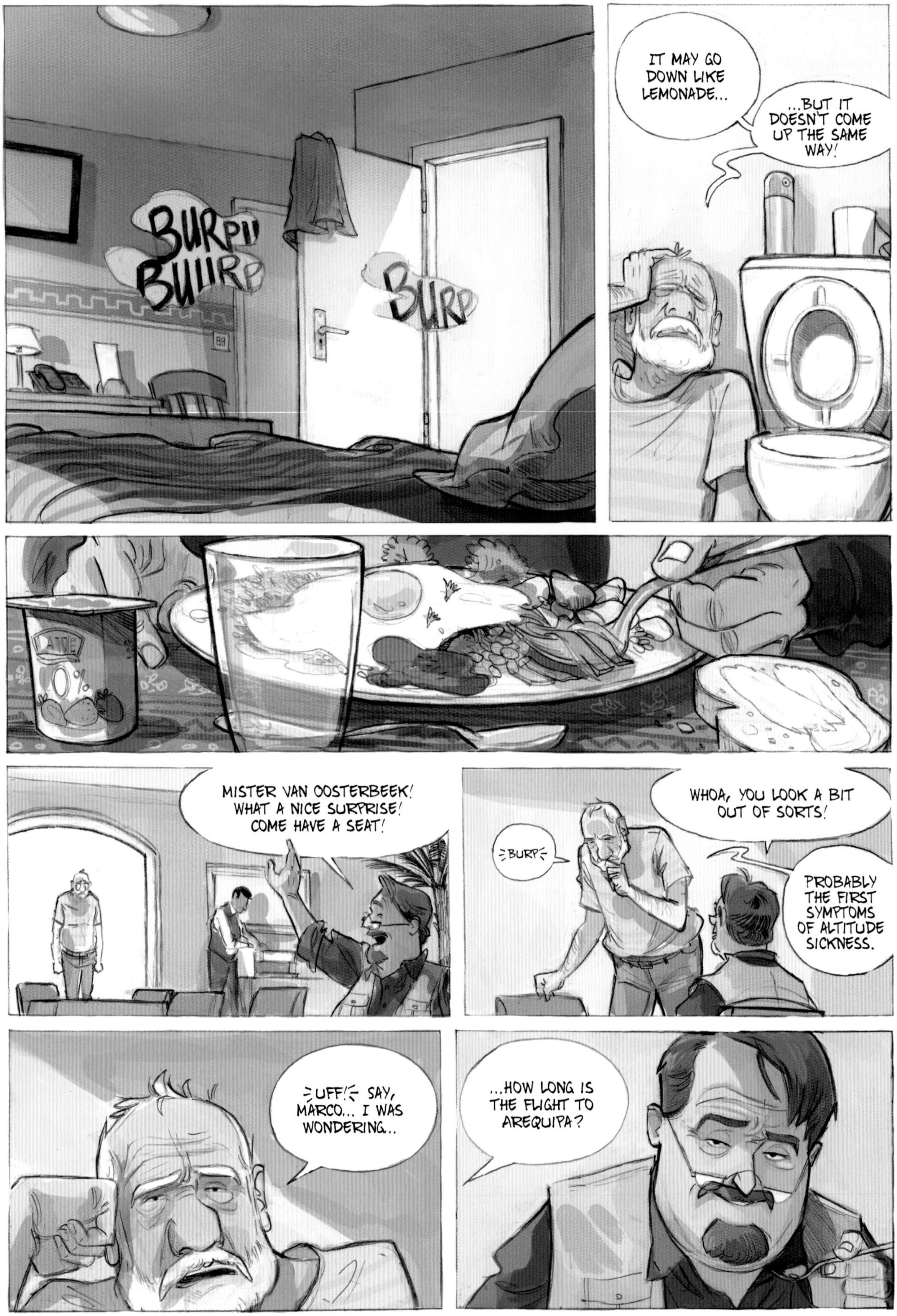
BURP!! BUIIRP
BURP
IT MAY GO DOWN LIKE LEMONADE...
...BUT IT DOESN'T COME UP THE SAME WAY!
MISTER VAN OOSTERBEEK! WHAT A NICE SURPRISE! COME HAVE A SEAT!
BURP
WHOA, YOU LOOK A BIT OUT OF SORTS!
PROBABLY THE FIRST SYMPTOMS OF ALTITUDE SICKNESS.
UFF! SAY, MARCO... I WAS WONDERING...
...HOW LONG IS THE FLIGHT TO AREQUIPA?

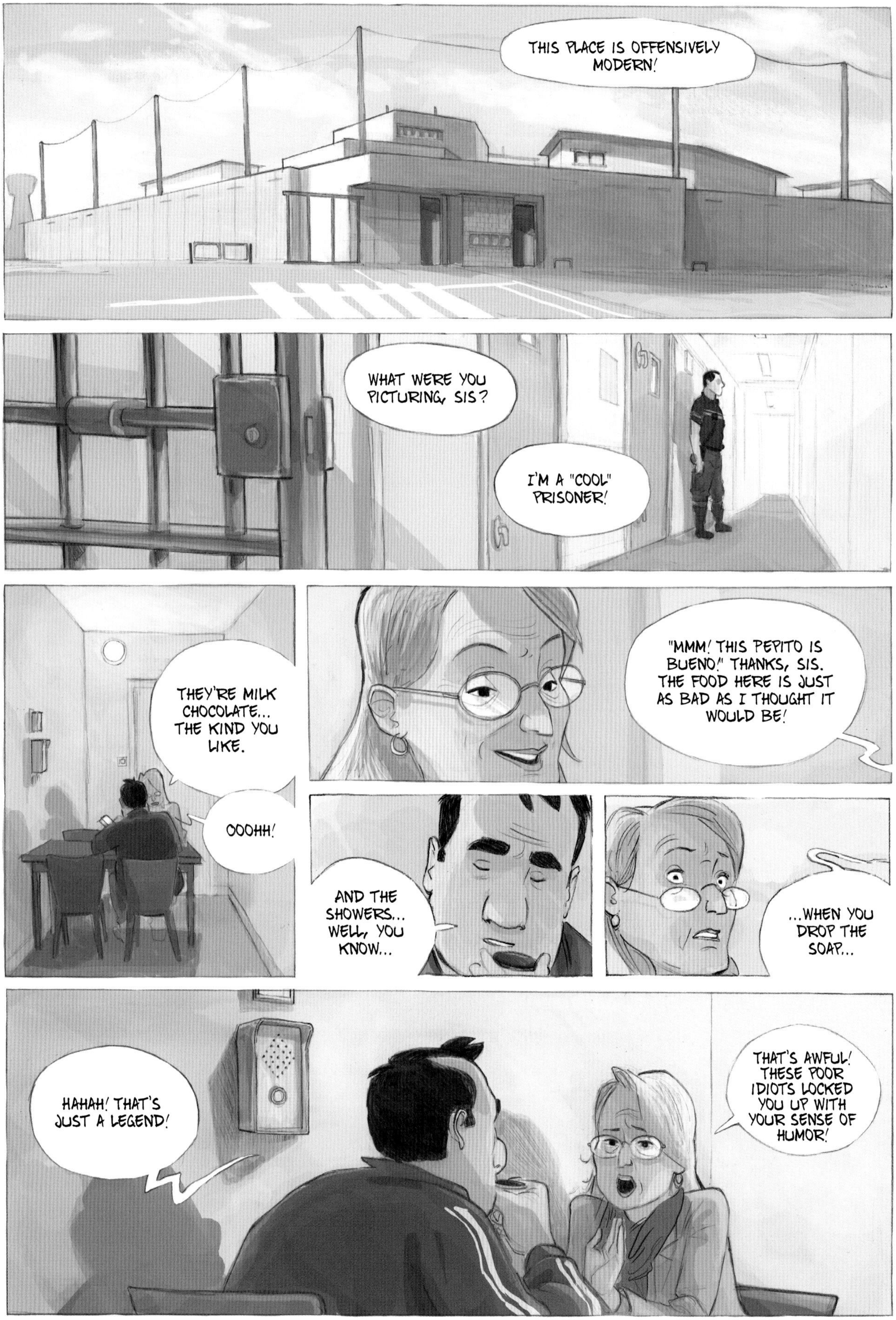
THIS PLACE IS OFFENSIVELY MODERN!
WHAT WERE YOU PICTURING, SIS?
I'M A "COOL" PRISONER!
THEY'RE MILK CHOCOLATE... THE KIND YOU LIKE.
OOOHH!
"MMM! THIS PEPITO IS BUENO!" THANKS, SIS. THE FOOD HERE IS JUST AS BAD AS I THOUGHT IT WOULD BE!
AND THE SHOWERS... WELL, YOU KNOW...
...WHEN YOU DROP THE SOAP...
HAHAH! THAT'S JUST A LEGEND!
THAT'S AWFUL! THESE POOR IDIOTS LOCKED YOU UP WITH YOUR SENSE OF HUMOR!

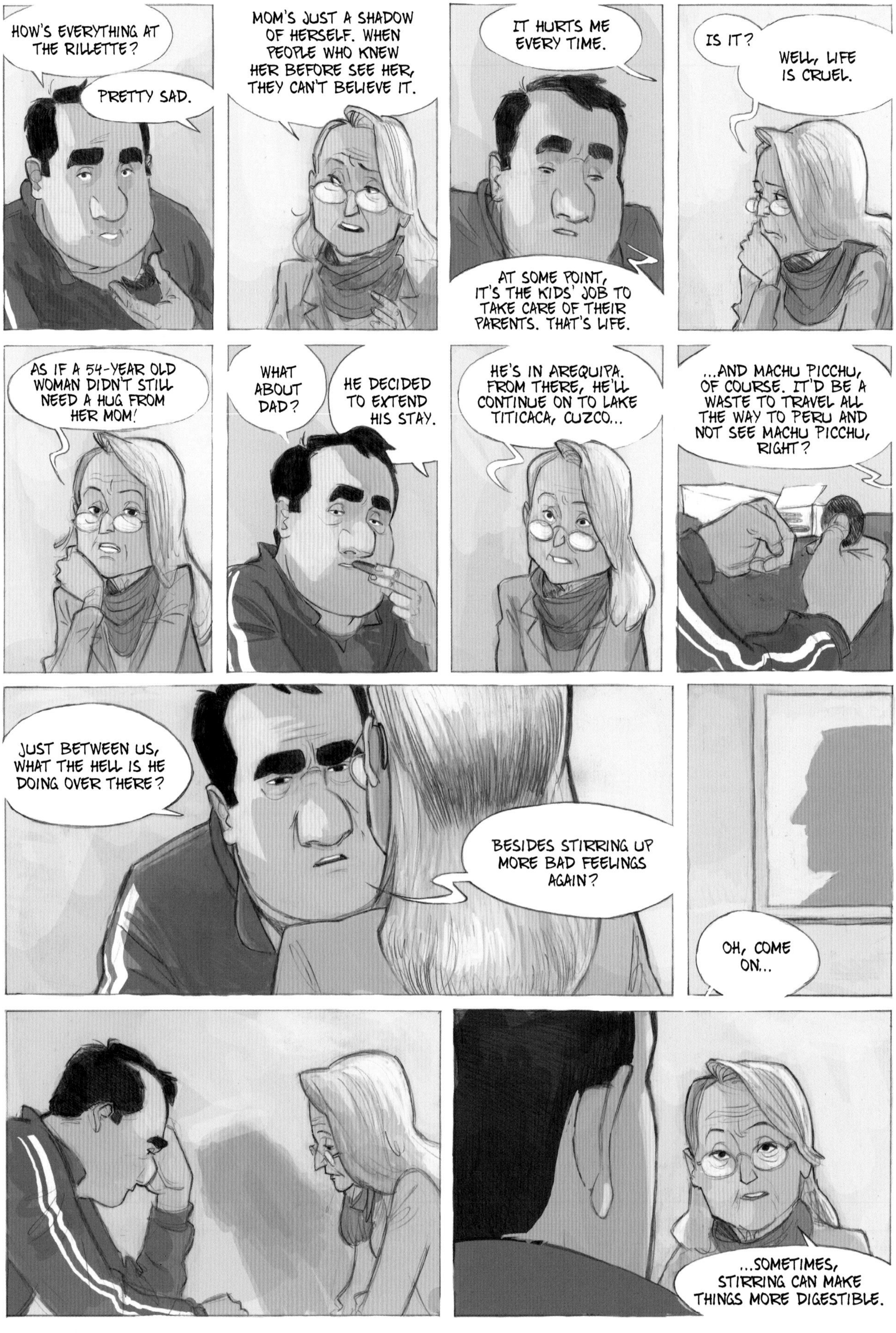
HOW'S EVERYTHING AT THE RILLETTE?
PRETTY SAD.
MOM'S JUST A SHADOW OF HERSELF. WHEN PEOPLE WHO KNEW HER BEFORE SEE HER, THEY CAN'T BELIEVE IT.
IT HURTS ME EVERY TIME.
AT SOME POINT, IT'S THE KIDS' JOB TO TAKE CARE OF THEIR PARENTS. THAT'S LIFE.
IS IT?
WELL, LIFE IS CRUEL.
AS IF A 54-YEAR OLD WOMAN DIDN'T STILL NEED A HUG FROM HER MOM!
WHAT ABOUT DAD?
HE DECIDED TO EXTEND HIS STAY.
HE'S IN AREQUIPA. FROM THERE, HE'LL CONTINUE ON TO LAKE TITICACA, CUZCO...
...AND MACHU PICCHU, OF COURSE. IT'D BE A WASTE TO TRAVEL ALL THE WAY TO PERU AND NOT SEE MACHU PICCHU, RIGHT?
JUST BETWEEN US, WHAT THE HELL IS HE DOING OVER THERE?
BESIDES STIRRING UP MORE BAD FEELINGS AGAIN?
OH, COME ON...
...SOMETIMES, STIRRING CAN MAKE THINGS MORE DIGESTIBLE.

YOU KNOW HE'S REFUSED TO HAVE ANY CONTACT WITH ME SINCE I GOT HERE?

NOT ONE VISIT...

NOT ONE LETTER...

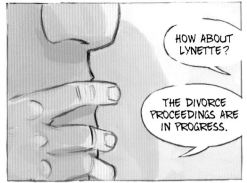

HOW ABOUT LYNETTE?

THE DIVORCE PROCEEDINGS ARE IN PROGRESS.

AT LEAST THE KIDS WON'T SUFFER.. SEEING AS WE DON'T HAVE ANY.

IN THE END, I DESERVED THIS. WHEN YOU SPIT IN THE SOUP, YOU SHOULDN'T BE SURPRISED WHEN NOBODY WANTS TO EAT AT YOUR TABLE!

HEY, I'M STILL HERE!

YEAH! AT LEAST YOU DIDN'T SWITCH PARTIES ON ME!

HOW HIGH ARE WE?

3800 METERS.

107

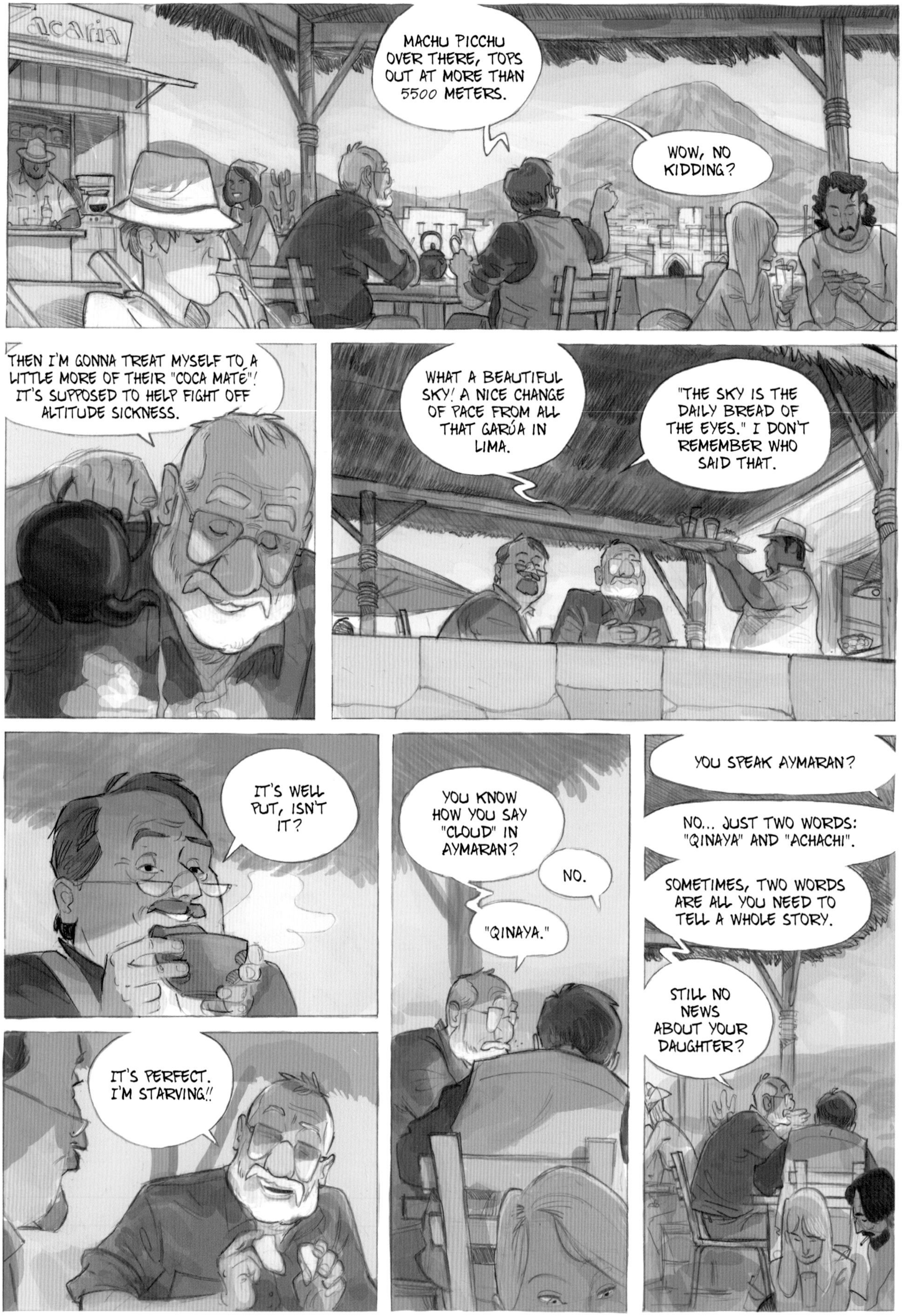
MACHU PICCHU OVER THERE, TOPS OUT AT MORE THAN 5500 METERS.
WOW, NO KIDDING?
THEN I'M GONNA TREAT MYSELF TO A LITTLE MORE OF THEIR "COCA MATÉ"! IT'S SUPPOSED TO HELP FIGHT OFF ALTITUDE SICKNESS.
WHAT A BEAUTIFUL SKY! A NICE CHANGE OF PACE FROM ALL THAT GARÚA IN LIMA.
"THE SKY IS THE DAILY BREAD OF THE EYES." I DON'T REMEMBER WHO SAID THAT.
IT'S WELL PUT, ISN'T IT?
IT'S PERFECT. I'M STARVING!!
YOU KNOW HOW YOU SAY "CLOUD" IN AYMARAN?
NO.
"QINAYA."
YOU SPEAK AYMARAN?
NO... JUST TWO WORDS: "QINAYA" AND "ACHACHI".
SOMETIMES, TWO WORDS ARE ALL YOU NEED TO TELL A WHOLE STORY.
STILL NO NEWS ABOUT YOUR DAUGHTER?

THE DNA TESTS ARE CONTINUING, SLOWLY BUT SURELY. THERE ARE STILL MORE THAN 3500 VICTIMS THAT HAVE YET TO BE IDENTIFIED...

THERE WERE TENS OF THOUSANDS OF BODIES, NOT TO MENTION THE MISSING! IT WAS A MESS. THE AUTHORITIES HAD TO HANDLE THINGS QUICKLY TO AVOID AN EPIDEMIC.

ARE YOU SAYING THEY... BURIED YOUR DAUGHTER IN A MASS GRAVE?

THEY HAD TO TAKE CARE OF THE LIVING FIRST. THE DEAD HAVE ALL THE PATIENCE IN THE WORLD. CLEARLY.

I CAN'T EVEN TELL YOU ALL THE PAPERWORK AND RED TAPE.

WHEN SOPHIE'S BODY HAS FINALLY BEEN IDENTIFIED, I'LL HAVE HER RETURNED TO BELGIUM SO SHE CAN REST AT HER MOTHER'S SIDE.

I WANT TO HAVE THE TWO OF THEM NEAR ME...

THAT'S WHY.

...

YOU KNOW, MARCO, THEY CAN LEAVE US, THEY CAN GROW OLD, BUT IT'S LIKE THEY'RE STILL HERE, RUNNING AROUND OUR FEET, JUST LIKE WHEN THEY WERE LITTLE TYKES.

EMERSON!!

IT WAS RALPH WALDO EMERSON WHO SAID "THE SKY IS THE DAILY BREAD OF THE EYES."

HEH HEH! WELL, I NEVER WOULDA GUESSED THAT!

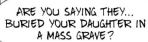

109

WHEN SHE WAS LITTLE, SOPHIE LOVED "THE SEVEN CRYSTAL BALLS" AND "PRISONERS OF THE SUN." DO YOU KNOW THE TINTIN COMICS?

THAT'S WHY!

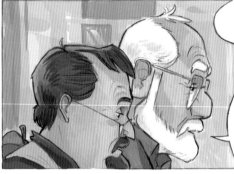

AND YOU, GABRIEL? WHY PERU?

WHY? BECAUSE I'M AN OLD IDIOT WHO STILL BELIEVES IN FAIRY TALES WHEN LIFE TENDS TO BEHAVE MORE LIKE THE EVIL WITCH.

IF THAT EMERSON OF YOURS WROTE ANYTHING NICE ABOUT DISENCHANTMENT...

...NOW'D BE A GOOD TIME TO PULL IT OUT...!

110

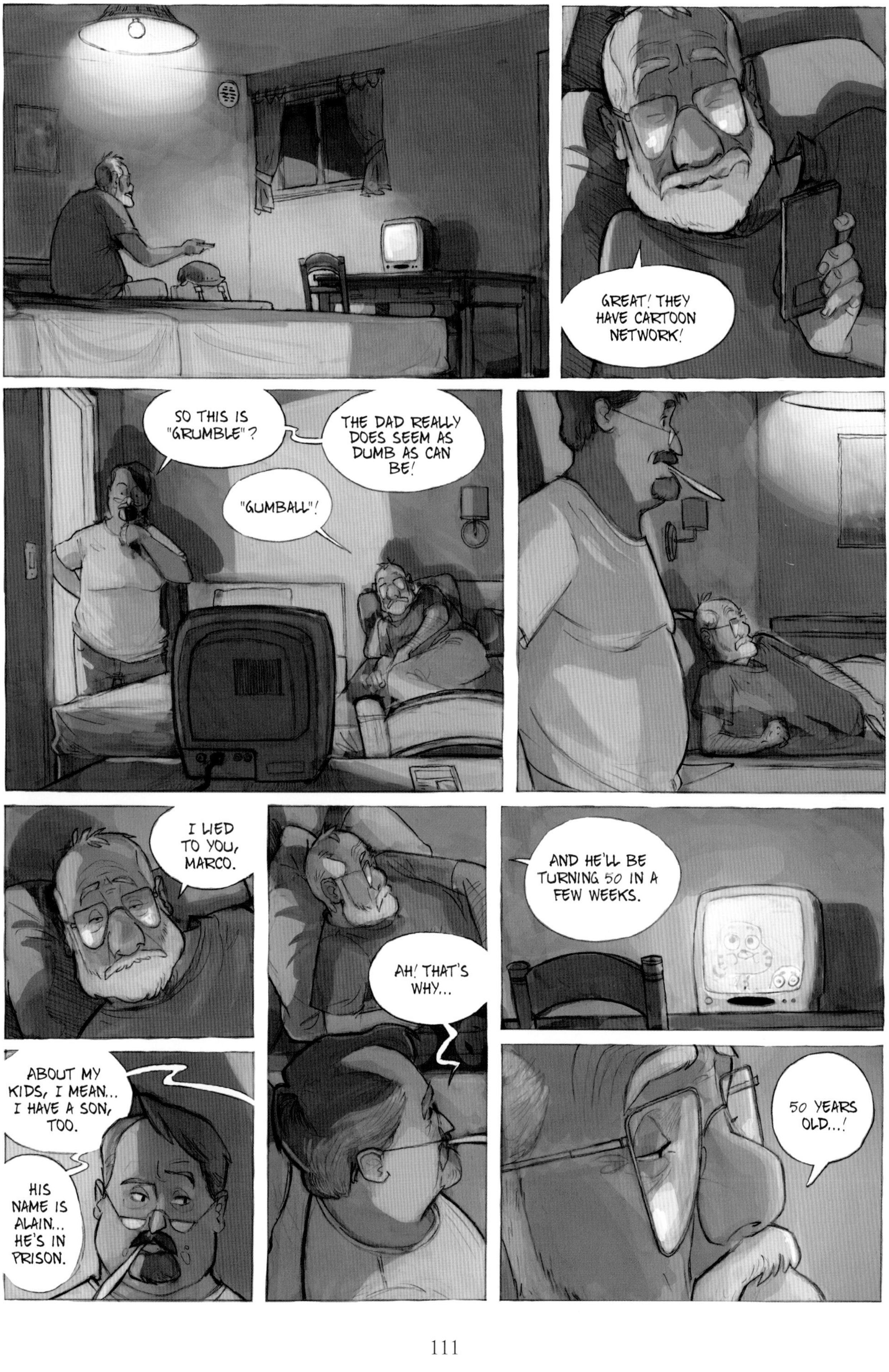
GREAT! THEY HAVE CARTOON NETWORK!
SO THIS IS "GRUMBLE"?
THE DAD REALLY DOES SEEM AS DUMB AS CAN BE!
"GUMBALL"!
I LIED TO YOU, MARCO.
ABOUT MY KIDS, I MEAN... I HAVE A SON, TOO.
HIS NAME IS ALAIN... HE'S IN PRISON.
AH! THAT'S WHY...
AND HE'LL BE TURNING 50 IN A FEW WEEKS.
50 YEARS OLD...!

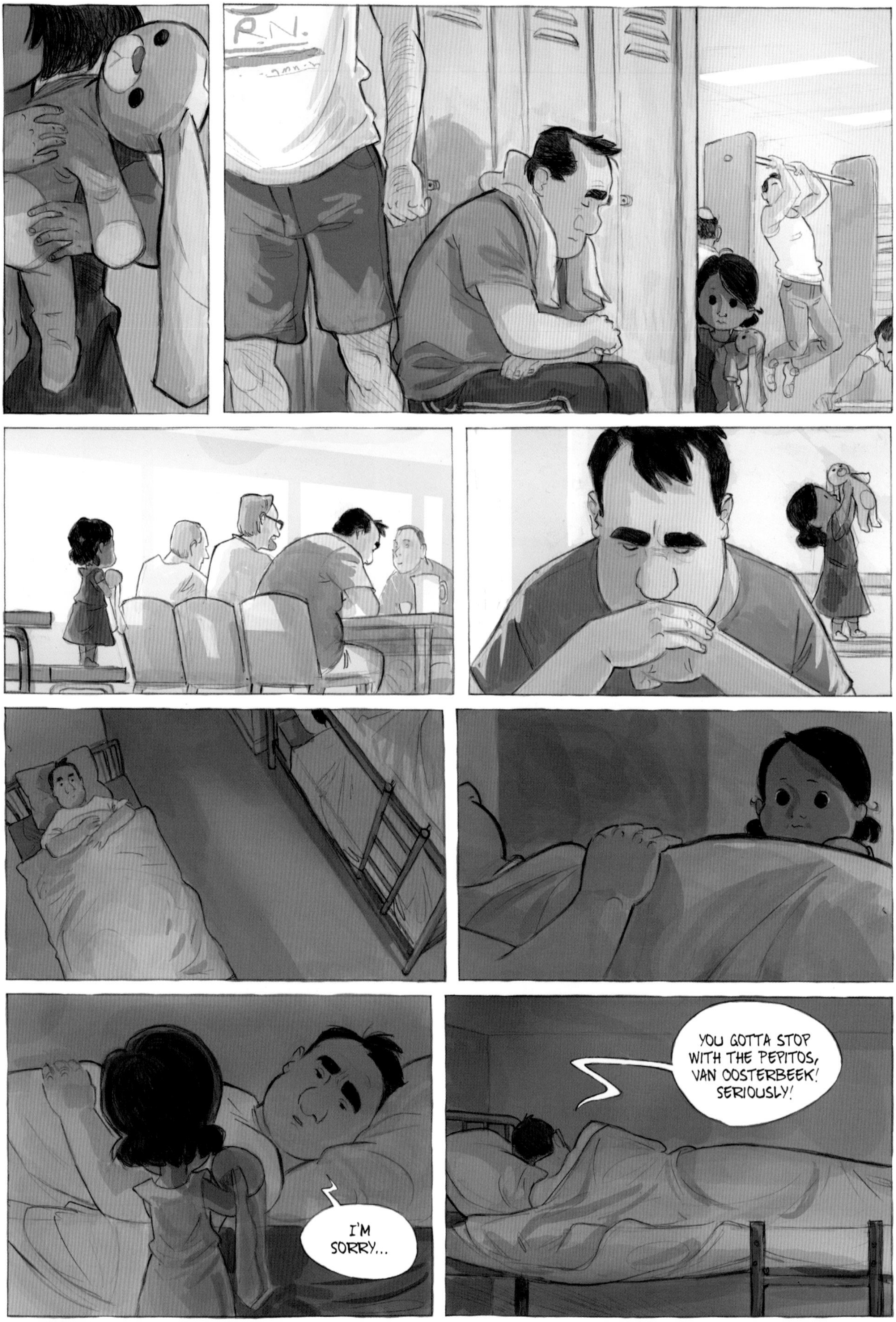
R.N.
I'M SORRY...
YOU GOTTA STOP WITH THE PEPITOS, VAN OOSTERBEEK! SERIOUSLY!

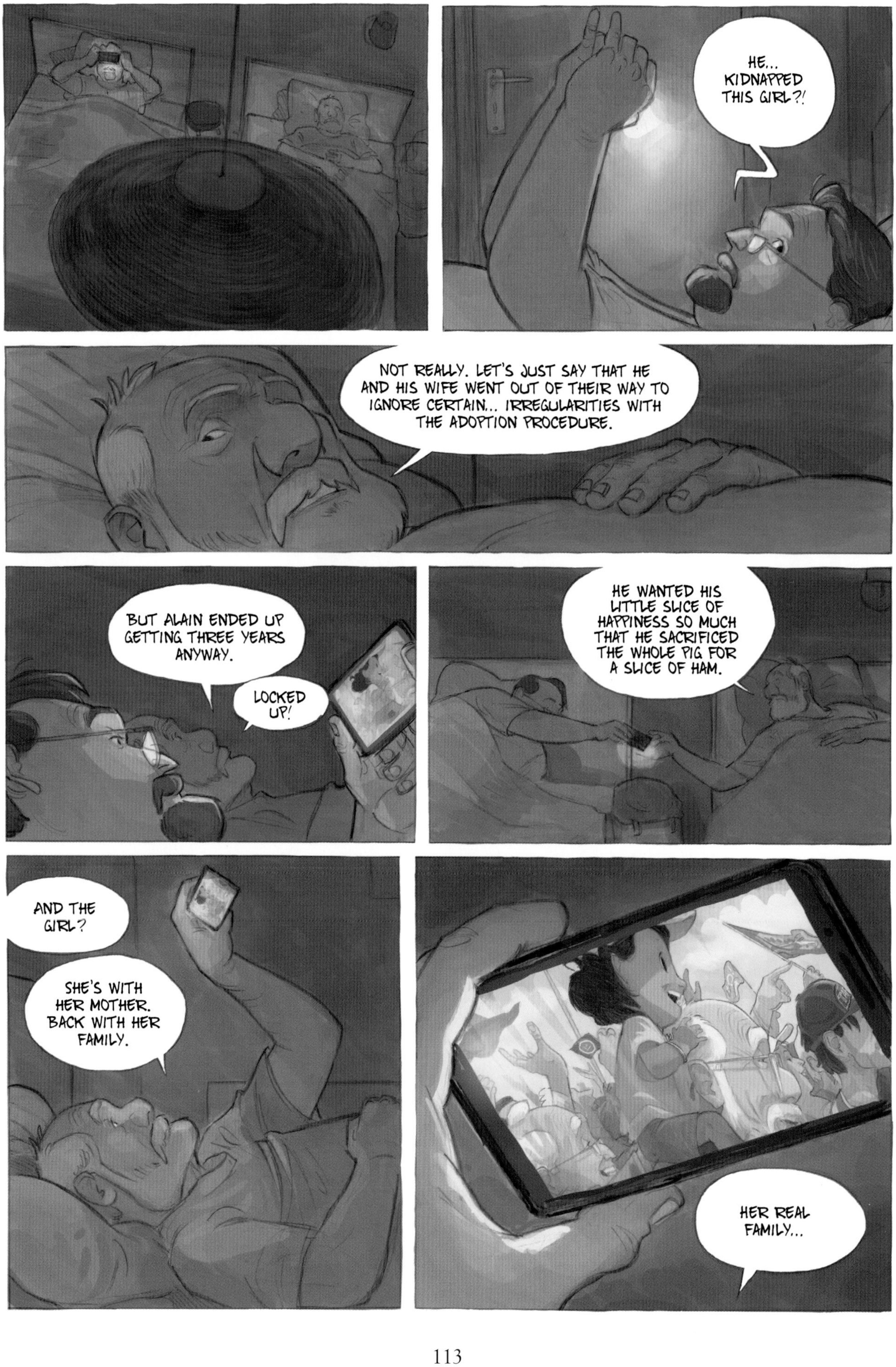
HE... KIDNAPPED THIS GIRL?!
NOT REALLY. LET'S JUST SAY THAT HE AND HIS WIFE WENT OUT OF THEIR WAY TO IGNORE CERTAIN... IRREGULARITIES WITH THE ADOPTION PROCEDURE.
BUT ALAIN ENDED UP GETTING THREE YEARS ANYWAY.
LOCKED UP!
HE WANTED HIS LITTLE SLICE OF HAPPINESS SO MUCH THAT HE SACRIFICED THE WHOLE PIG FOR A SLICE OF HAM.
AND THE GIRL?
SHE'S WITH HER MOTHER. BACK WITH HER FAMILY.
HER REAL FAMILY...

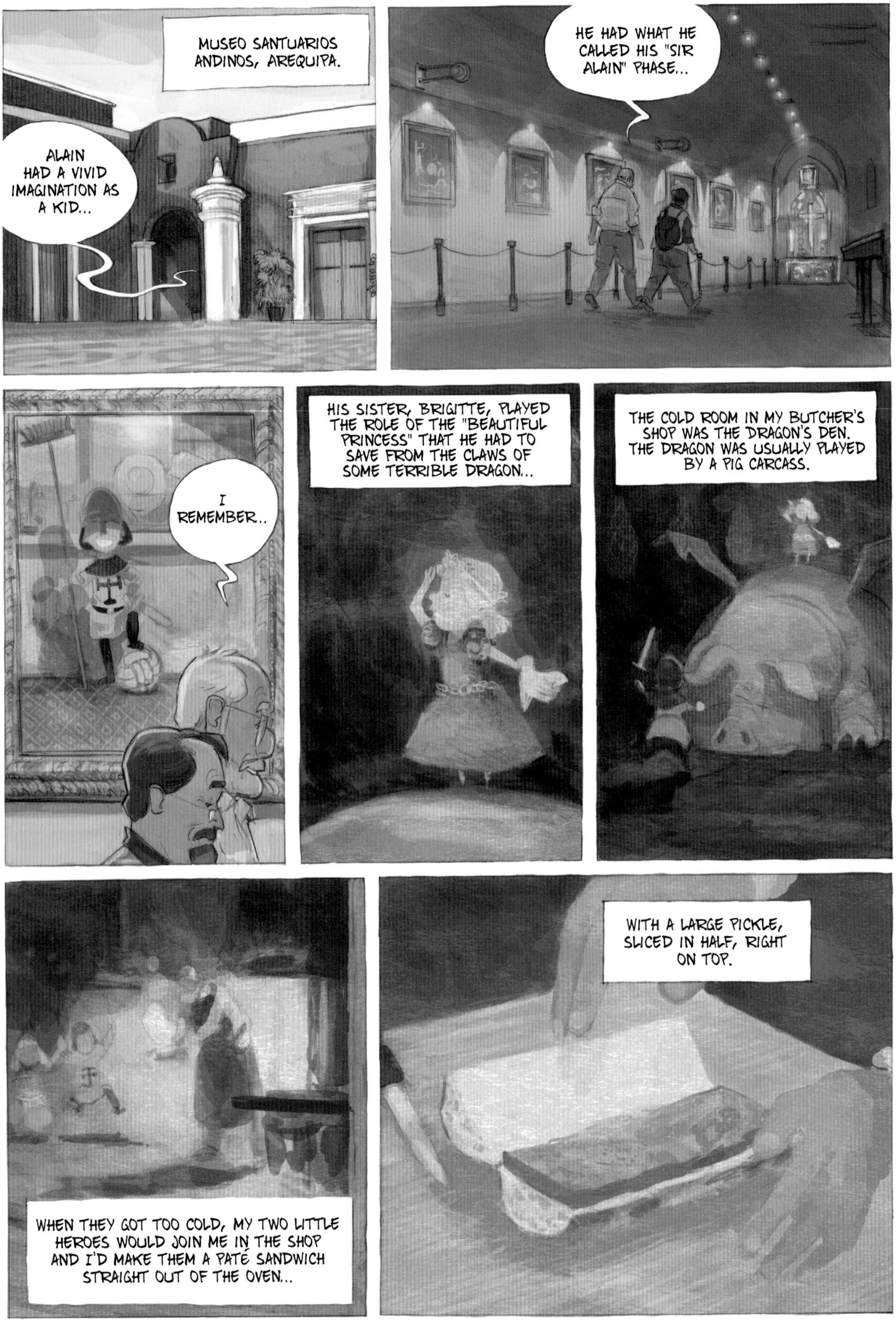
MUSEO SANTUARIOS ANDINOS, AREQUIPA.
ALAIN HAD A VIVID IMAGINATION AS A KID...
HE HAD WHAT HE CALLED HIS "SIR ALAIN" PHASE...
I REMEMBER..
HIS SISTER, BRIGITTE, PLAYED THE ROLE OF THE "BEAUTIFUL PRINCESS" THAT HE HAD TO SAVE FROM THE CLAWS OF SOME TERRIBLE DRAGON...
THE COLD ROOM IN MY BUTCHER'S SHOP WAS THE DRAGON'S DEN. THE DRAGON WAS USUALLY PLAYED BY A PIG CARCASS.
WHEN THEY GOT TOO COLD, MY TWO LITTLE HEROES WOULD JOIN ME IN THE SHOP AND I'D MAKE THEM A PATÉ SANDWICH STRAIGHT OUT OF THE OVEN...
WITH A LARGE PICKLE, SLICED IN HALF, RIGHT ON TOP.

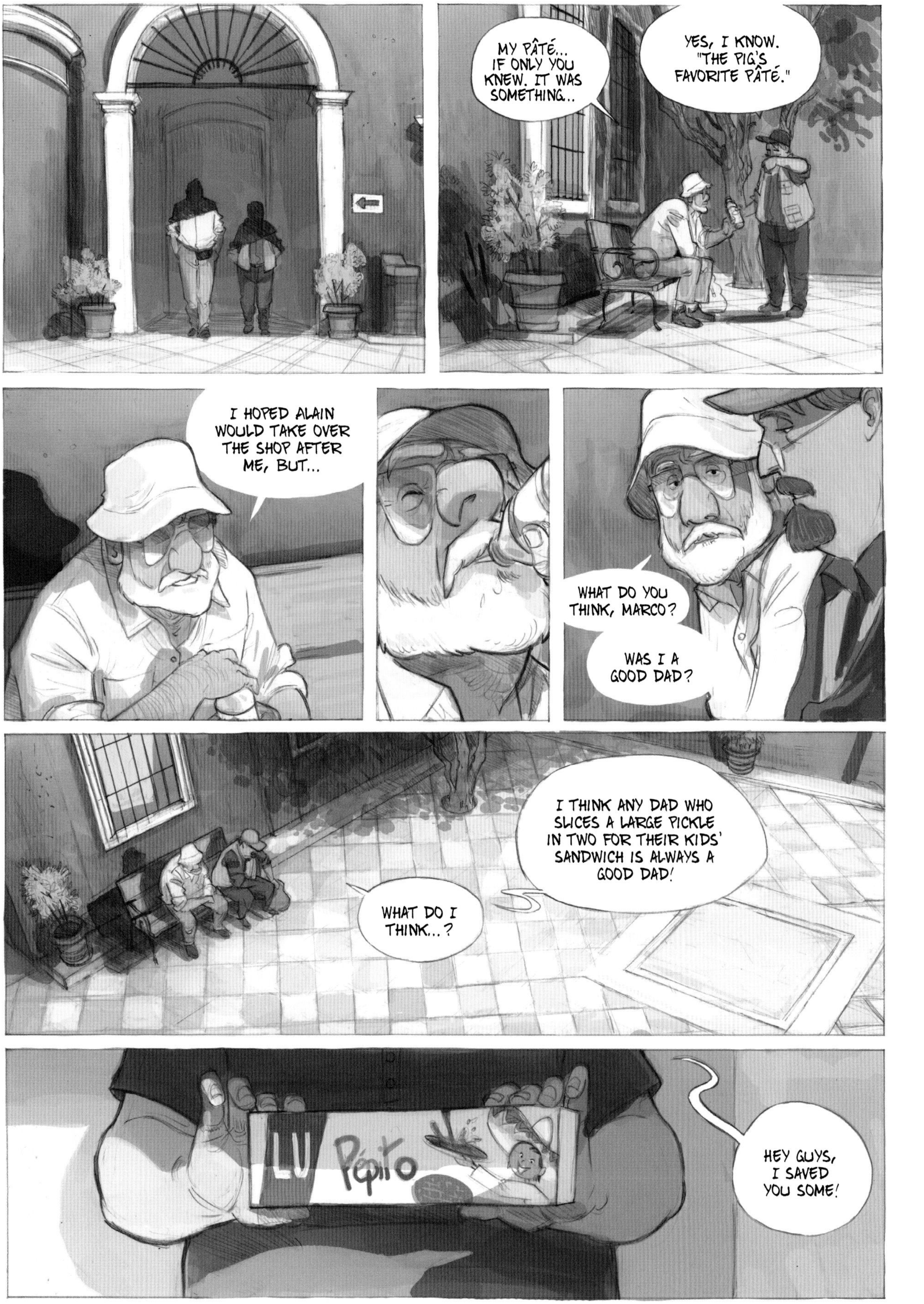
MY PÂTÉ... IF ONLY YOU KNEW. IT WAS SOMETHING...
YES, I KNOW. "THE PIG'S FAVORITE PÂTÉ."
I HOPED ALAIN WOULD TAKE OVER THE SHOP AFTER ME, BUT...
WHAT DO YOU THINK, MARCO?
WAS I A GOOD DAD?
WHAT DO I THINK...?
I THINK ANY DAD WHO SLICES A LARGE PICKLE IN TWO FOR THEIR KIDS' SANDWICH IS ALWAYS A GOOD DAD!
LU
Pépito
HEY GUYS, I SAVED YOU SOME!

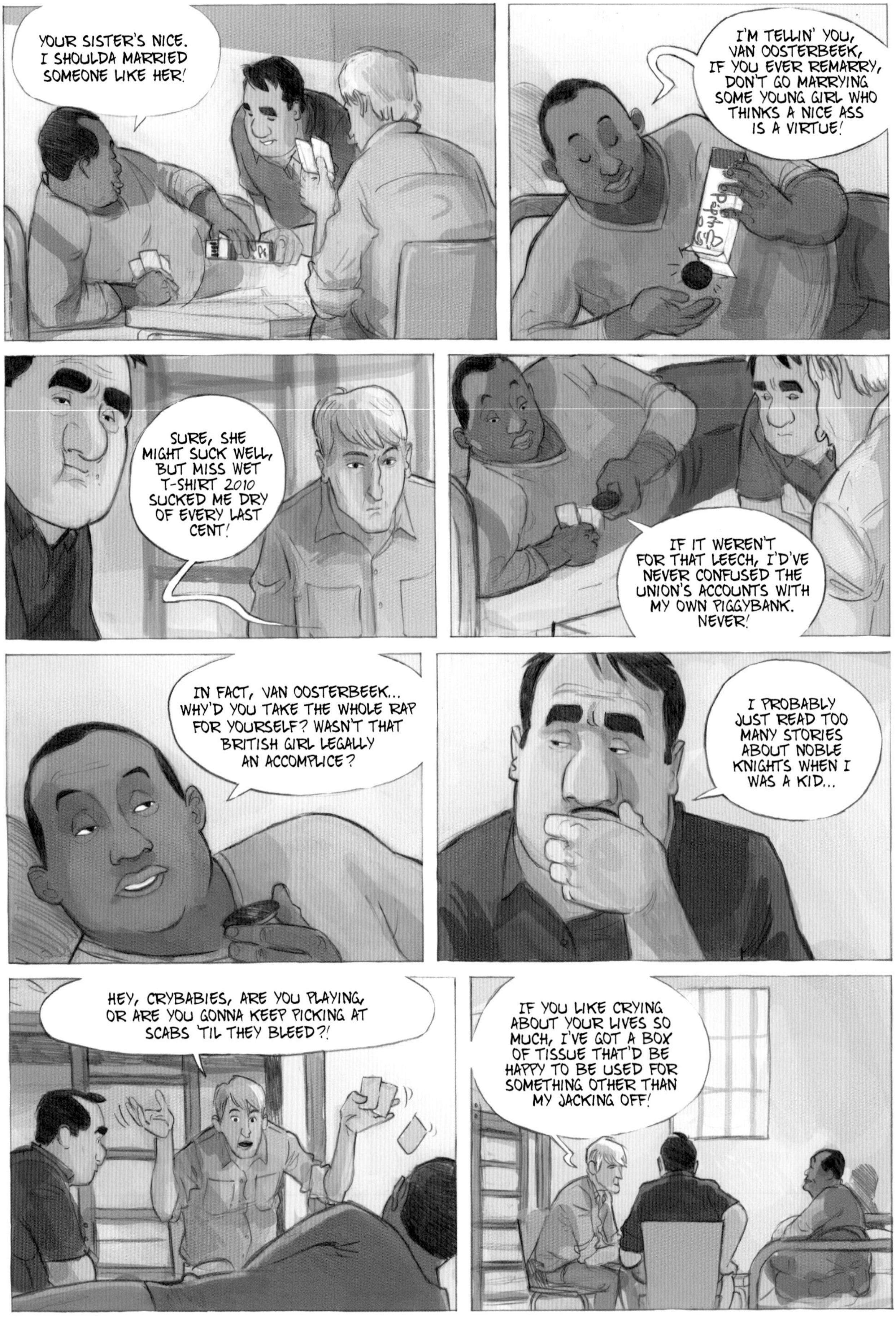
YOUR SISTER'S NICE. I SHOULDA MARRIED SOMEONE LIKE HER!
I'M TELLIN' YOU, VAN OOSTERBEEK, IF YOU EVER REMARRY, DON'T GO MARRYING SOME YOUNG GIRL WHO THINKS A NICE ASS IS A VIRTUE!
SURE, SHE MIGHT SUCK WELL, BUT MISS WET T-SHIRT 2010 SUCKED ME DRY OF EVERY LAST CENT!
IF IT WEREN'T FOR THAT LEECH, I'D'VE NEVER CONFUSED THE UNION'S ACCOUNTS WITH MY OWN PIGGYBANK. NEVER!
IN FACT, VAN OOSTERBEEK... WHY'D YOU TAKE THE WHOLE RAP FOR YOURSELF? WASN'T THAT BRITISH GIRL LEGALLY AN ACCOMPLICE?
I PROBABLY JUST READ TOO MANY STORIES ABOUT NOBLE KNIGHTS WHEN I WAS A KID...
HEY, CRYBABIES, ARE YOU PLAYING, OR ARE YOU GONNA KEEP PICKING AT SCABS 'TIL THEY BLEED?!
IF YOU LIKE CRYING ABOUT YOUR LIVES SO MUCH, I'VE GOT A BOX OF TISSUE THAT'D BE HAPPY TO BE USED FOR SOMETHING OTHER THAN MY JACKING OFF!

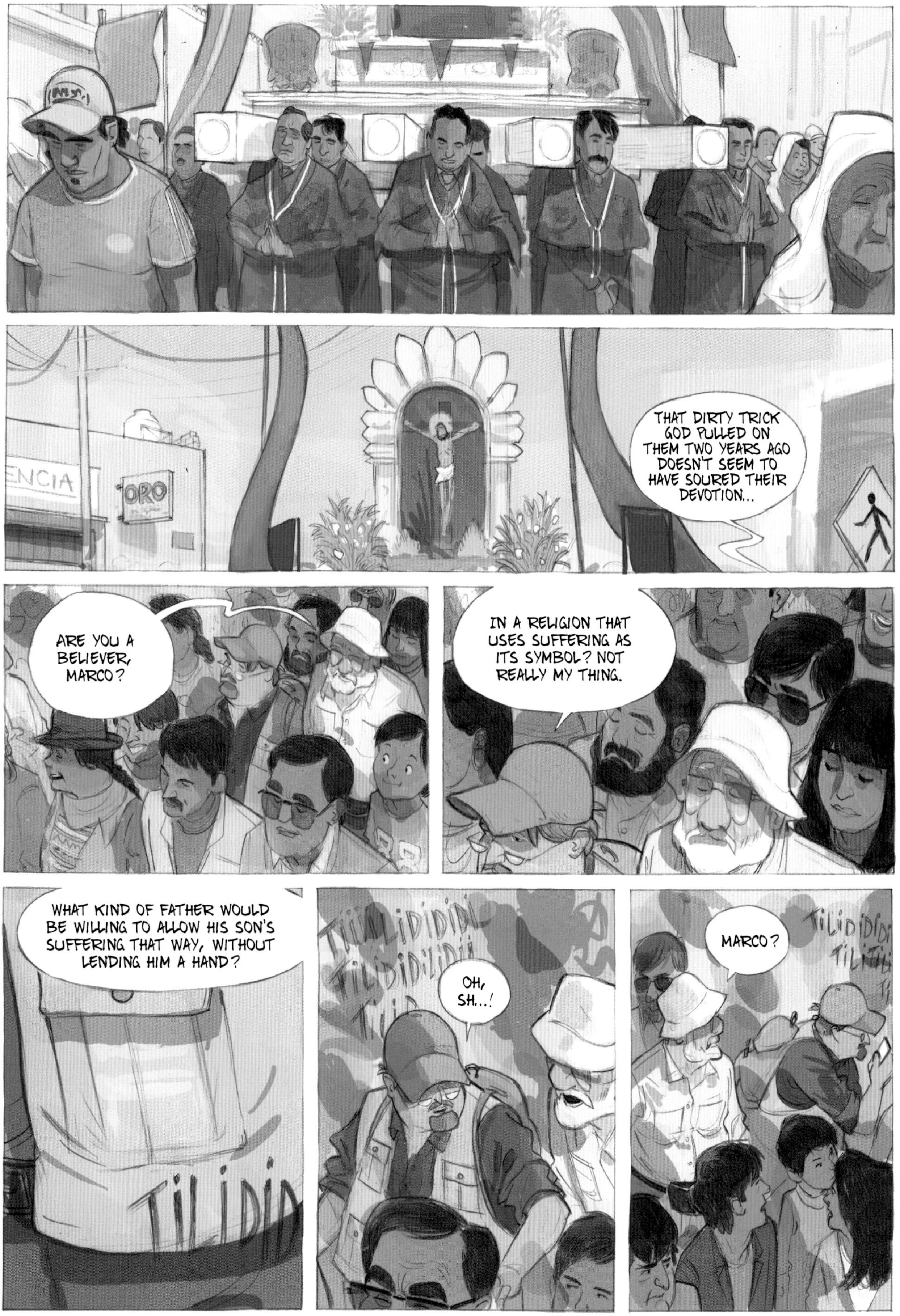

THAT DIRTY TRICK GOD PULLED ON THEM TWO YEARS AGO DOESN'T SEEM TO HAVE SOURED THEIR DEVOTION...
ARE YOU A BELIEVER, MARCO?
IN A RELIGION THAT USES SUFFERING AS ITS SYMBOL? NOT REALLY MY THING.
WHAT KIND OF FATHER WOULD BE WILLING TO ALLOW HIS SON'S SUFFERING THAT WAY, WITHOUT LENDING HIM A HAND?
TILIDID
TILIDIDIDI
TILIDIDILIDIDI
OH, SH...!
MARCO?
TILIDIDIDI

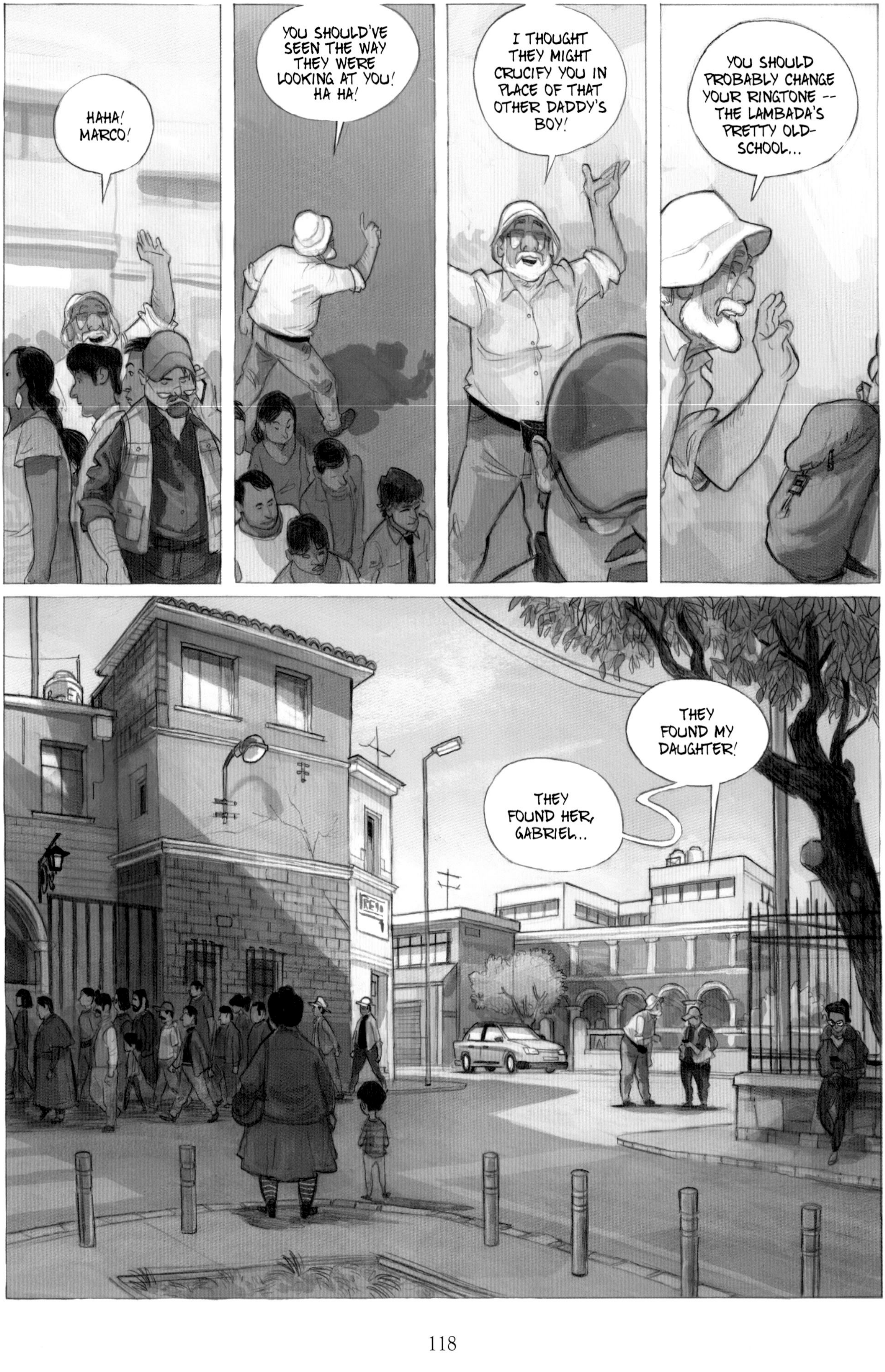
HAHA! MARCO!
YOU SHOULD'VE SEEN THE WAY THEY WERE LOOKING AT YOU! HA HA!
I THOUGHT THEY MIGHT CRUCIFY YOU IN PLACE OF THAT OTHER DADDY'S BOY!
YOU SHOULD PROBABLY CHANGE YOUR RINGTONE -- THE LAMBADA'S PRETTY OLD-SCHOOL...
THEY FOUND MY DAUGHTER!
THEY FOUND HER, GABRIEL...

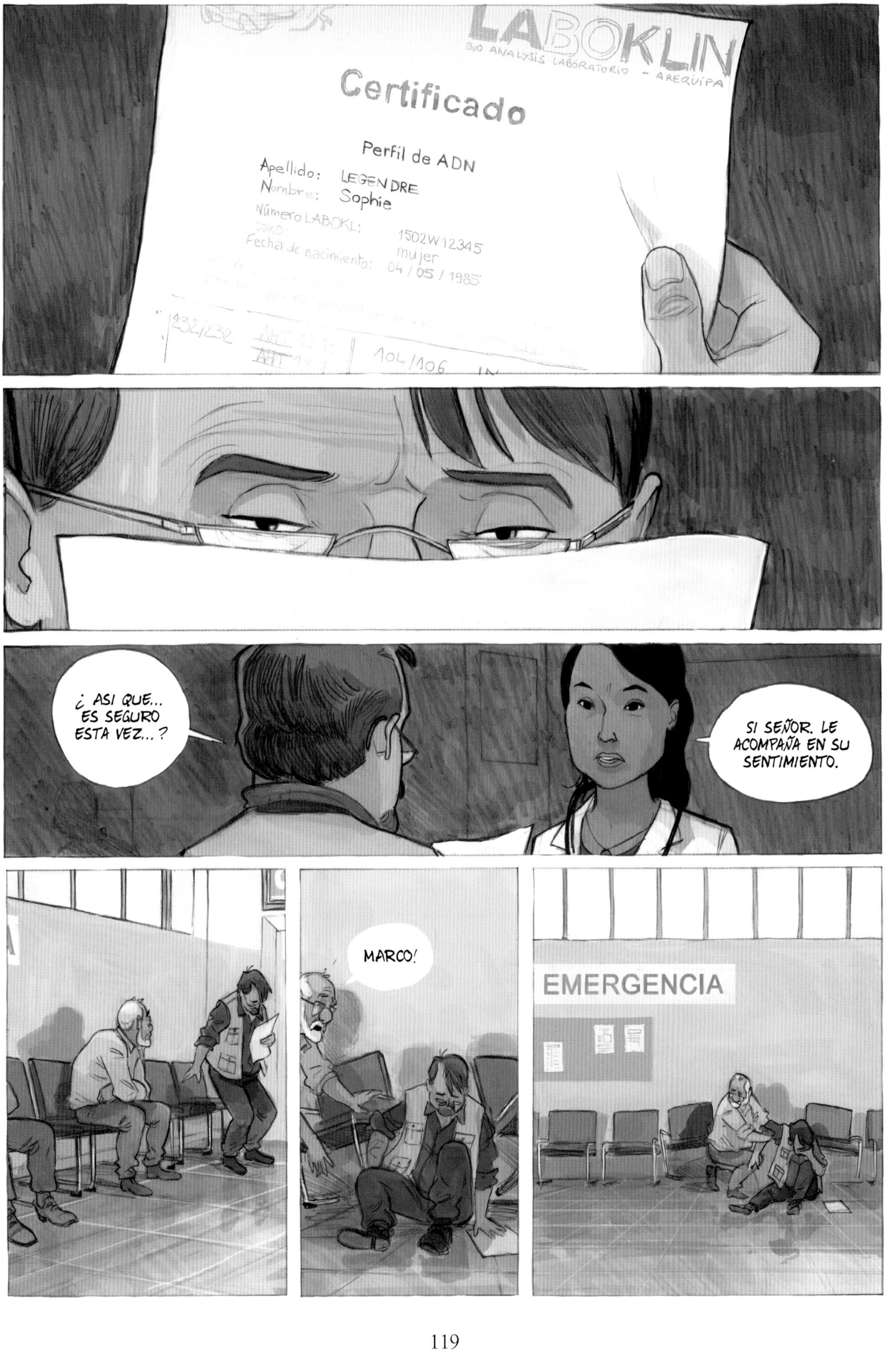
LABOKLIN
BIO ANALYSIS LABORATORIO - AREQUIPA
Certificado
Perfil de ADN
Apellido: LEGENDRE
Nombre: Sophie
Número LABOKL: 1502W12345
Sexo: mujer
Fecha de nacimiento: 04 / 05 / 1985
¿ ASI QUE... ES SEGURO ESTA VEZ... ?
SI SEÑOR. LE ACOMPAÑA EN SU SENTIMIENTO.
MARCO!
EMERGENCIA

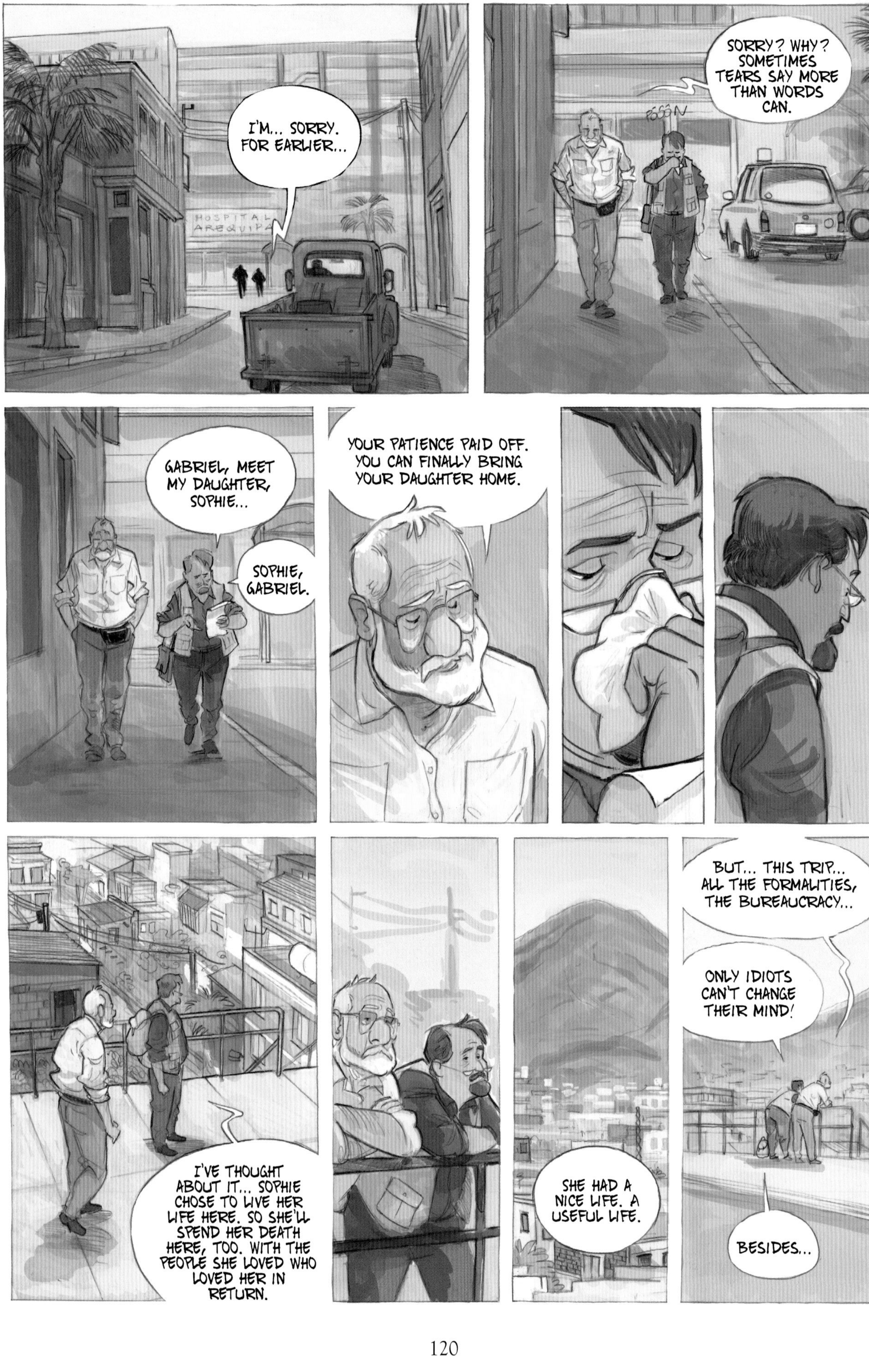
I'M... SORRY. FOR EARLIER...
HOSPITAL AREQUIPA
SORRY? WHY? SOMETIMES TEARS SAY MORE THAN WORDS CAN.
GABRIEL, MEET MY DAUGHTER, SOPHIE...
SOPHIE, GABRIEL.
YOUR PATIENCE PAID OFF. YOU CAN FINALLY BRING YOUR DAUGHTER HOME.
I'VE THOUGHT ABOUT IT... SOPHIE CHOSE TO LIVE HER LIFE HERE. SO SHE'LL SPEND HER DEATH HERE, TOO. WITH THE PEOPLE SHE LOVED WHO LOVED HER IN RETURN.
SHE HAD A NICE LIFE. A USEFUL LIFE.
BUT... THIS TRIP... ALL THE FORMALITIES, THE BUREAUCRACY...
ONLY IDIOTS CAN'T CHANGE THEIR MIND!
BESIDES...

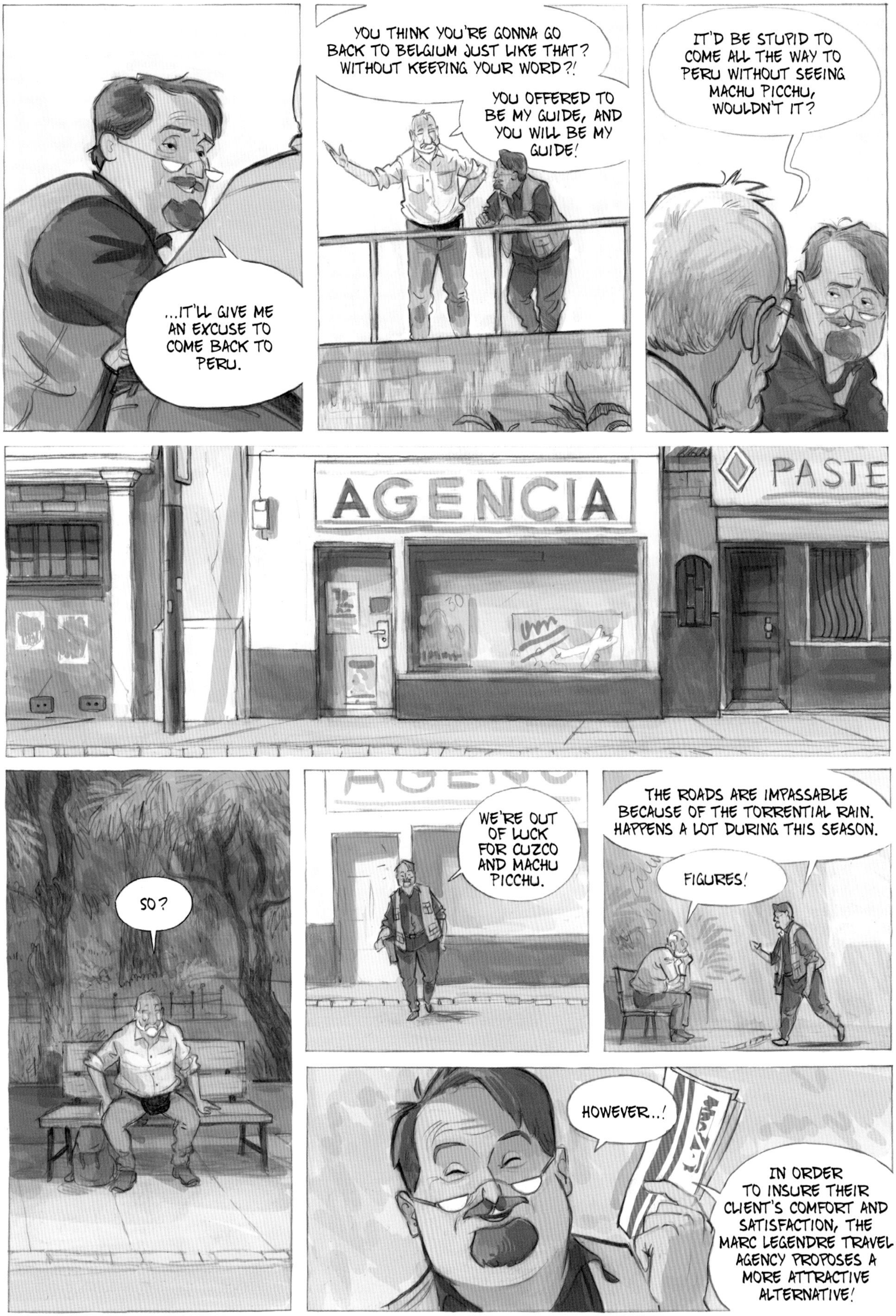
...IT'LL GIVE ME AN EXCUSE TO COME BACK TO PERU.
YOU THINK YOU'RE GONNA GO BACK TO BELGIUM JUST LIKE THAT? WITHOUT KEEPING YOUR WORD?!
YOU OFFERED TO BE MY GUIDE, AND YOU WILL BE MY GUIDE!
IT'D BE STUPID TO COME ALL THE WAY TO PERU WITHOUT SEEING MACHU PICCHU, WOULDN'T IT?
AGENCIA
PASTE
SO?
WE'RE OUT OF LUCK FOR CUZCO AND MACHU PICCHU.
THE ROADS ARE IMPASSABLE BECAUSE OF THE TORRENTIAL RAIN. HAPPENS A LOT DURING THIS SEASON.
FIGURES!
HOWEVER...!
IN ORDER TO INSURE THEIR CLIENT'S COMFORT AND SATISFACTION, THE MARC LEGENDRE TRAVEL AGENCY PROPOSES A MORE ATTRACTIVE ALTERNATIVE!

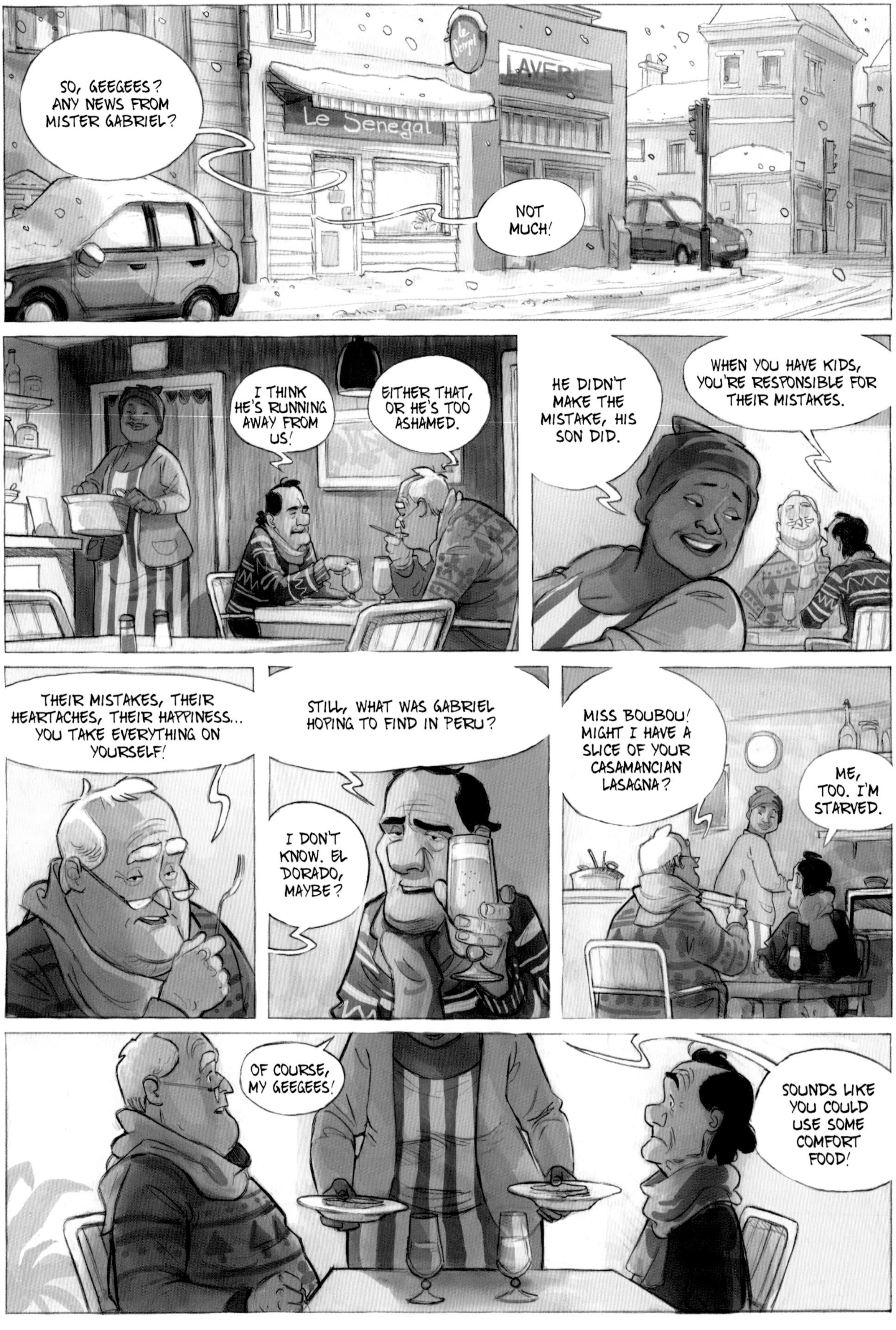
Le Senegal
LAVERIE
SO, GEEGEES? ANY NEWS FROM MISTER GABRIEL?
NOT MUCH!
I THINK HE'S RUNNING AWAY FROM US!
EITHER THAT, OR HE'S TOO ASHAMED.
HE DIDN'T MAKE THE MISTAKE, HIS SON DID.
WHEN YOU HAVE KIDS, YOU'RE RESPONSIBLE FOR THEIR MISTAKES.
THEIR MISTAKES, THEIR HEARTACHES, THEIR HAPPINESS... YOU TAKE EVERYTHING ON YOURSELF!
STILL, WHAT WAS GABRIEL HOPING TO FIND IN PERU?
I DON'T KNOW. EL DORADO, MAYBE?
MISS BOUBOU! MIGHT I HAVE A SLICE OF YOUR CASAMANCIAN LASAGNA?
ME, TOO. I'M STARVED.
OF COURSE, MY GEEGEES!
SOUNDS LIKE YOU COULD USE SOME COMFORT FOOD!

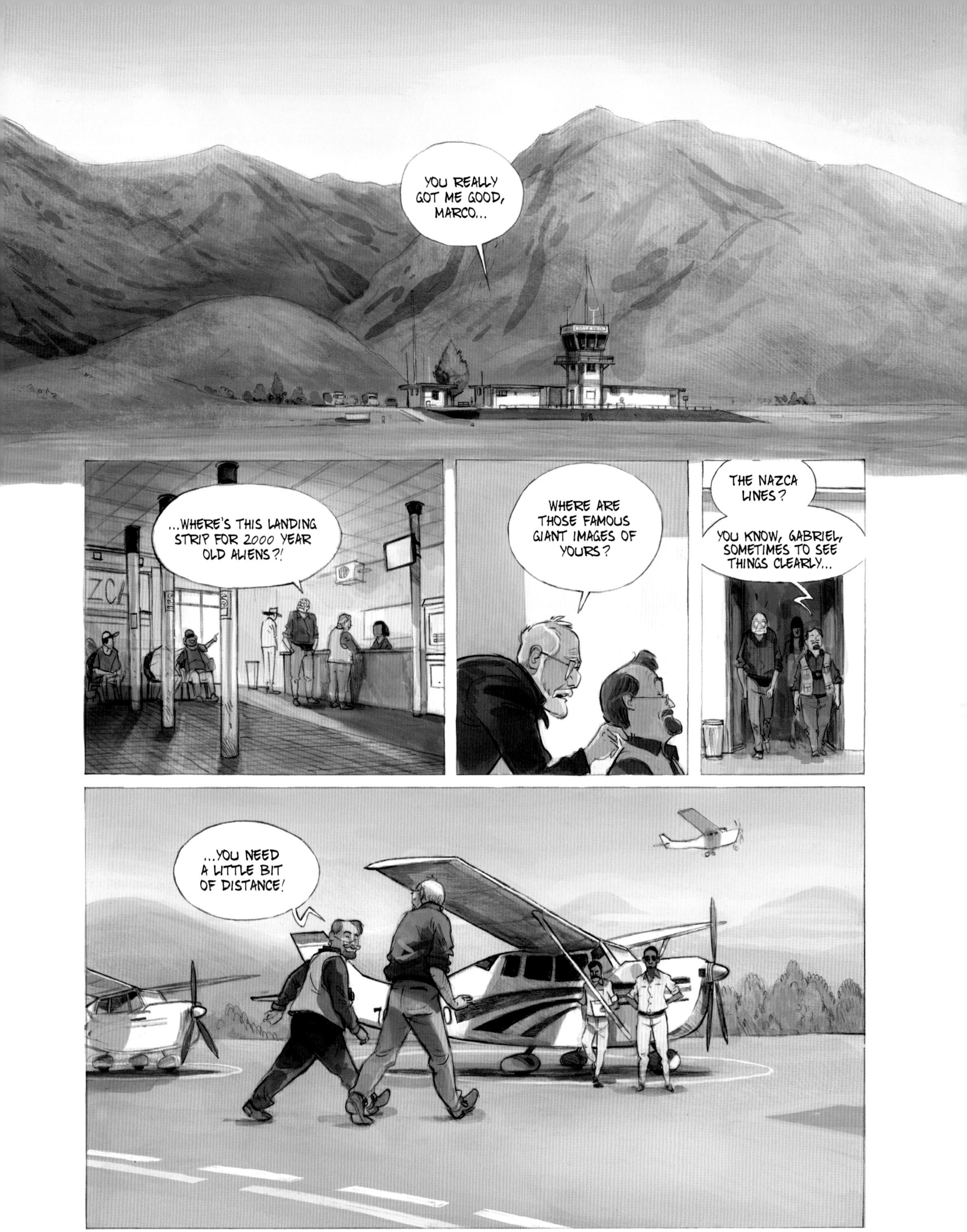
YOU REALLY GOT ME GOOD, MARCO...
...WHERE'S THIS LANDING STRIP FOR 2000 YEAR OLD ALIENS?!
WHERE ARE THOSE FAMOUS GIANT IMAGES OF YOURS?
THE NAZCA LINES?
YOU KNOW, GABRIEL, SOMETIMES TO SEE THINGS CLEARLY...
...YOU NEED A LITTLE BIT OF DISTANCE!

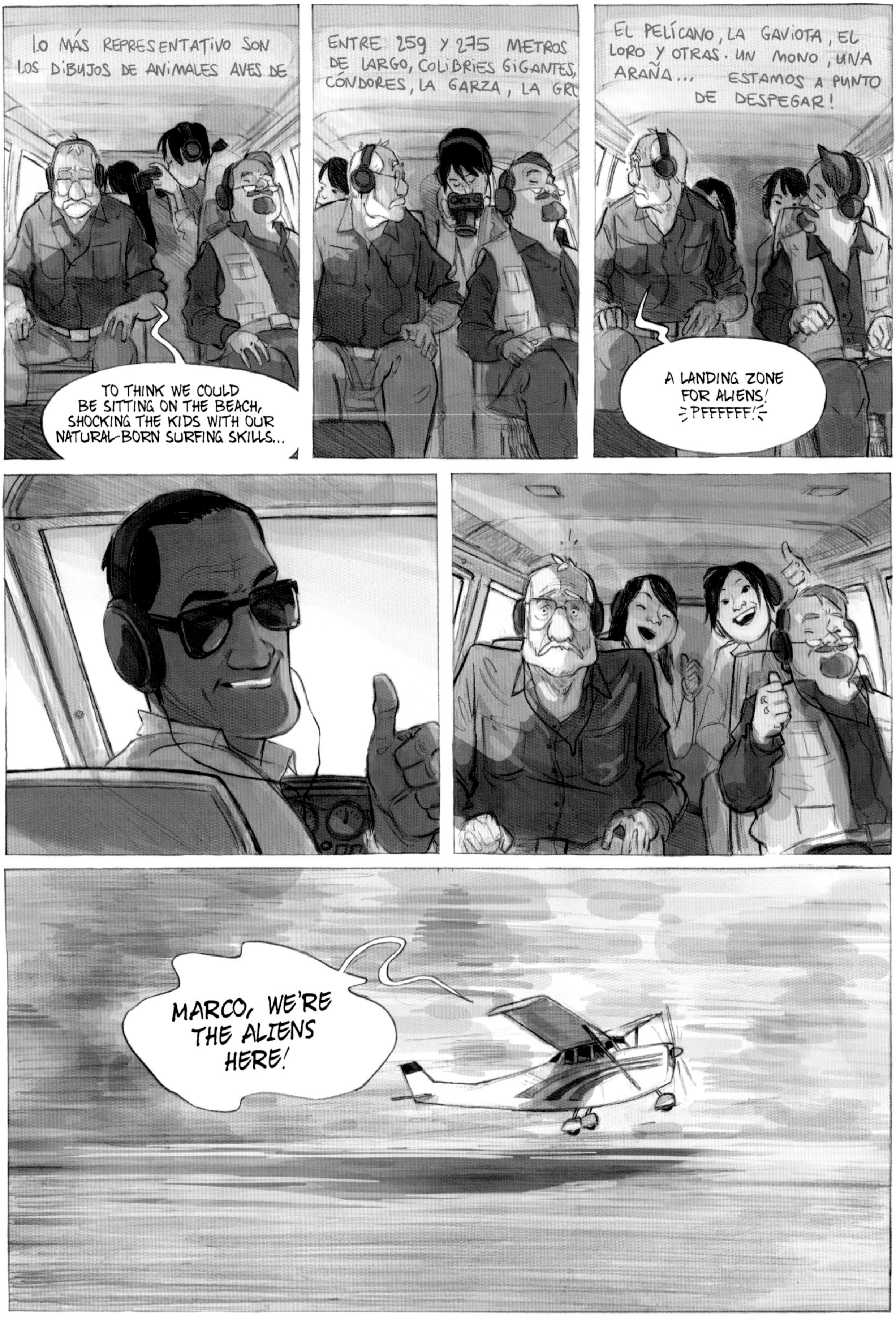
LO MÁS REPRESENTATIVO SON LOS DIBUJOS DE ANIMALES AVES DE
TO THINK WE COULD BE SITTING ON THE BEACH, SHOCKING THE KIDS WITH OUR NATURAL-BORN SURFING SKILLS...
ENTRE 259 Y 275 METROS DE LARGO, COLIBRÍES GIGANTES, CÓNDORES, LA GARZA, LA GRU
EL PELÍCANO, LA GAVIOTA, EL LORO Y OTRAS. UN MONO, UNA ARAÑA... ESTAMOS A PUNTO DE DESPEGAR!
A LANDING ZONE FOR ALIENS!
PFFFFFF!
MARCO, WE'RE THE ALIENS HERE!

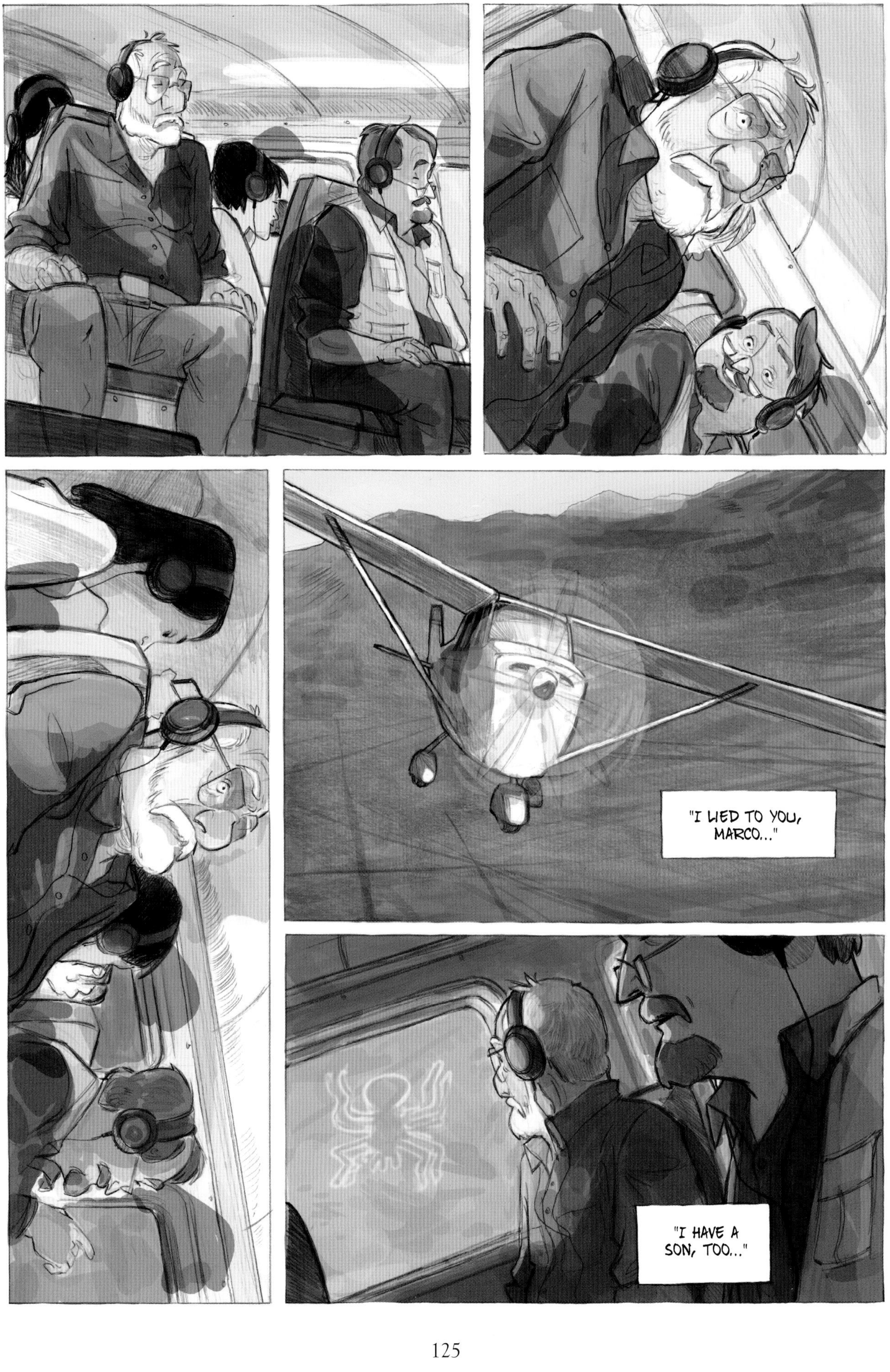
"I LIED TO YOU, MARCO..."
"I HAVE A SON, TOO..."

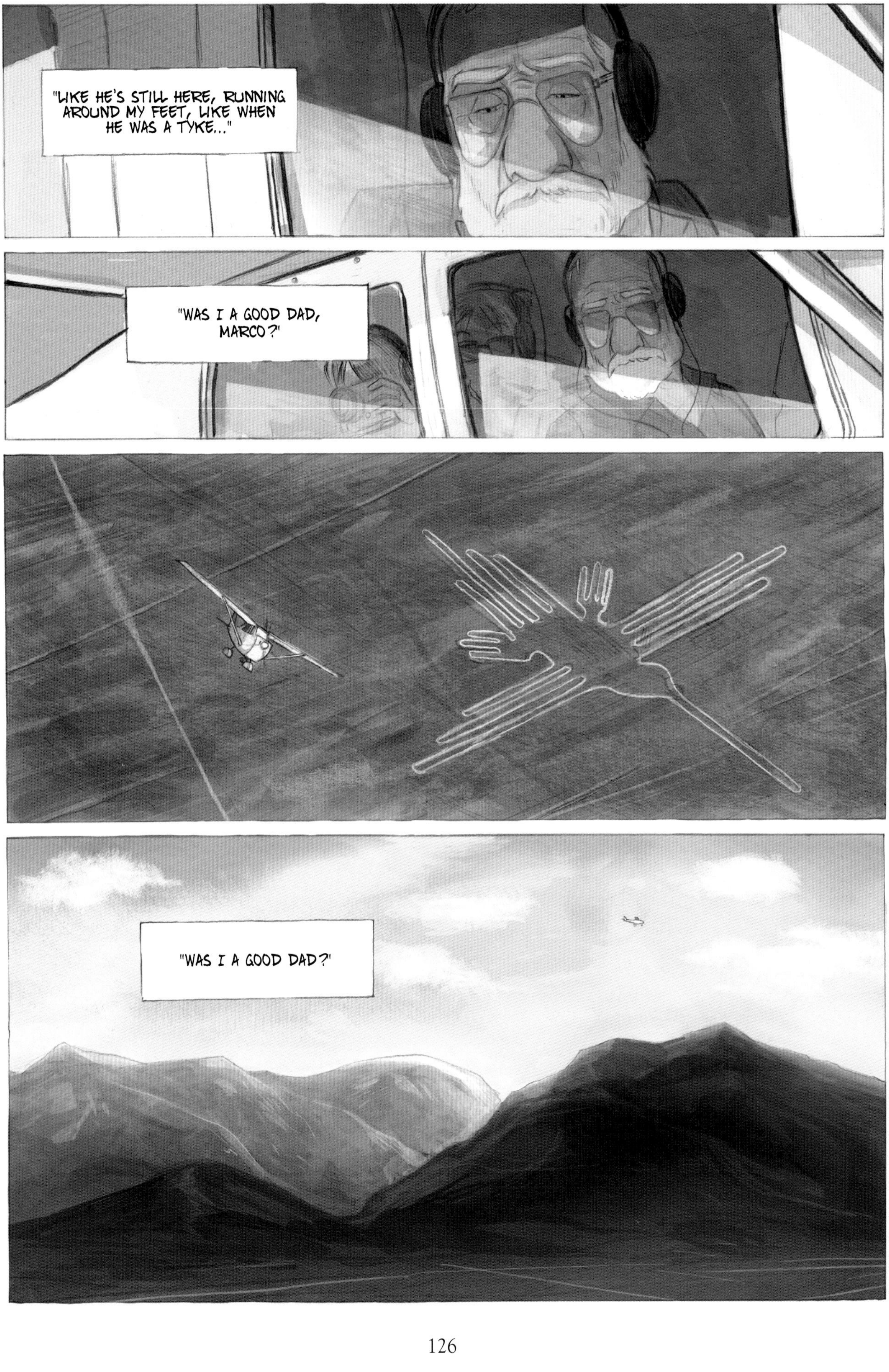
"LIKE HE'S STILL HERE, RUNNING AROUND MY FEET, LIKE WHEN HE WAS A TYKE..."
"WAS I A GOOD DAD, MARCO?"
"WAS I A GOOD DAD?"

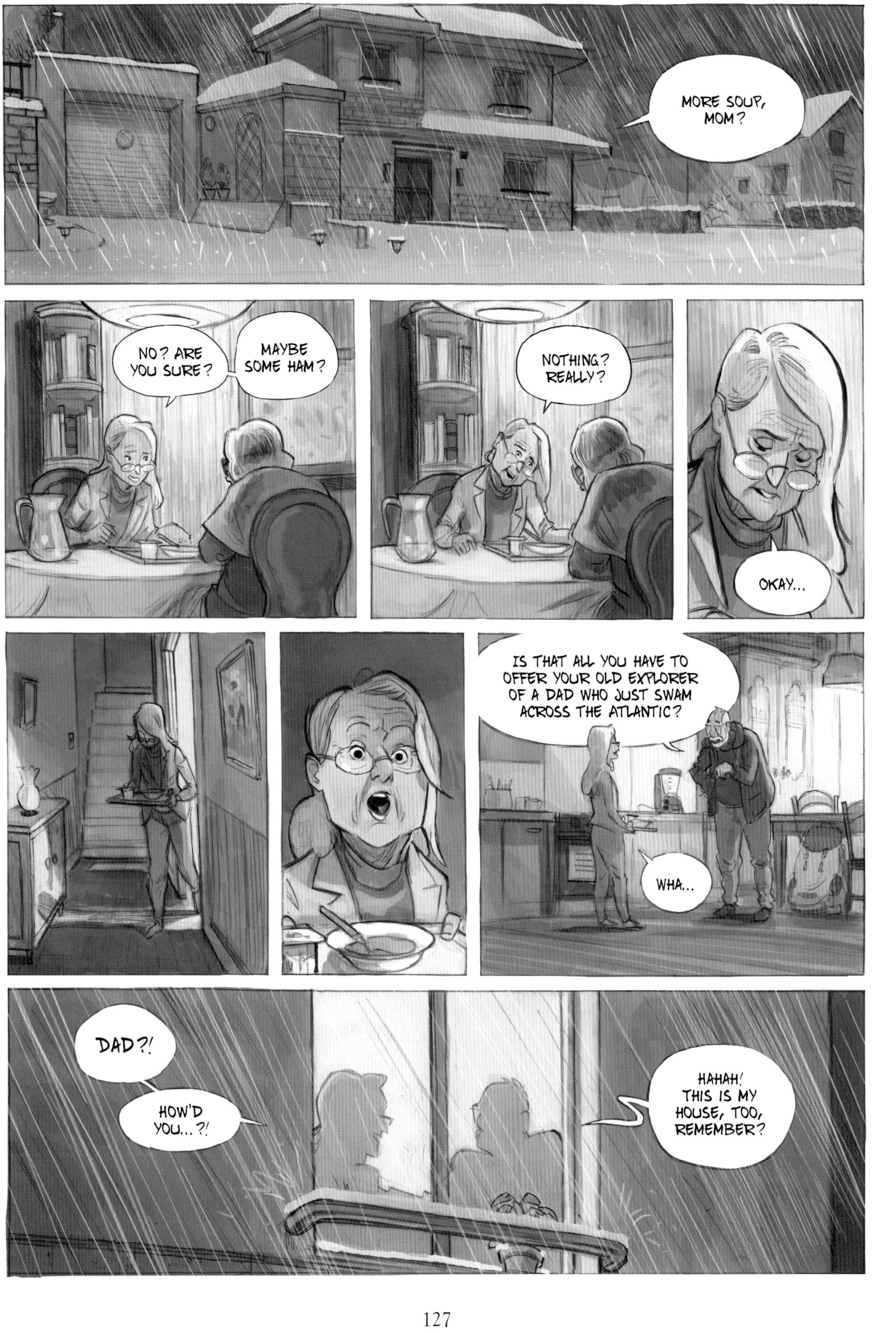
MORE SOUP, MOM?
NO? ARE YOU SURE?
MAYBE SOME HAM?
NOTHING? REALLY?
OKAY...
IS THAT ALL YOU HAVE TO OFFER YOUR OLD EXPLORER OF A DAD WHO JUST SWAM ACROSS THE ATLANTIC?
WHA...
DAD?!
HOW'D YOU...?!
HAHAH! THIS IS MY HOUSE, TOO, REMEMBER?

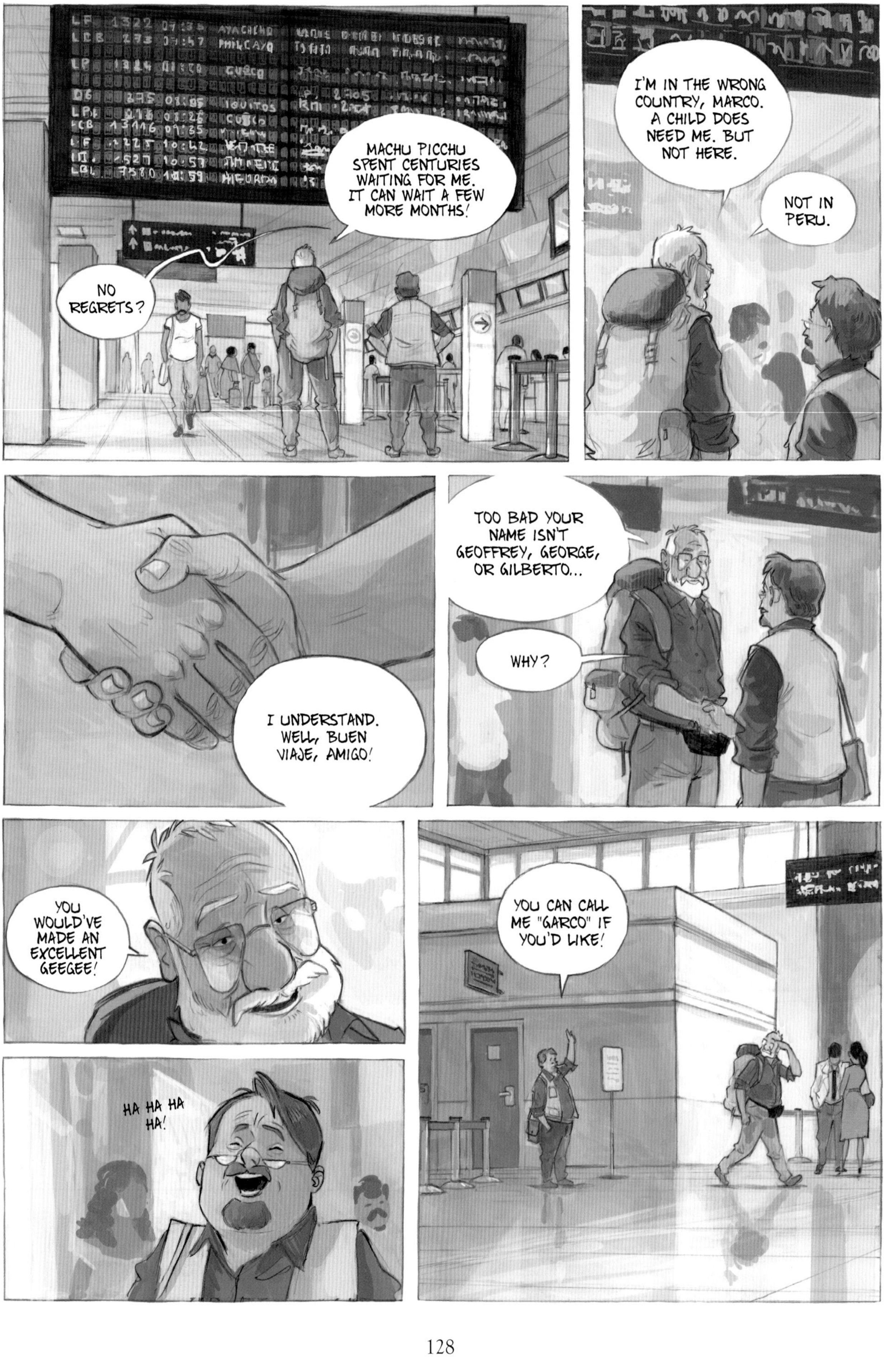
MACHU PICCHU SPENT CENTURIES WAITING FOR ME. IT CAN WAIT A FEW MORE MONTHS!
NO REGRETS?
I'M IN THE WRONG COUNTRY, MARCO. A CHILD DOES NEED ME. BUT NOT HERE.
NOT IN PERU.
I UNDERSTAND. WELL, BUEN VIAJE, AMIGO!
TOO BAD YOUR NAME ISN'T GEOFFREY, GEORGE, OR GILBERTO...
WHY?
YOU WOULD'VE MADE AN EXCELLENT GEEGEE!
HA HA HA HA!
YOU CAN CALL ME "GARCO" IF YOU'D LIKE!

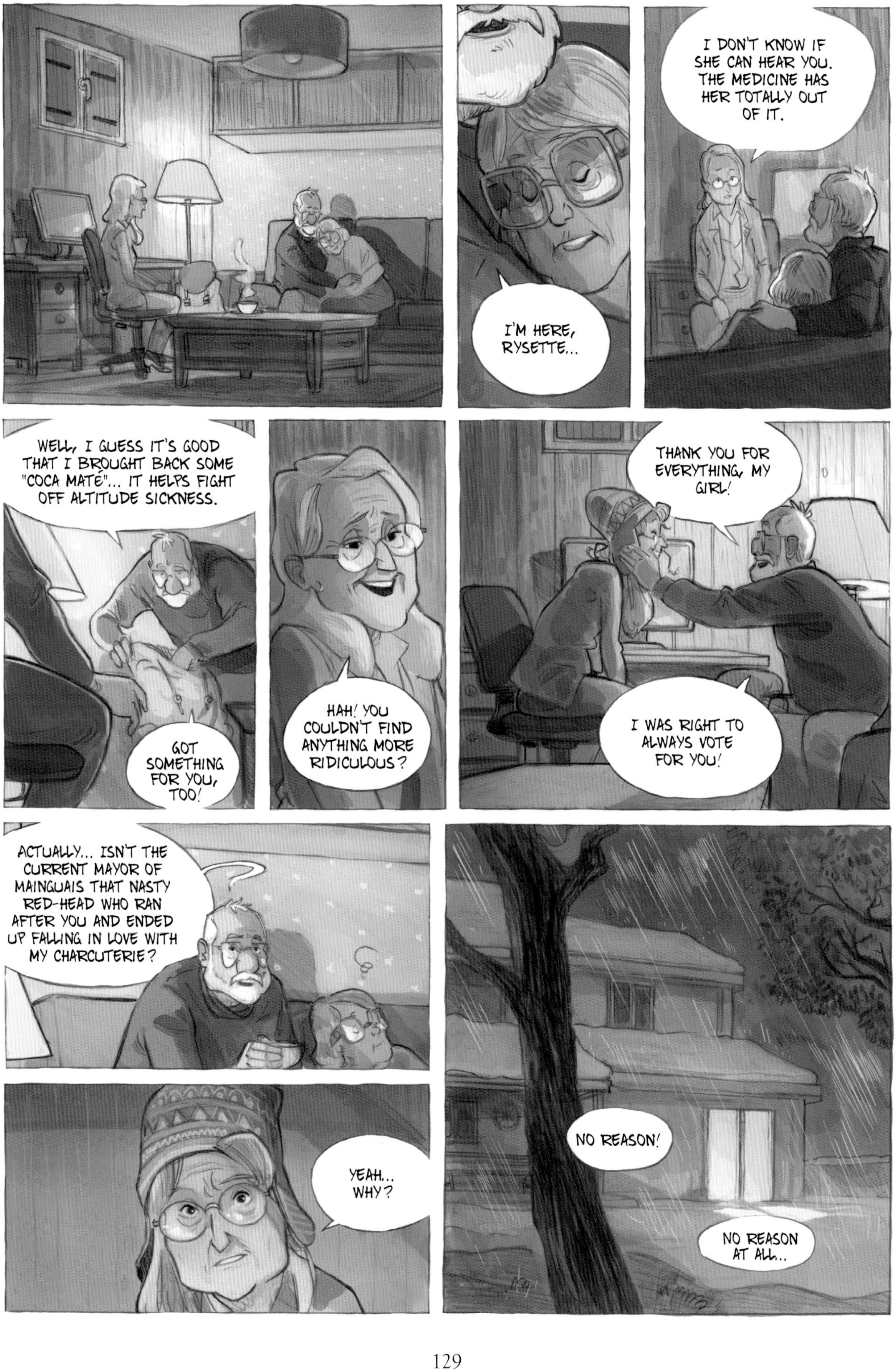
I'M HERE, RYSETTE...
I DON'T KNOW IF SHE CAN HEAR YOU. THE MEDICINE HAS HER TOTALLY OUT OF IT.
WELL, I GUESS IT'S GOOD THAT I BROUGHT BACK SOME "COCA MATÉ"... IT HELPS FIGHT OFF ALTITUDE SICKNESS.
GOT SOMETHING FOR YOU, TOO!
HAH! YOU COULDN'T FIND ANYTHING MORE RIDICULOUS?
THANK YOU FOR EVERYTHING, MY GIRL!
I WAS RIGHT TO ALWAYS VOTE FOR YOU!
ACTUALLY... ISN'T THE CURRENT MAYOR OF MAINGUAIS THAT NASTY RED-HEAD WHO RAN AFTER YOU AND ENDED UP FALLING IN LOVE WITH MY CHARCUTERIE?
YEAH... WHY?
NO REASON!
NO REASON AT ALL...

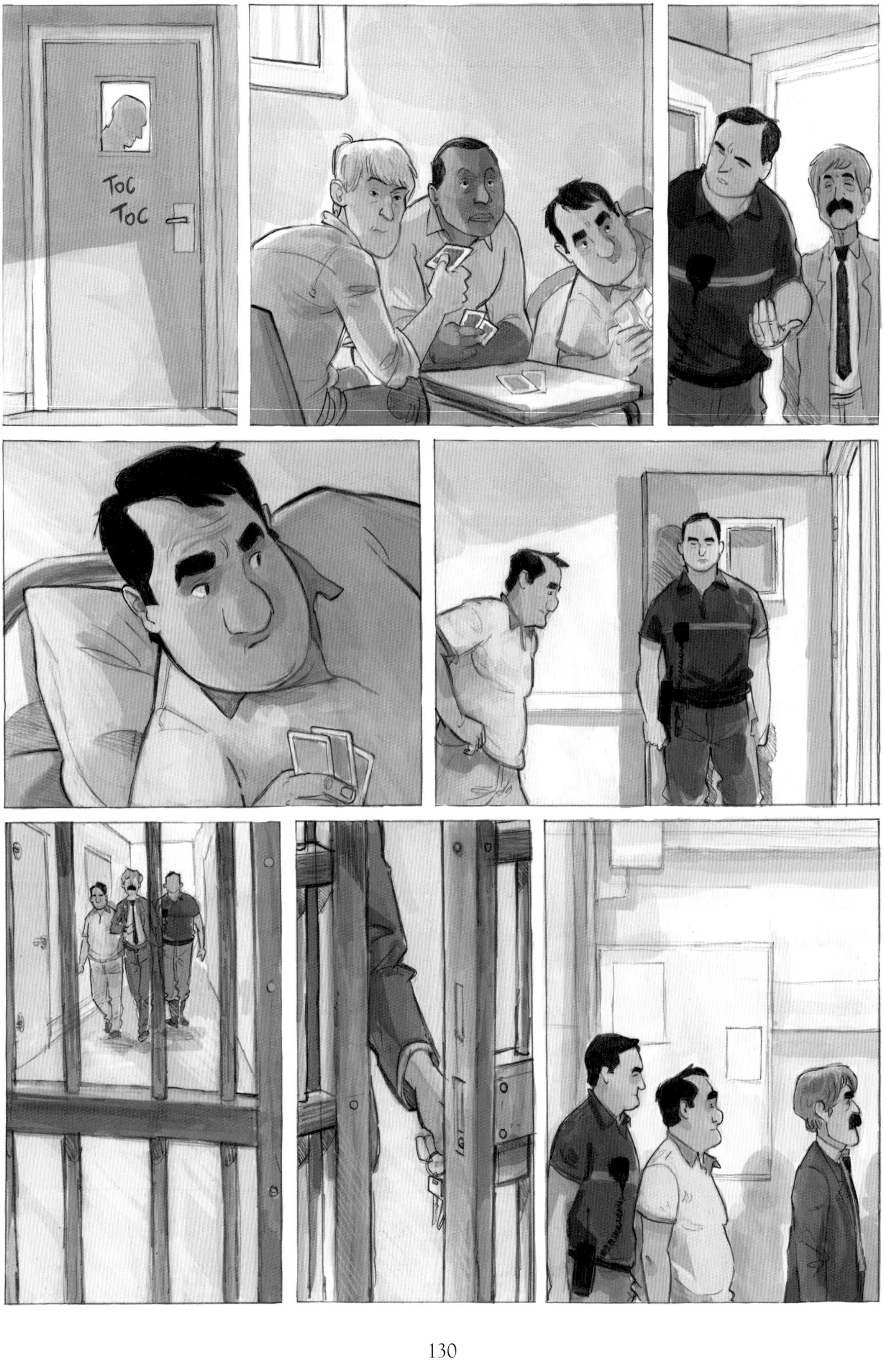
TOC
TOC

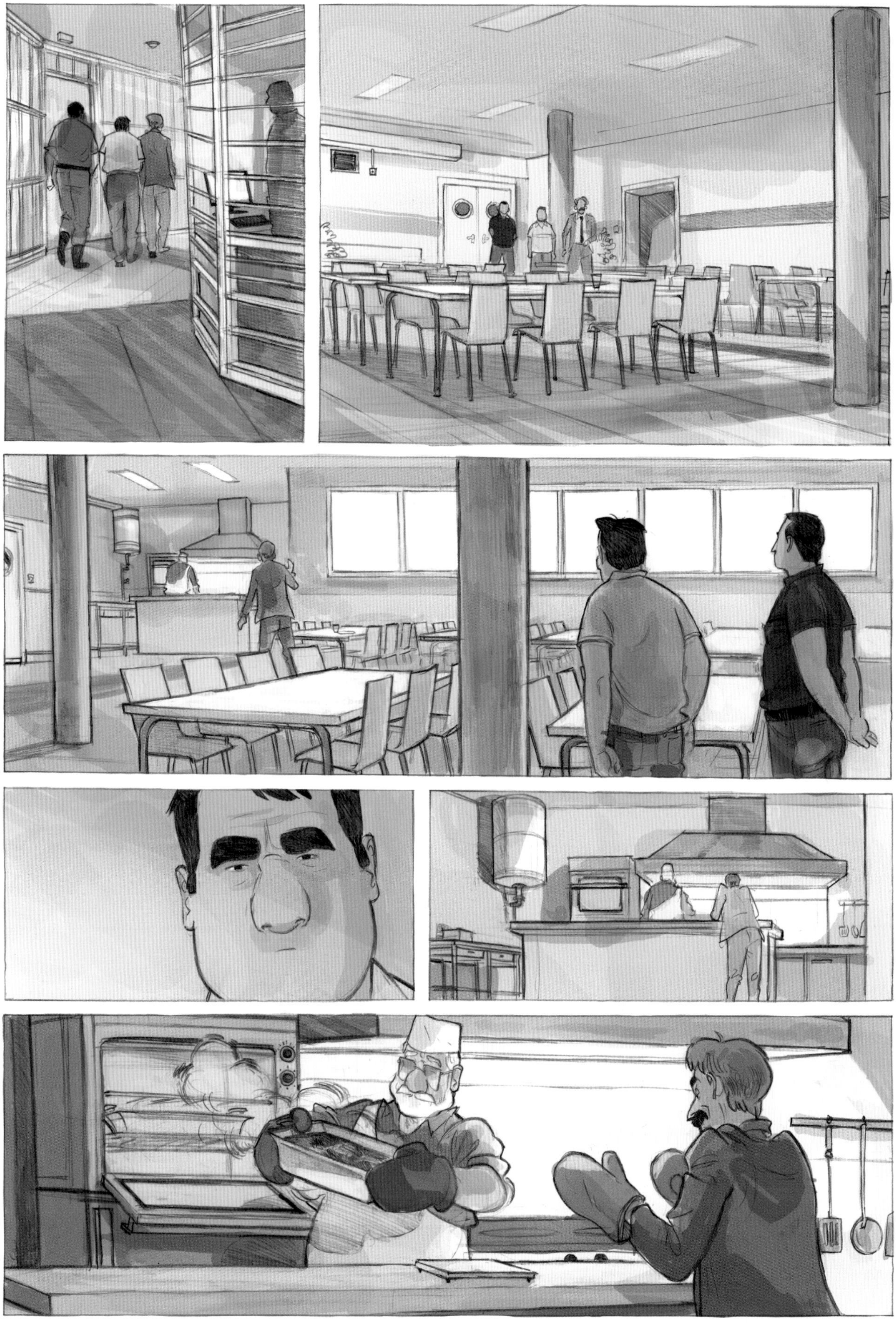

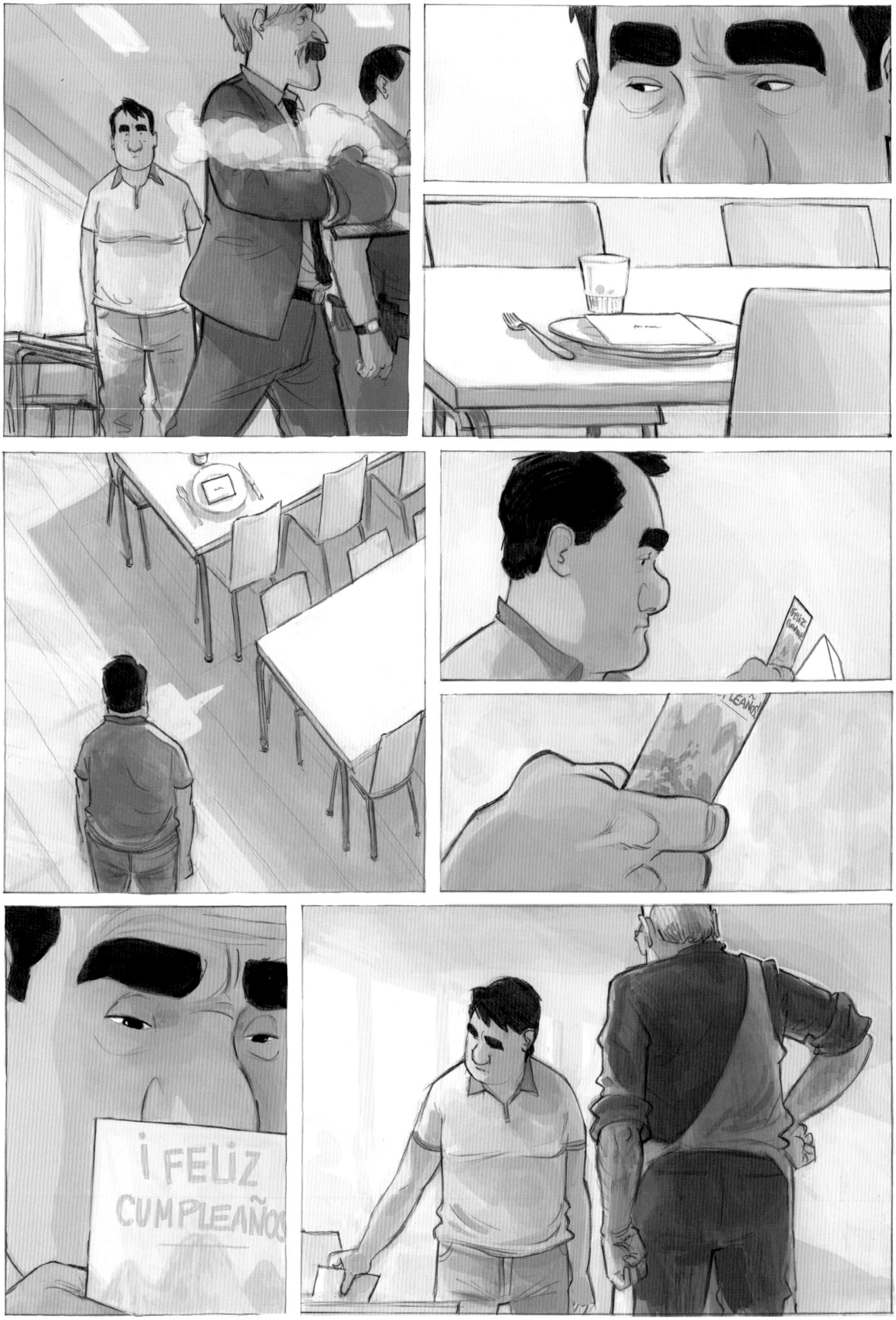
¡FELIZ
CUMPLEAÑOS

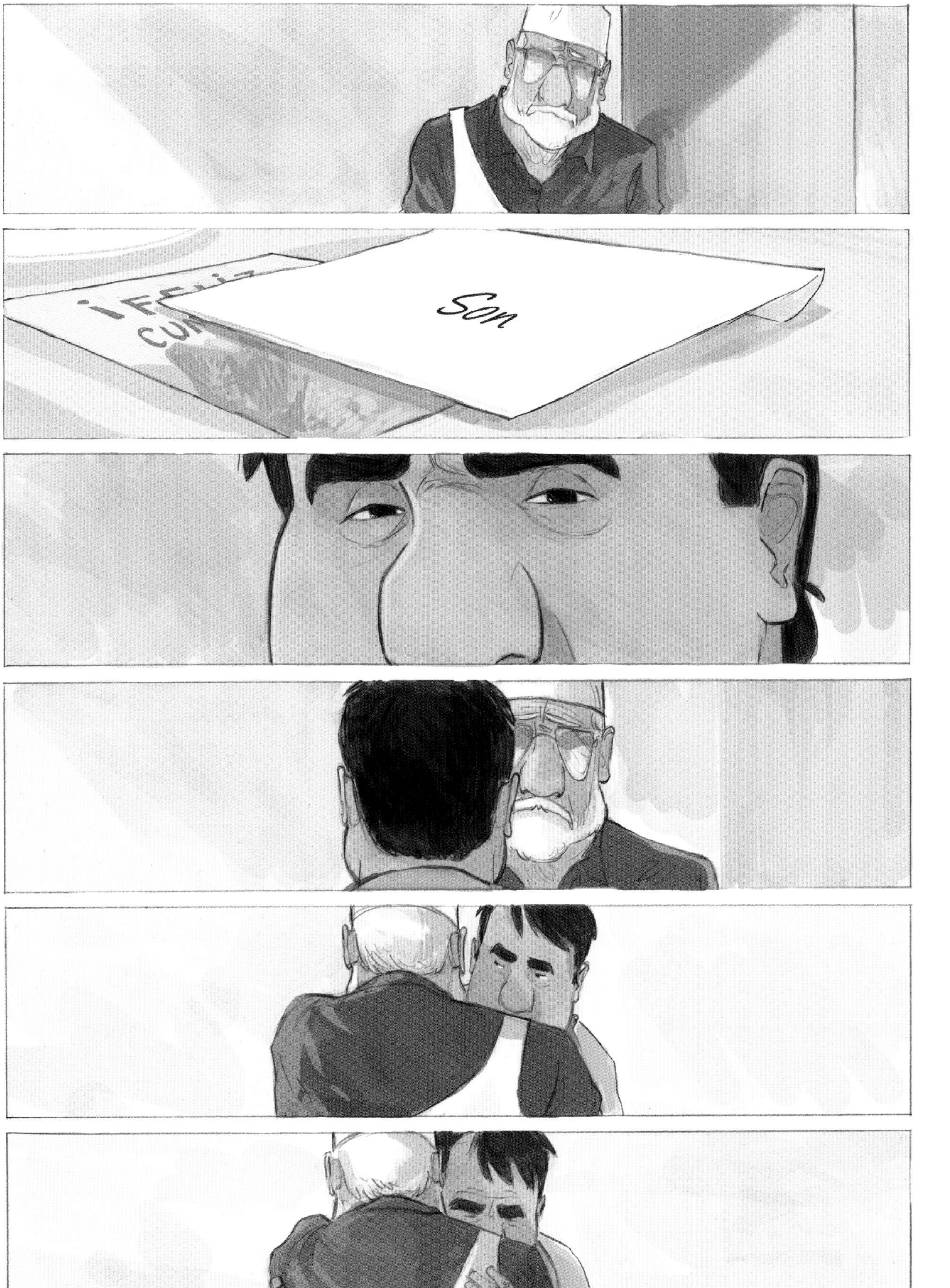
Son

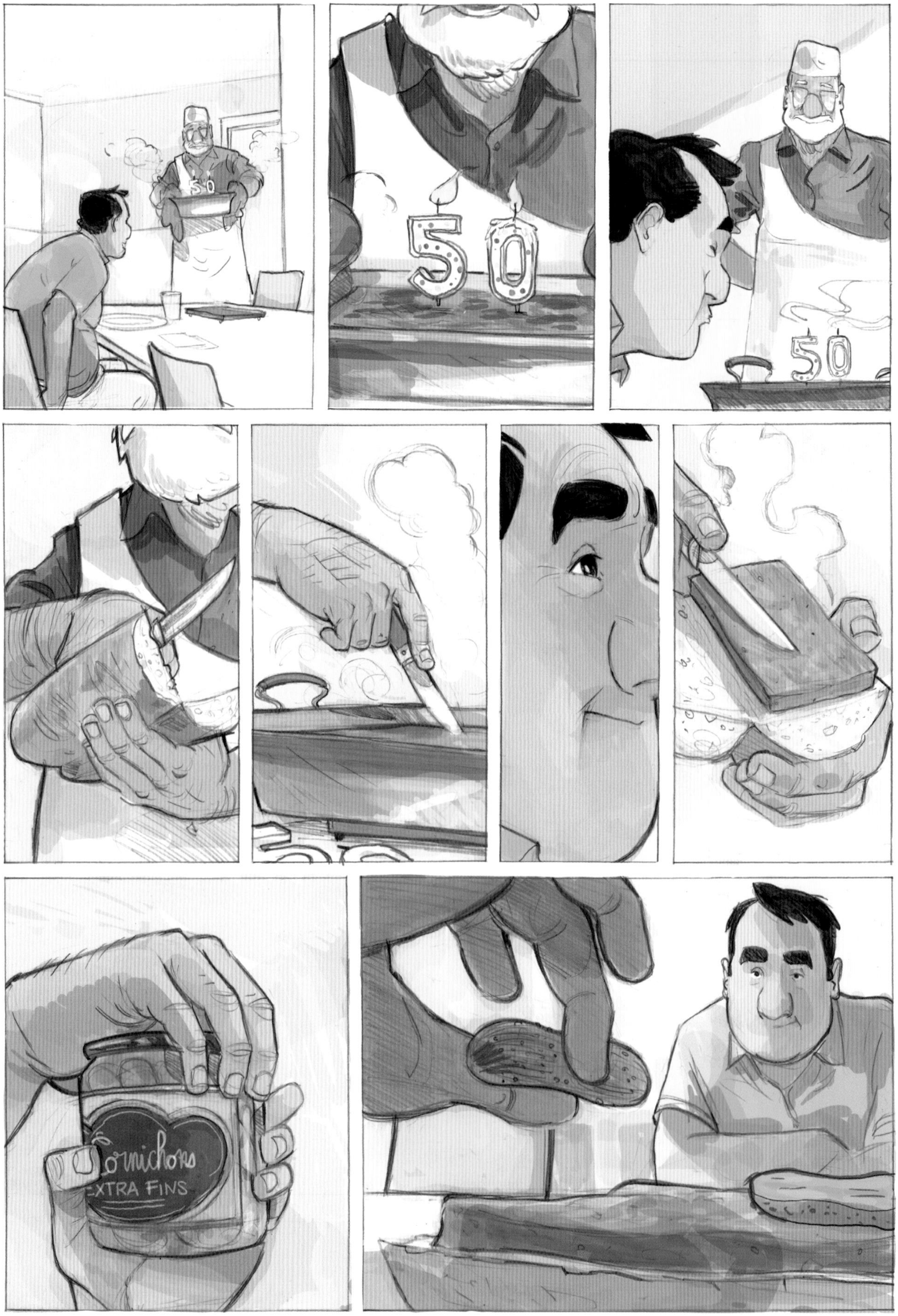
50
50
50
EXTRA FINS

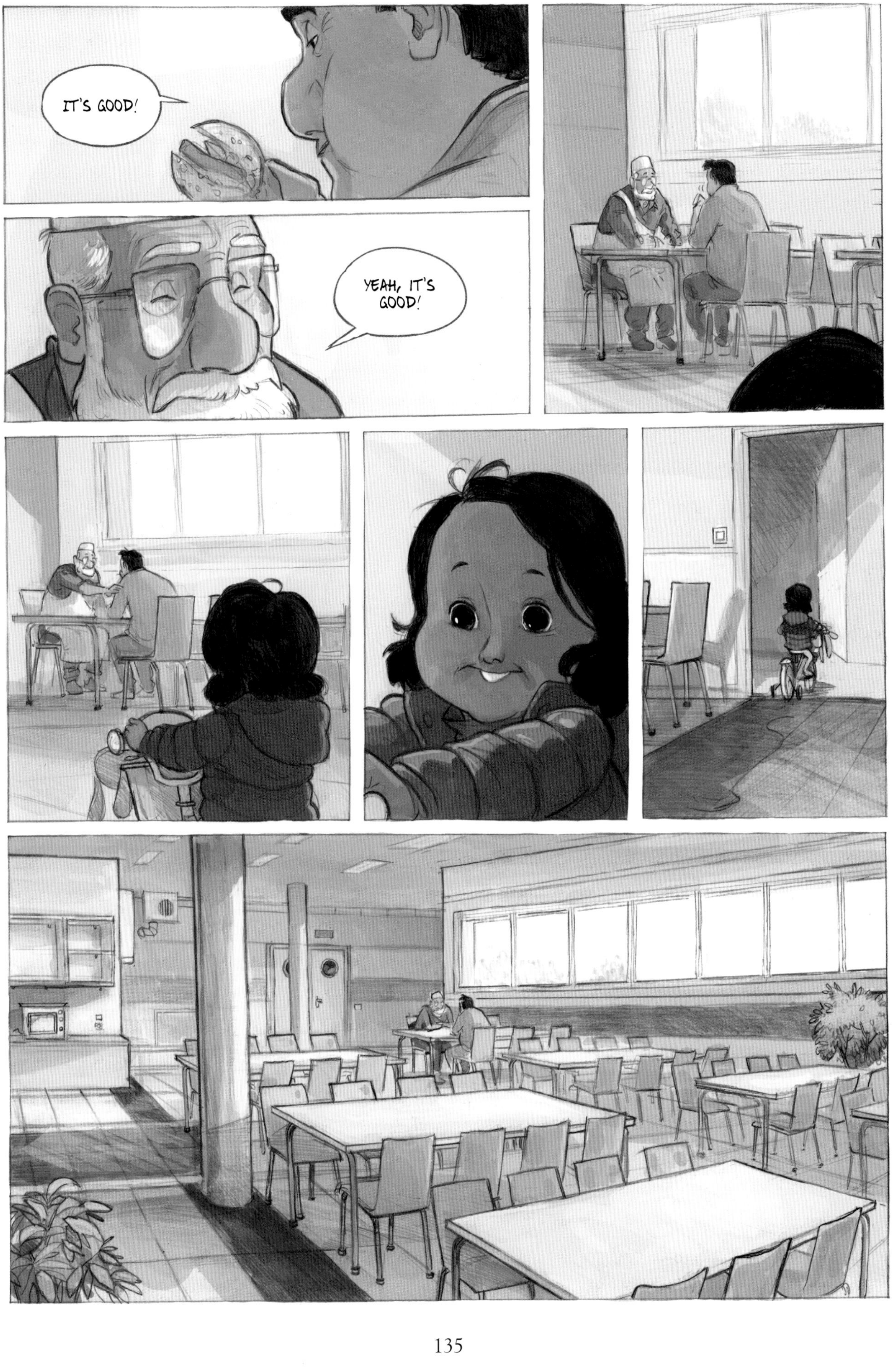
IT'S GOOD!
YEAH, IT'S GOOD!

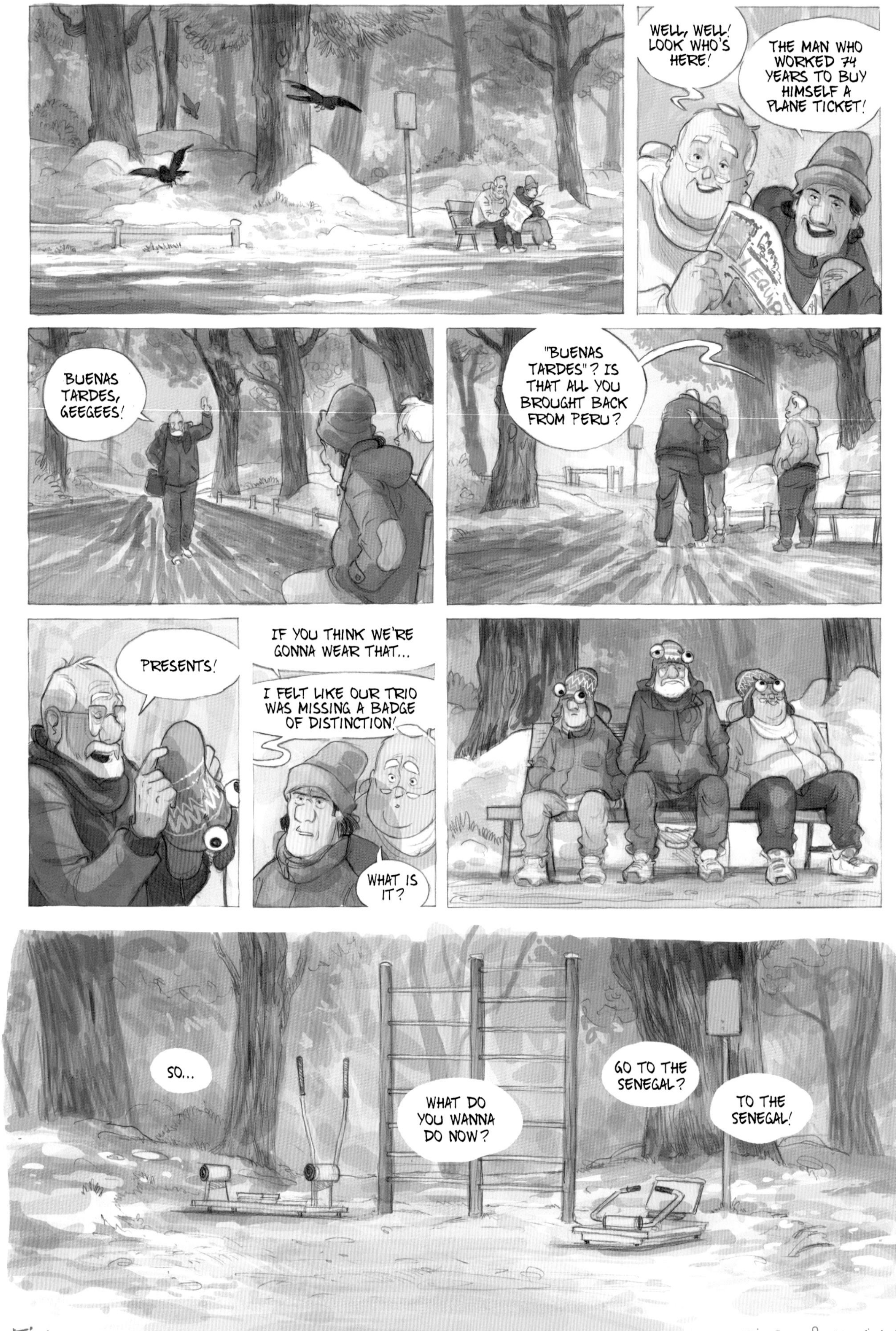
WELL, WELL! LOOK WHO'S HERE!
THE MAN WHO WORKED 74 YEARS TO BUY HIMSELF A PLANE TICKET!
BUENAS TARDES, GEEGEES!
"BUENAS TARDES"? IS THAT ALL YOU BROUGHT BACK FROM PERU?
PRESENTS!
IF YOU THINK WE'RE GONNA WEAR THAT...
I FELT LIKE OUR TRIO WAS MISSING A BADGE OF DISTINCTION!
WHAT IS IT?
SO...
WHAT DO YOU WANNA DO NOW?
GO TO THE SENEGAL?
TO THE SENEGAL!

FIN.

ZIDROU & MONIN 2017

SKETCHBOOK

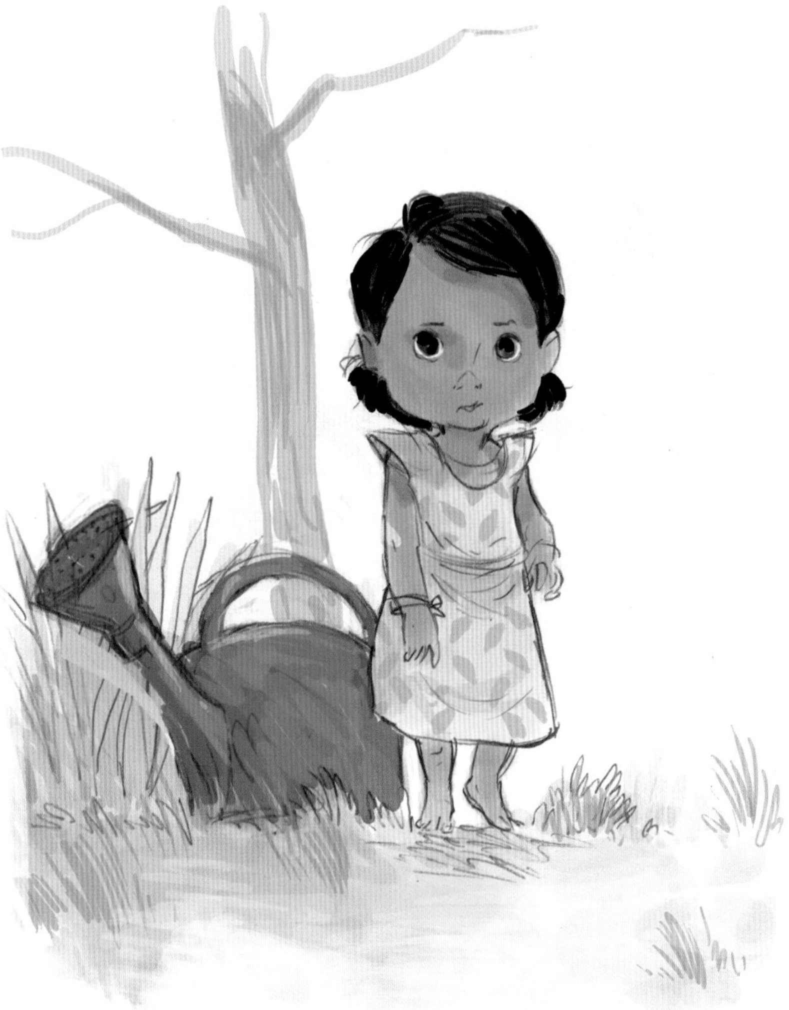

Illustrations by ARNO MONIN

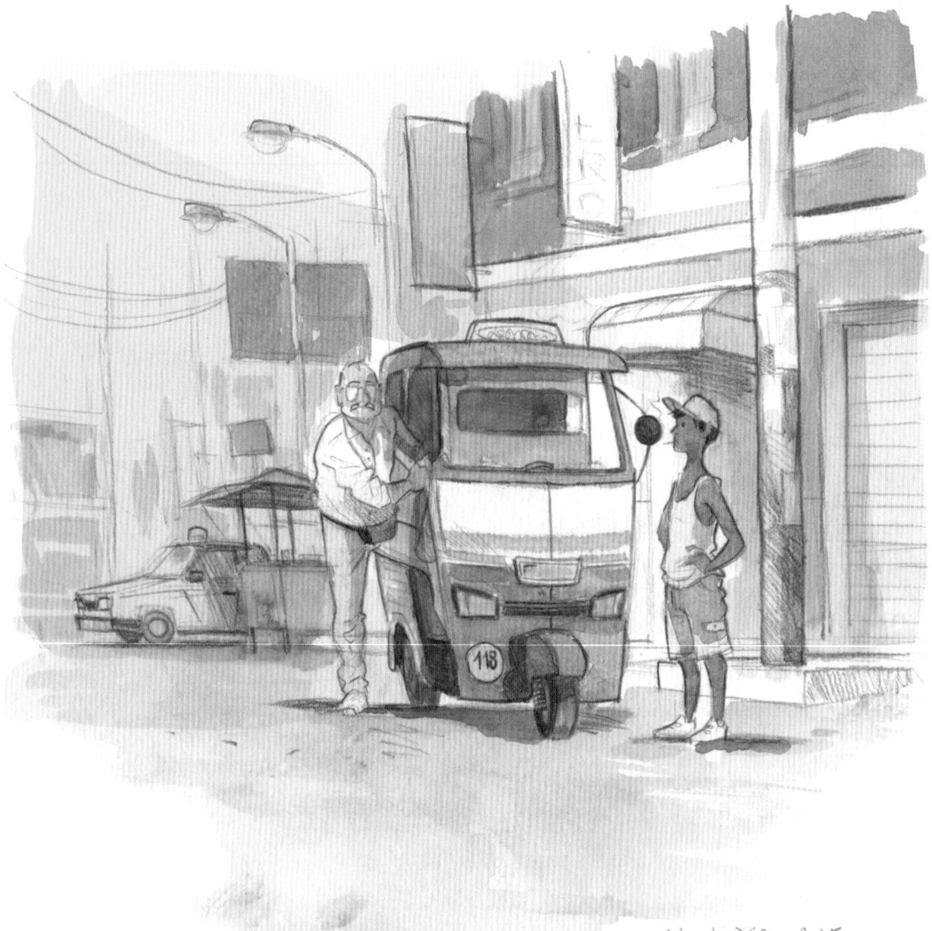
118

Gabriel, PÉROU 2015.

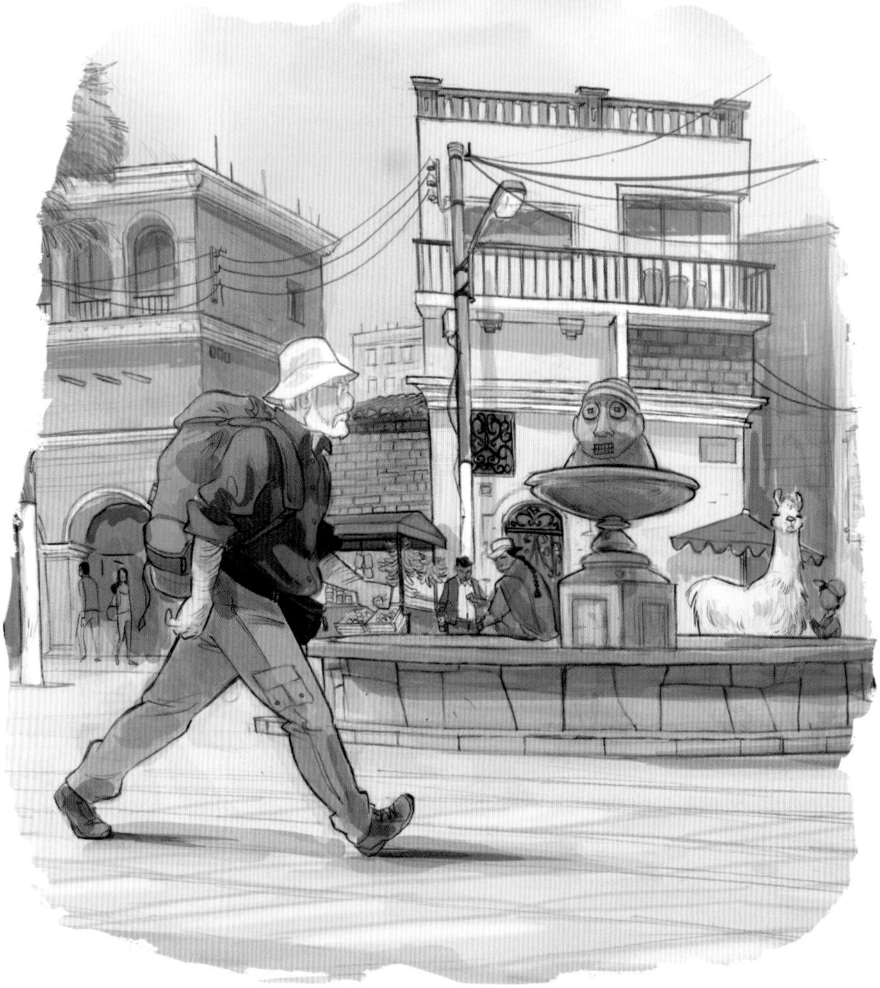

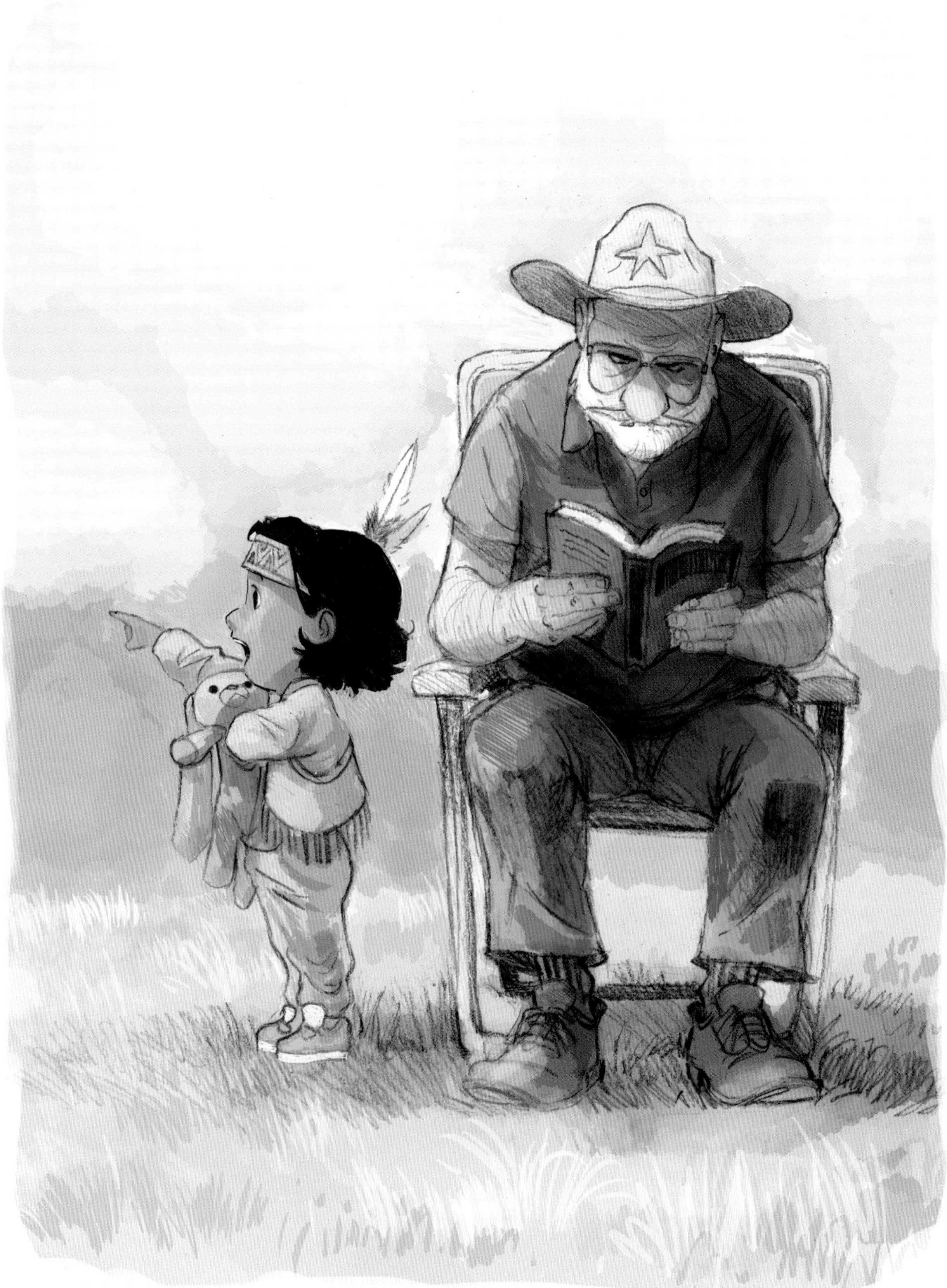

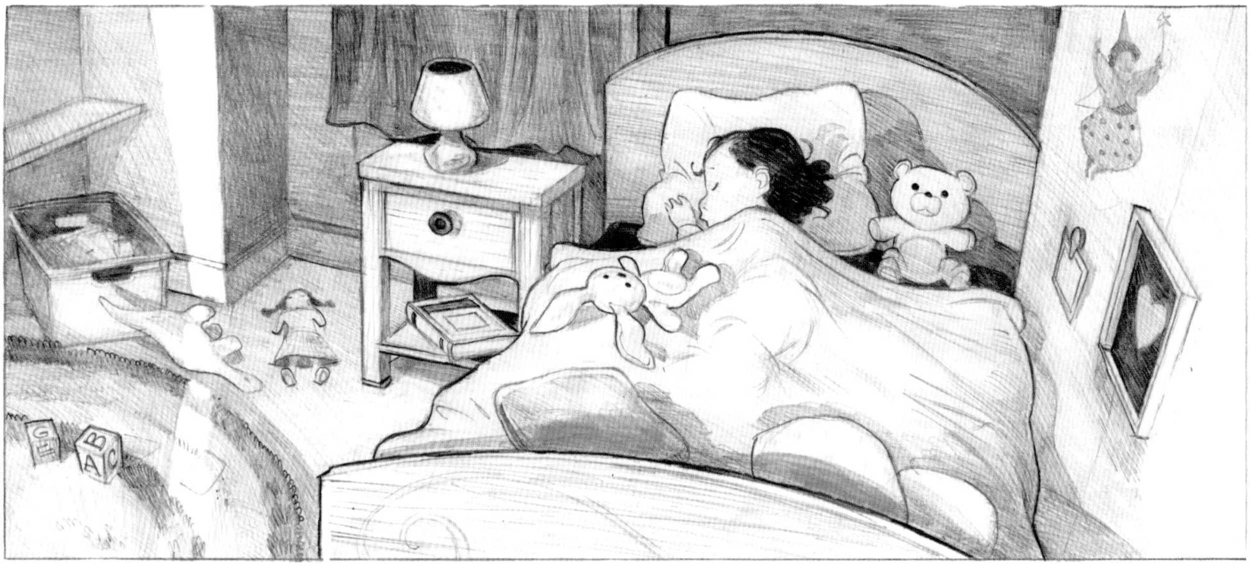

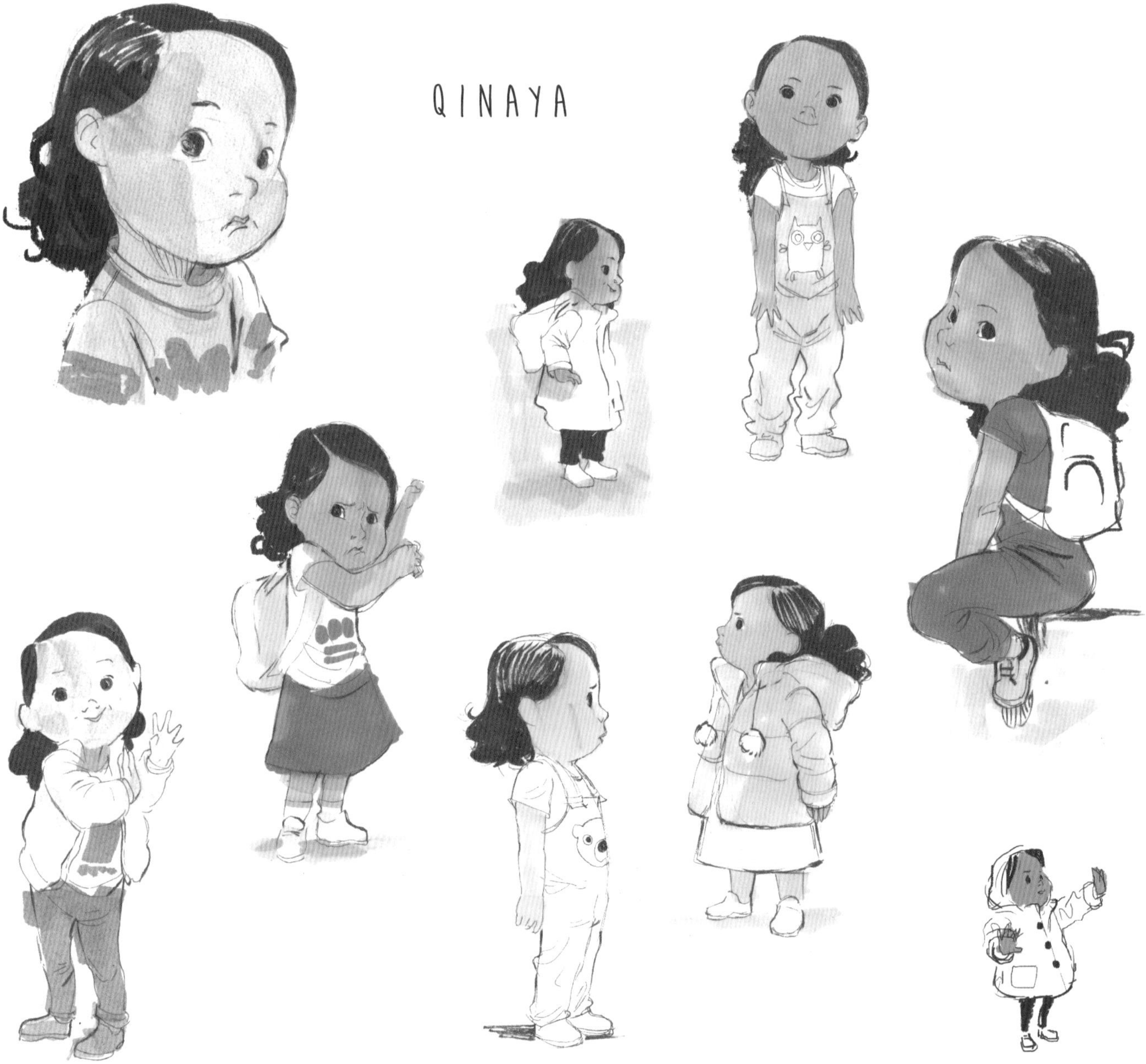
QINAYA

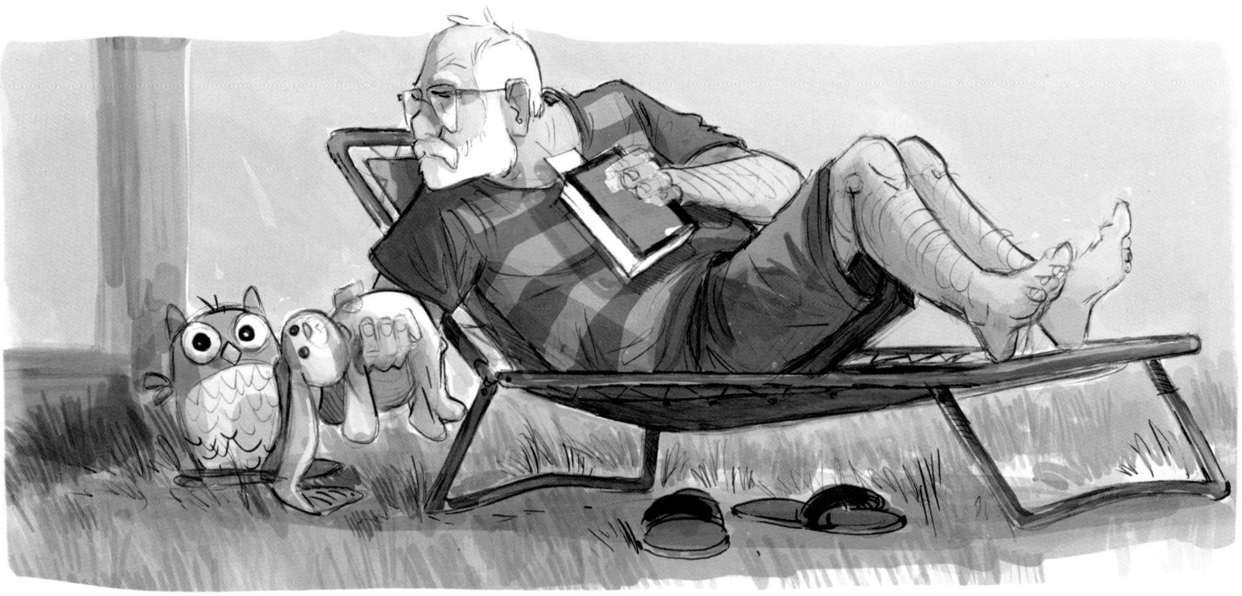

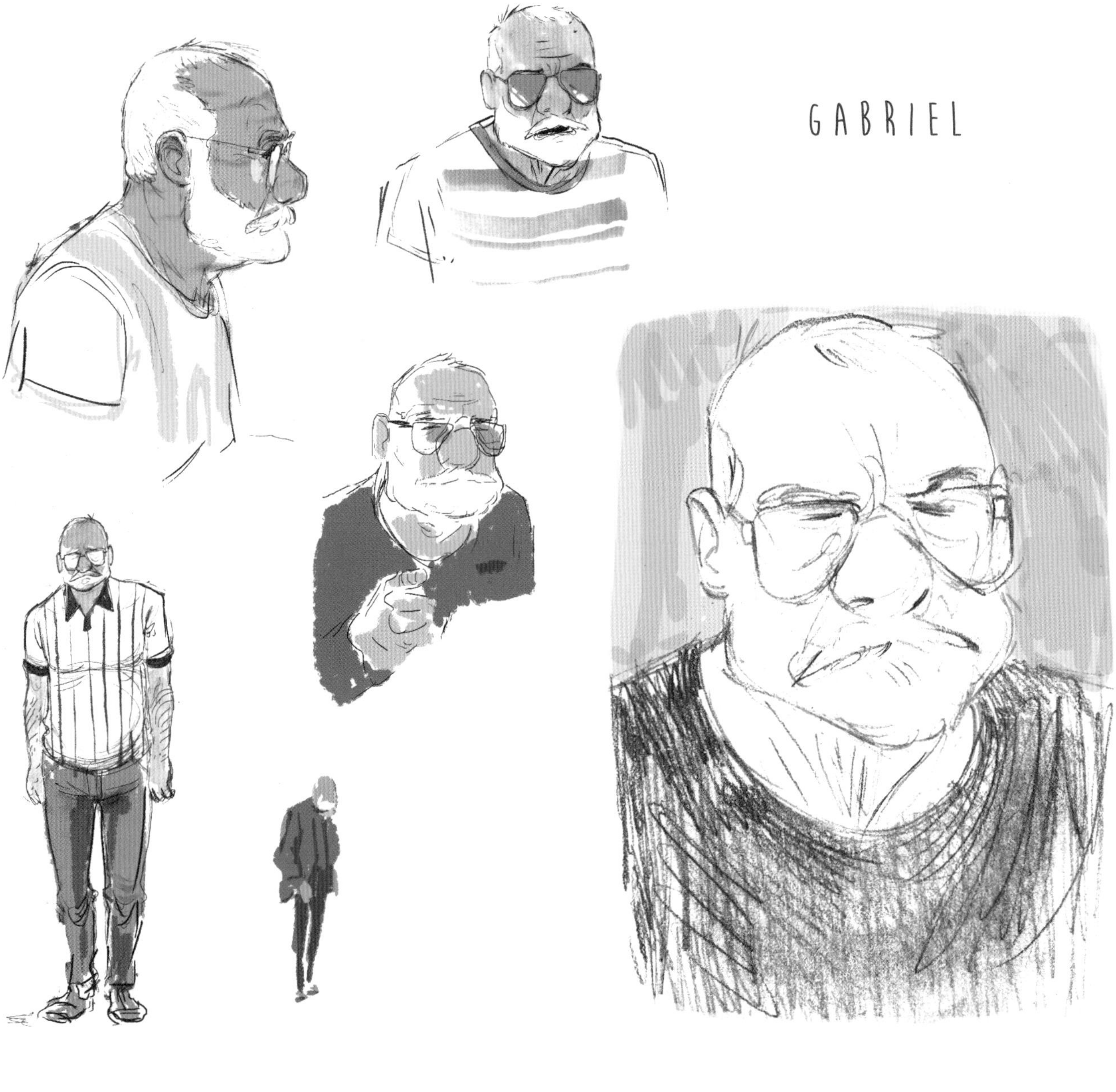
GABRIEL

MARCO

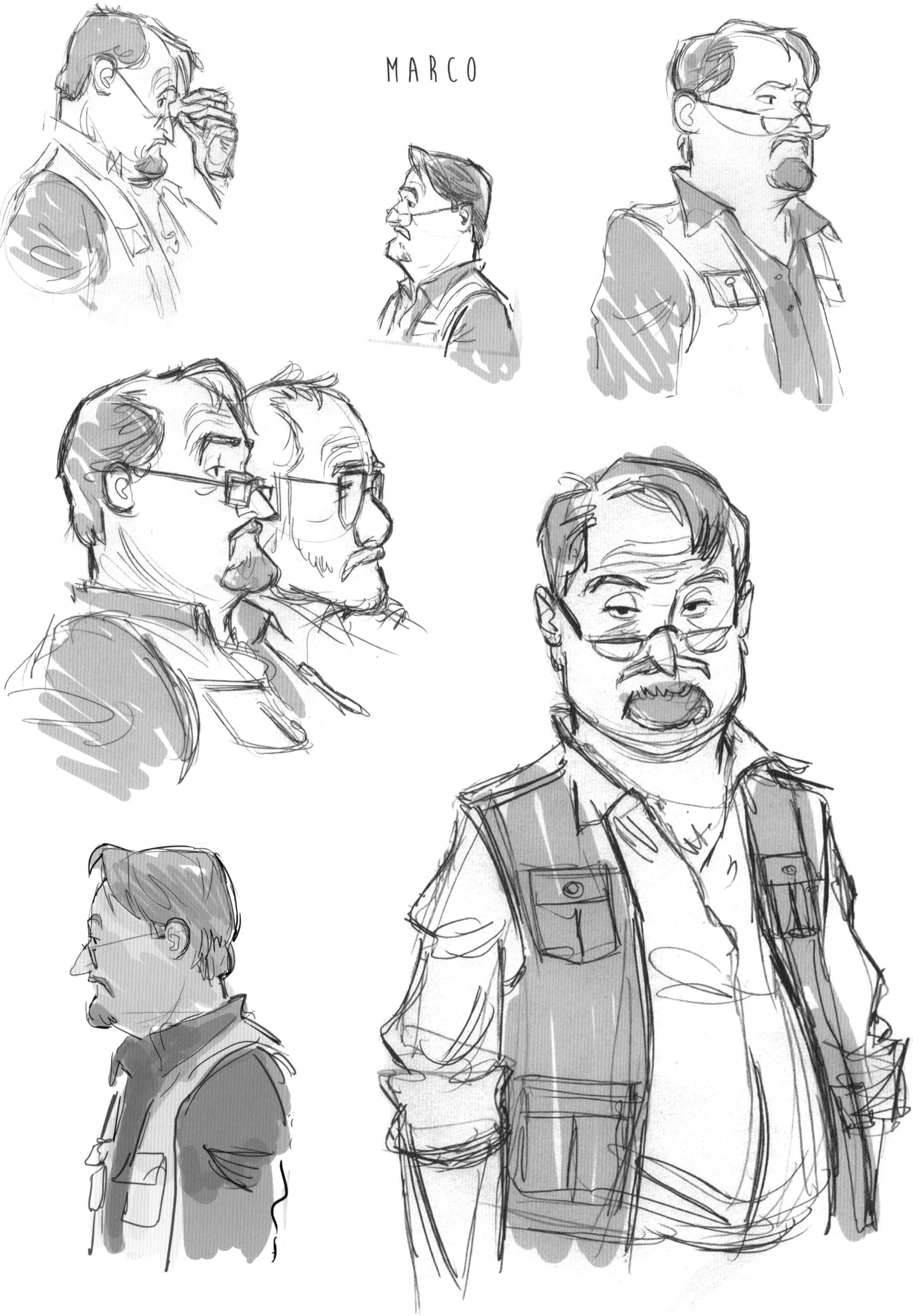

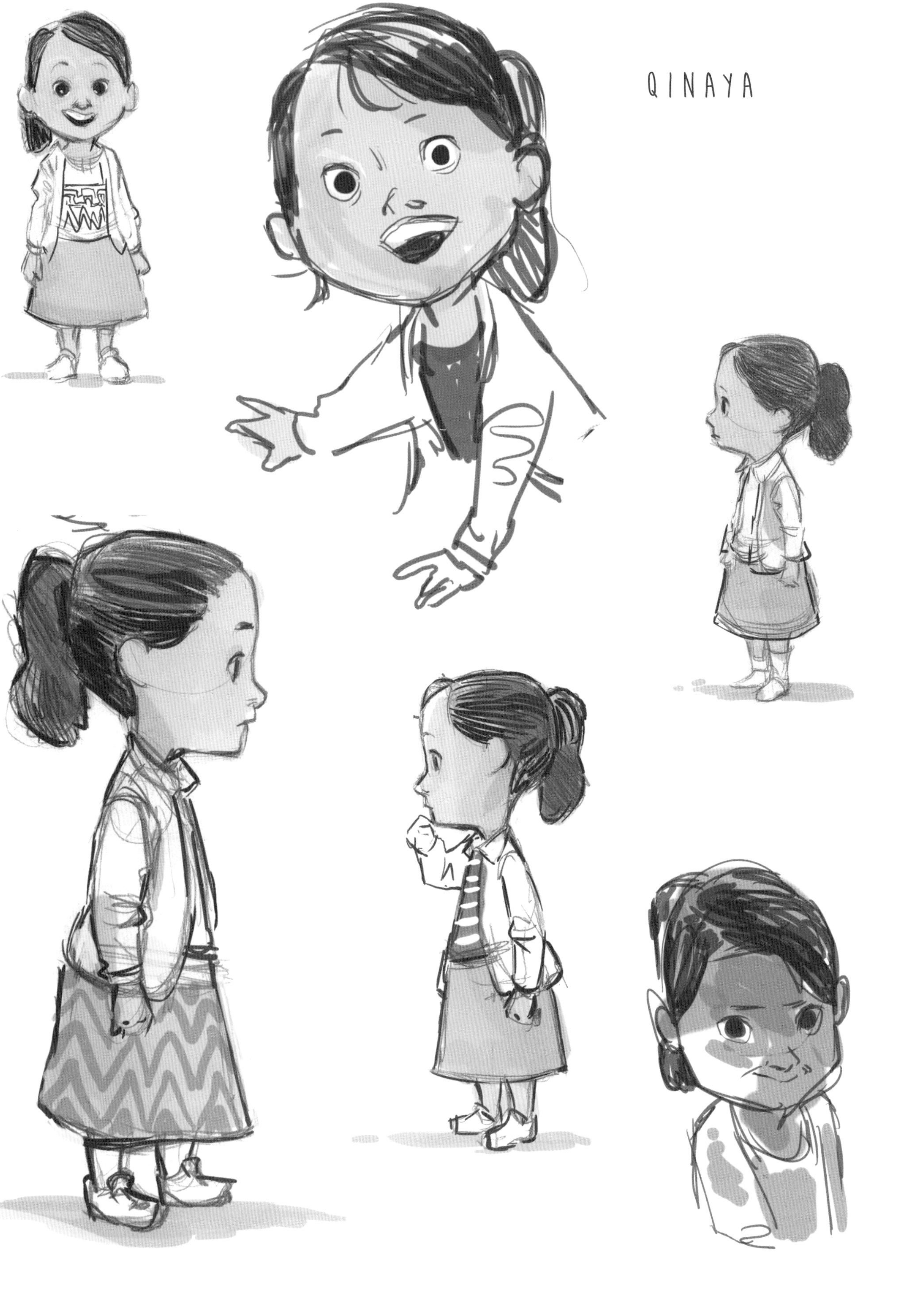
QINAYA